THE LAST DAYS COLLECTION

A Treasury of Articles from Last Days Ministries

PRETTY GOOD PUBLISHING
BOX 40, LINDALE, TX 75771-0040

Cover art by Larry DeGraff

Illustrations by Larry DeGraff and Terry DeGraff except for "Zeal–Love Ablaze" by Joe Zucker and Bible illustrations by Gustave Doré.

Scripture quotations are taken from the following sources:
> Amplified New Testament, ©The Lockman Foundation, 1958.
>
> King James Version
>
> The Living Bible, ©Tyndale House Publishers, 1971.
>
> Modern Language Bible: The Berkeley Version in Modern English, ©Zondervan Publishing House, 1969.
>
> New American Standard Bible, ©The Lockman Foundation, 1977.
>
> New International Version, ©International Bible Society, 1984.
>
> The New King James Version, ©Thomas Nelson Inc., Publishers, 1985.
>
> Revised Standard Version, ©National Council of the Churches of Christ in the U.S.A., Division of Christian Education, 1971.
>
> Weymouth New Testament In Modern Speech, ©Kregel Publications.

Specific scripture references are listed with their sources on page 215.

Copyright ©1986, 1988
Last Days Ministries
All Rights Reserved

Published by Pretty Good Publishing
A Division of Last Days Ministries
Box 40, Lindale, TX 75771-0040

Printed in the United States of America by Pretty Good Printing

ISBN   0-961-30020-5

CONTENTS

Introduction 11

The Authors 13

Articles

Breaking Up The Fallow Ground	*Charles G. Finney*	19
Music Or Missions?	*Keith Green*	26
The Holy Bible – Wholly True	*Winkie Pratney*	30
In Search Of Mr. Right	*Keith Green*	36
Gossip	*Melody Green*	41
Total Commitment (Communism vs. Christianity)	*Keith Green*	47
Do You Feel Like Giving Up?	*David Wilkerson*	54
Forgiveness – Forgive Or Forget It!	*Keith Green*	59
Zeal – Love Ablaze!	*Leonard Ravenhill*	64
Will You Be Bored In Heaven?	*Keith Green*	69
The Backslider In Heart	*Charles G. Finney*	75
Uncovering The Truth About Modesty	*Melody Green*	82
Christmas Mourning	*Keith Green*	90
Where Are The Elijahs Of God?	*Leonard Ravenhill*	95
Who Cares?	*William Booth*	100
How To Witness... For The Right Side!	*Charles G. Finney*	106

What's Wrong With The Gospel? Section 1: "The Missing Parts" .... *Keith Green*	113
What's Wrong With The Gospel? Section 2: "The Added Parts" .... *Keith Green*	122
Being A Christian At Home .... *Melody Green*	132
Aggressive Christianity .... *Catherine Booth*	140
God Comes To New York .... *Charles G. Finney*	148
Be Ye Not Angry And Sin Not .... *Leonard Ravenhill*	156
Creation Or Evolution? Part 1 .... *Winkie Pratney*	162
Creation Or Evolution? Part 2: The Historical Record .... *Winkie Pratney*	172
Creation Or Evolution? Part 3: The Fossil Record .... *Winkie Pratney*	178
How To Overcome Sin .... *Charles G. Finney*	188
Love vs. Romance... Fact Or Fantasy? .... *Kathleen Dillard*	194
Everything You Should Know *Before* You Get A Divorce .... *Keith Green*	200
"Devotions" Or Devotion? .... *Charles G. Finney*	209
Scripture Reference Sources	215
Ministry Materials For Whatever You Can Afford	217

INTRODUCTION

There we were, a rather interesting assortment of almost seventy people, stuffed into seven houses in a conservative Los Angeles suburb. In 1975 when my late husband Keith and I became Christians, we started filling our home with anyone who showed even a glimmer of interest in Jesus. Later, we rented several other houses in the neighborhood and even bought the house next door from our neighbor Harvey. We cut a hole through the fence for easy access and filled Harvey's house with girls – which is how the girls' dorm acquired the unlikely name of "Harvey's House."

We held Bible studies almost every night, potlucks on Friday, and an outreach to kids on drugs. We baptized people in anything that held water from bathtubs to jacuzzis to the Pacific Ocean. Our neighbors were wary, but our hearts were enthusiastic, wondering who we could share the Lord with next. And so in 1977, Last Days Ministries was born.

And in 1978, in the garage of "The School House" (it was across the street from a school), we set up some *very* used equipment and our first small printing press. And what a press it was! That Multi 1250 was stubborn, lazy, and loud – and in spite of the fact that no one really knew exactly how to run it, the job always got done!

The memories are still vivid... those freezing January nights when Keith and some of the other guys would huddle over that cranky press – trying to keep the ink and themselves warm in the rays of a rusty heat lamp. Then there were those blistering San Fernando Valley summer afternoons when the stifling heat made it a major step of faith to believe you could draw another breath. There were many memorable experiences in those very first days of Last Days, like the time the fellows wondered what they should do with the five screws left over from a "do-it-yourself" overhaul on the press. But the abundant grace of God, an understanding of purpose, and a good sense of humor kept us going no matter what happened.

In those early days we never would have guessed where the Lord was leading us. Our first few Last Days Newsletters (now The Last Days Magazine) were all folded and stapled by hand. Our first tract, "Breaking Up The Fallow Ground" was simply a paraphrased chapter from a book by Charles Finney that we inserted in the center of the Newsletter. God had used it so mightily in our lives, we were eager to share it with others.

When people began ordering extra copies of the Newsletter to give to their friends, we reprinted the whole newsletter at first. Then we realized they really only wanted copies of the main articles, and so to save money we simply reprinted those in pamphlet form. And so, our tract ministry was born. From there we just kept growing – writing articles ourselves and asking others we knew and loved to minister God's heart.

In 1979 we moved to Lindale, Texas, and as the requests for literature increased, we upgraded to more colorful and cooperative presses. And by November 1988 we'd printed and mailed over 58 million tracts – and distributed all of them on a "whatever you can afford" basis.

I am continually blessed that from a small house on Dolorosa St., so much has come to pass. Even the name of that street is meaningful. The Via Dolorosa in Spanish is known as The Way Of Suffering – the road Jesus walked to Calvary. Last Days Ministries has known some suffering, but we have also known abundant joy as we've seen the Lord use our efforts to reach out to a hurting world with His love. Literally tens of thousands of letters have poured in over the years- reports of how an article touched a heart or changed a life. I think my favorite stories are the unlikely ones – when someone finds a tract stuck on their windshield or lying in the street or picks one up that had been carelessly discarded on a public restroom floor. And upon reading it, comfort floods a wounded heart, a marriage is saved, an abortion is cancelled, a desperate prayer is answered, or a new life in Jesus is found.

As the years have gone by, we've also received many letters asking us to figure out a way to make the tracts easier to refer to on a daily basis. "Maybe you could put them into a book or something..."

And so, here it is. For me, this book is like flipping through a family album – each message marking a season, a particular truth God was underscoring in my life at that time. Truths I sometimes need to be reminded of. I hope this collection of articles will encourage you in your walk with the Lord. I pray that as you read, God will make every word come alive in your heart with the power of His Spirit and the wonder of His ever faithful love.

> Yours in Him,
> Melody Green
> President, Last Days Ministries
> November 1988

THE AUTHORS

Keith Green was a man known for his uncompromising Christian stance. He gave his life to Jesus in 1975 and was "sold out" for the Lord right from the very start. Keith's energy and passion for reaching people through music and ministry was unprecedented, and lives around the world are still being changed as his ministry continues to go forth. Last Days Ministries was born in 1977 as Keith and his wife Melody began reaching out to others with the Gospel and taking needy people into their home.

On July 28, 1982, at the age of 28, Keith and two of their young children, Josiah and Bethany, were in a small plane crash and went to be with Jesus. Although Keith was one of America's best-selling Christian musicians and songwriters, recording 5 albums in his lifetime with over 1.5 million in distribution, Keith considered himself first and foremost a servant of Jesus. He often said that when he died he only wanted to be remembered as having been worthy to bear the name "Christian."

Melody Green is president of Last Days Ministries and the director of the pro-life arm of Last Days, Americans Against Abortion. As a speaker who is much in demand, Melody travels frequently each year challenging her audiences with messages from the Lord's heart. She has written some of the best loved songs in contemporary music, as well as a variety of stirring articles, including the widely acclaimed treatise on abortion, "Children – Things We Throw Away?" Over 9 million copies of this article have been distributed, and it has been responsible for saving countless babies' lives and sparing mothers the trauma of abortion.

Melody is editor-in-chief of *The Last Days Magazine*, which reaches hundreds of thousands of people worldwide. Melody's special insight and godly example have been an encouragement to many all over the world. She lives in Lindale, Texas, with her two daughters, Rebekah and Rachel.

Winkie Pratney is a well-known evangelist, author, and conference speaker. Originally from New Zealand, Winkie, along with his wife Faye and son Billy, share their home life between New Zealand

and the U.S. After meeting Jesus, he gave up a promising career in research chemistry to begin a full-time globetrotting ministry, lecturing and teaching about the One who called him.

Leonard Ravenhill is a powerful preacher and the noted author of many stirring books, including the classic, "Why Revival Tarries." Born and raised in England, he became one of that country's foremost outdoor evangelists, drawing traffic-stopping crowds. His heart is filled with a burning desire to see God's people walk in purity and holy zeal. Leonard and his wife Martha live in Lindale, Texas.

David Wilkerson, president of World Challenge, is an internationally known evangelist and author. He is probably best known as the founder of Teen Challenge, and as the author of the best-selling book, *The Cross and the Switchblade*. His commitment to see holiness and purity restored to the Church is reflected in his writings and teachings, as well as in his very life. He is the senior pastor of Times Square Church in New York City, where he ministers to the homeless and needy.

William Booth (1829-1921) founded The Salvation Army in 1865. His passion for the lost, especially those considered "irredeemable" by the established church, was legendary. His whole life can be summed up in his own words, "Go for souls – and go for the worst!" The Salvation Army declared "Salvation War," first in the London slums, then all over Europe, and eventually on every continent.

Catherine Booth (1829-1890) the wife of William, was known as "the mother of the Salvation Army." Intent on saving others to the end, Catherine stepped out boldly in ways that many women (even in our day) are reluctant to go. Her life made such an impression that at her death over 50,000 people flocked to Congress Hall in London to pay tribute to her. Catherine authored six books, as well as many powerful pamphlets and articles that deeply affected the people of England. She and William raised eight dedicated Christian children, founded and ran The Salvation Army, and preached the Gospel worldwide.

Charles G. Finney (1792-1875), often called "America's foremost revivalist," led a tremendous awakening in America which literally altered the course of our national history. Under his direction, Oberlin College was a major cultivation ground for the early movement to end slavery. Finney's logical, clear cut presentation of the Gospel reached thousands with the renewing power and love of Jesus Christ. His writings continue to challenge many to live a life holy and pleasing to God.

Kathleen Dillard came to Last Days Ministries in 1978, and in 1982 helped establish the Intensive Christian Training School. She is a gifted woman of God who continues to lend frequent leadership, not only to the school, but also to the staff at Last Days Ministries. Kathleen, her husband Wayne, and daughter Julia, live in Lindale, TX.

Breaking Up The Fallow Ground

AN OUTLINE FOR REPENTENCE

by Charles G. Finney

Edited and Paraphrased by
Keith and Melody Green

This article is for Christians who have had trouble finding the true peace that is promised with conversion. For those who are frustrated because they are constantly struggling with weakness and sin, this could well be the very help they've been praying for. Charles Finney saw countless tens of thousands of true conversions—and all before the days of radio, TV, or mass publications. We thank God for continuing to anoint and use his writings. Many thousands have been helped by this article to break through to God's precious forgiveness. Remember one thing as you read this—God loves you so much, and is waiting for you to be thoroughly cleansed by His grace through repentance.

The Jews were a nation of farmers, and it is therefore a common thing for God to refer, in the Scriptures, to scenes from their daily lives as illustrations. Hosea addresses them as a nation of backsliders, but uses words that farmers and shepherds are familiar with. He rebukes them for their idolatry and sharply warns them of the impending judgments of God.

Fallow ground is ground which has once been tilled, but has gotten hard and now lies waste. It needs to be broken up and made soft again, before it is ready to receive seed. If you mean to break up the fallow ground of your heart, you must begin by looking at your heart—examine carefully the state of your mind and see where you are. Many people never even seem to think about doing this. They pay no attention to their own hearts, and never know whether they are doing well in their walk with the Lord or not—whether they are bearing fruit or are totally barren. Now you must draw off your attention from all other things and look into this right now! Make a business of it, do not be in a hurry.

Self-examination consists of looking at your life, considering your motives and actions... calling up your past and seeing its true character. Look back over your past history. Take up your individual sins one by one, and look at them. This doesn't mean that you just take a casual glance at your past life, see that it has been full of sin, and then go to God and make a sort of general confession, asking forgiveness. General confessions of sin are not good enough. Your sins were committed one by one; and as much as you are able, they ought to be reviewed and repented of one by one. It's a good idea to take a pen and some paper as you go over them, and write them down as they come to mind.

Go over them as carefully as a businessman goes over his books; and as often as a sin comes to your memory, write it down! Now begin, and start with what are usually, but improperly, called **sins of omission** (i.e. things you didn't do that you should have!).

1) Ingratitude (Unthankfulness). Take this sin, for example, and write down under this heading all the times you can remember where you have received great blessings and favors from God for which you have never given thanks. How many cases can you remember? Some remarkable protection where your life was spared, some wonderful turn of events that saved you from ruin. Write down the instances of God's goodness to you when you were still in sin, before your conversion, for which you have never been half-thankful enough—and the uncountable mercies you have received since. How long the list of times where your ingratitude has been so black that you are forced to hide your face in shame! Get on your knees and confess them one by one to God, and ask Him to forgive you.

As you're confessing these, they will immediately remind you of others…write them down too. Go over them three or four times in this way, and see what an incredible number of times God has given you mercy for which you have never thanked Him!

2) Lack of Love for God. Think how grieved and alarmed you'd be, if you suddenly realized a great lack of affection for you in your wife, husband, or children—if you saw that someone else had captured their hearts, thoughts, and time. Perhaps in such a case you would almost die with a just and holy jealousy. Now, God calls Himself a jealous God. Have you not given your heart to other loves and infinitely offended Him?

3) Neglect of the Bible. Put down the cases where for perhaps weeks or longer, God's Word was not a pleasure to you. Some people, indeed, read over whole chapters in such a way that afterwards they could not tell you what they had been reading. If that is so with you, no wonder your life has no direction, and your relationship with God is in such a miserable state.

4) Unbelief. Recall the instances in which you have virtually charged the God of truth with lying, by your unbelief of His express promises and declarations. If you have not believed or expected to receive the blessings which God has clearly promised, **you have called Him a liar.**

5) Lack of Prayer. Think of all the times you have neglected private prayer, family prayer, and group prayer meetings; or you've prayed in such a way as to grieve and offend God more than if you hadn't prayed at all.

6) Neglect of Fellowship. When you have allowed yourself to make small and foolish excuses that have prevented you from attending meetings. When you have neglected and poured contempt upon the gathering of the saints merely because you "didn't like church"!

7) The Manner in which You have Performed Spiritual Duties. Think of all the times when you have spoken about God with such a lack of feeling and faith, in such a worldly frame of mind, that your words were nothing more than the mere chattering of a wretch who didn't deserve that God should listen to him at all. When you have fallen down upon your knees and "said your prayers" in such an unfeeling and careless way that if you had been put under oath five minutes later, you could not say what you had been praying for.

8) Lack of Love for Souls. Look around at all your friends and relatives, and think of how little compassion you have felt for them. You have stood by and seen them going straight to hell, and it seems as though you didn't even care! How many days have there been when you have failed to make their wretched condition the subject of even one single fervent prayer, or to prove any real desire for their salvation?

9) Lack of Care for the Poor and Lost in Foreign Lands. Perhaps you have not cared enough about them to even attempt to learn of their condition. Do you avoid missions magazines? How much do you really know or care about the unconverted masses of the world? Measure your desire for their salvation by the self-denial you practice in giving from your substance to send them the Gospel.

Do you deny yourself even the hurtful excesses of life, such as tobacco or alcohol? Do you defend your standard of living? Will you not suffer yourself **any** inconvenience to save them? Do you daily pray for them in private? Are you setting aside funds to put into the treasury of the Lord when you go up to pray? (As in the story of the widow's mite—*Mark 12:41-44*.) If your soul is not agonized for the poor and lost of this world, then why are you such a hypocrite as to pretend to be a Christian? (See *Matt. 25:31-46*.)

10) Neglect of Family Duties. Think of how you have lived before your family, how you have prayed, what an example you have set before them. What direct efforts do you habitually make for their spiritual welfare?

11) Lack of Watchfulness Over Your Witness. How many times have you failed to take your words and actions seriously? How often have you entirely neglected to watch your conduct and speech, and having been off your guard, you have sinned before the world, the church, and before God!

12) Neglect to Watch Over Your Brethren. How often have you broken your covenant that you would watch over them in the Lord? How little do you know or care about the state of their souls? And yet you are under a solemn duty to watch over them. What have you done to get to know them better? How many times have you seen them falling into sin, and you let them go on? And you pretend to love them? Would you watch your wife or child going into disgrace, or falling into a fire, and hold your peace?

13) Neglect of Self-Denial. There are many professing Chistians who are willing to do almost anything in religion **that does not require self-denial.** They think they are doing a great deal for God, and doing about as much as He ought to reasonably ask, but they are not willing to deny themselves any comfort or convenience whatsoever for the sake of serving the Lord.

They will not willingly suffer reproach for the name of Christ. Nor will they deny themselves the luxuries of life to save a world from hell. They are so far from realizing that self-denial is a condition of discipleship, that they do not even know what it is! They have never really denied themselves a ribbon or a pin for Christ and the Gospel. Some are giving from their abundance, and giving a lot—and will even complain that others do not give more—when in truth, they are not giving **anything** that they need, or anything that they would enjoy if they kept it. **They only give from their surplus wealth!**

"Break up your fallow ground, for it is time to seek the Lord until He comes to rain righteousness on you..." —Hosea 10:12

Now we turn to **sins of commission...**

14) Love of Things and Possessions. What has been the state of your heart concerning your earthly possessions? Have you looked at them as really yours—as if you had a right to use or dispose of them as your own? If you have, write it down! If you have loved property and sought after it for its **own** sake, or to gratify ambition, you have sinned and must repent.

15) Vanity. How many times have you spent more time decorating your body to go to church, than you have in preparing your heart and mind for the worship of God? You have cared more about how you appeared outwardly to men than how your soul appeared in the sight of God. You sought to divide the worship of God's house, to draw off the attention of God's people, to look at your pretty appearance. And you pretend that you do not care anything about having people look at you? Be honest about it! Would you take all this pain about your looks if every person were blind?

16) Envy. Look at the cases in which you were jealous of those who were in a higher position than you. Or perhaps you have envied those who have been more talented or more useful than yourself. Have you not so envied some, that it has caused you pain to hear them praised? It has pleased you more to dwell upon their faults than upon their virtues...upon their failures rather than their successes. Be honest with yourself, and if you have harbored this spirit of hell, then repent deeply before God.

17) Bitterness. Recall all the instances in which you have harbored a grudge or a bitter spirit toward someone, or have spoken of Christians in a manner completely devoid of charity and love. Love "hopes all things," but you have given no benefit of doubt, and have suspected the worst.

18) Slander (Gossip). Think of all the times you have spoken behind people's backs of their faults (real or supposed) unnecessarily and without cause. This is slander. You need not lie to be guilty of slander–to tell the truth with the intent to injure is slander.

19) Levity (A spirit of excessive humor). How often have you joked before God, as you would not have dared in the presence of an earthly dignitary or important official. You have either been an atheist and forgotten that God existed–or you have had less respect for Him and His presence than you would have had for a mere judge on earth.

20) Lying. Now understand what lying is. Any form of designed deception is lying. If you purpose to make an impression other than the naked truth, you lie. Put down all those cases you can recollect. Do not call them by any soft names. God calls them lies and charges you with lying, so you'd better charge yourself correctly! Think of all your words, looks, and actions designed to make an impression on others contrary to the truth, for selfish reasons.

21) Cheating. Set down all the cases where you have dealt with anyone in a way you yourself would not like at all. That is cheating. God has said that we should treat all men in the same manner we would like to be treated. *(Matt. 7:12)* **That is the rule.** And if you have not done so you are a cheat! God did not say that you should do what you would **expect** them to do, for if that were the rule it would allow for all kinds of wickedness in our actions. But it says, do what you would **want** them to do to you! *(Have you cheated the government? i.e., unemployment insurance, welfare, food stamps, social security, student loans, etc., gained by fraud?)*

22) Hypocrisy. For instance, in your prayers and confessions to God, set down all the times in which you have prayed for things you didn't really want. How many times have you confessed sins that you never intended to stop doing? Yes, you have confessed sins when you knew in your heart you as much expected to go and repeat them, as you expected to live!

23) Robbing God. Think of all the instances in which you have totally misspent your time, squandering the hours which God gave you to serve Him, and save souls. Precious time wasted in vain amusement or worthless conversation, in reading worldly novels, or **even doing nothing;** cases where you have misused your talents and ability to think. Think of how you have squandered God's money on your lusts, or spent it for things which you really didn't need, which did not contribute to your health, comfort, or usefulness. **Think of a professing believer using God's money to poison himself with tobacco or intoxicating drink!**

24) Bad Temper. Perhaps you have abused your wife, or your children, or your family, or employees, or neighbors. Write it all down!

25) Hindering Others from Being Useful. You have not only robbed God of your own talents, but tied the hands of somebody else. What a wicked servant is he who not only is useless himself, but hinders the rest! This is done sometimes by taking their time needlessly. Thus you have played into the hands of Satan, and not only proved yourself to be an idle vagabond, but prevented others from working also.

26) Idols and Other Religions. *(I found as I was sitting down to write out my sins, that there were whole categories of sins that are common* *today, that would never even have been spoken of to the church in Finney's day. Some of these include fornication and sexual sins, the whole area of false peace induced by drugs, and occult involvement—including astrology, witchcraft, meditation, yoga, and the whole gamut of Eastern religions and philosophies, etc.—Keith)*

Some Important Guidelines To Follow

1) If you find you have committed a fault against anyone, and that person is within your reach, go and confess it immediately and get that out of the way. If they are too far away for you to go and see them, sit down and write them a letter (or better yet call them), confessing the injury you have committed against them. If you have defrauded anybody, send the money— **the full amount *and* the interest.**

2) As you go over the catalogue of your sins, be sure to resolve upon **immediate** and **entire** reformation. Wherever you find anything wrong, commit yourself at once, **in the strength of God,** to sin no more in that way. It will be of no benefit to examine yourself unless you determine to change, in every aspect, that which you find wrong in heart, temper, or conduct.

3) Go thoroughly to work in all this! Go now! Do not put it off—**that** will only make matters worse. Confess to God those sins that have been committed against God, and to man those sins that have been committed against man. Do not think about getting off easy by going around the stumbling blocks. Take them up out of the way. In breaking up your fallow ground, you must remove every obstacle. Things may be left that you may think are little things, and you may wonder why you don't have your peace with God, when the reason is your proud and carnal mind has covered up something which God has required you to confess and remove.

Unless you take up your sins in this way, and consider them in detail, one by one, you can form no idea of the amount or weight of them. **You should go over the list as thoroughly and as carefully and as solemnly as if you were preparing yourself for the Judgment!** *(I Cor. 11:31)*

This article is available in tract form as LD#1.

MUSIC OR MISSIONS?

BY KEITH GREEN

Today, so many people ask me if I can tell them how they can start or enter into a music ministry. At concerts I get countless questions about this, and I get lots of letters and even some long-distance phone calls from so many people who feel they are just "called" into the music ministry. One day, I began to ask myself why so few have ever asked me how to become a missionary, or even a local street preacher, or how to disciple a new believer. Everyone, it seems, would prefer the "bright lights" of what they think a music ministry would be, rather than the mud and obscurity of the mission field or the streets of the ghetto, or even the true spiritual sweetness of just being a nobody whom the Lord uses mightily.

ARE YOU WILLING?

My answer to their question is almost always the same. "Are you willing to never play music again? Are you willing to be a nothing? Are you willing to go anywhere, and do anything for Christ? Are you willing to stay right where you are and let the Lord do great things through you, though nobody seems to care or notice at all?" They all seem to always answer each of these questions with a quick "yes!" But I really doubt if they know what their answer entails.

STAR STRUCK

My dearest family in Jesus...Why are we so star struck? Why do we idolize Christian singers and speakers? We go from glorifying musicians in the world, to glorifying Christian musicians. It's all idolatry! Can't you see that? It's true that there are many men and women of God who are so anointed to call down the Spirit of God on His people and on the unsaved. But Satan is getting a great

---

"So of course, what we idolize, we ourselves desire to become, sometimes with our whole hearts."

---

victory as we seem to worship these ministers on tapes and records, and clamor to get their autographs in churches and concert halls from coast to coast.

Can't you see that you are hurting these ministers? They try desperately to tell you that they don't deserve to be praised, and because of this you squeal with delight and praise them all the more. You're smothering them, making it almost impossible for them to see that it's really Jesus. They keep telling themselves that, but you keep telling them that it's really them, crushing their humility and grieving the Spirit that is trying to keep their eyes on Jesus.

So of course, what we idolize, we ourselves desire to become, sometimes with our whole heart. So a lot of people want to be just like their favorite gospel singer and performer, and they seek after it with the same fervor that the Lord demands we seek after Him! And again, we insult the Spirit of grace and try to make a place for ourselves, rather than a place for Jesus.

A THANKLESS JOB

How come no one idolizes or praises the missionaries who give up everything and live in poverty, endangering their lives and their families with every possible danger that the American dream has almost completely eliminated? How come no one lifts up and exalts the ghetto and prison ministers and preachers who never can take up an offering, for if they did they would either laugh (or cry) for what they'd receive? How come? Because (1) we're taught from very early on that comfort is our goal and security... and (2) that we should always seek for a lot of people to like us. Who lives more comfortably and has more "fans" than the latest bright and shining gospel star? Who has lived less comfortably and has had fewer friends and supporters than the selfless people who have died untimely, premature deaths trying to conquer souls and whole nations for the whole glory of God as missionaries and soul winners?

Do you really believe we're living in the very last times? Then why do you spend more money on gospel records and concerts than you give to organizations that feed the poor, or to the missionaries your church is supporting?

There are ministries all over the world where people who have nothing to "tithe" on are being saved and transformed. Broken people with nothing to hold them back except not having anyone to hold their hand during the times when it all looks completely hopeless.

I repent of ever having recorded one single song, and ever having played even one concert, if my music and (more importantly) my life has not provoked you in godly jealousy *(Rom. 11:11)* to sell out completely to Jesus!

Quit trying to make gods out of music ministers, and quit desiring to become like those gods. The Lord commands you, *"Deny yourself, take up your cross daily, and follow Me." (Luke 9:23)* My piano is not my cross, it is my tool. I'd never play the thing again if God would show me a more effective tool for proclaiming His Gospel.

CONCLUSION

To finish, let me say that the only music ministers to whom the Lord will say, "Well done, thou good and faithful servant," are the ones whose lives prove what their lyrics are saying, and the ones to whom music is the least important part of their life–glorifying the only worthy One has to be the most important!

Let's all repent of idolatry, and seeking a comfortable, rewarding life while we are passing through like strangers and pilgrims in this world. *(Heb. 11:13)* For our reward is in heaven...and our due service to the Lord is *"not only to believe in Him, but also to suffer for His sake." (Phil. 1:29)*

Amen...Let us die graciously together and endure to the end like brave soldiers who give their lives, without a thought, for our noble and glorious King of Light.

This article is available in tract form as LD#2.

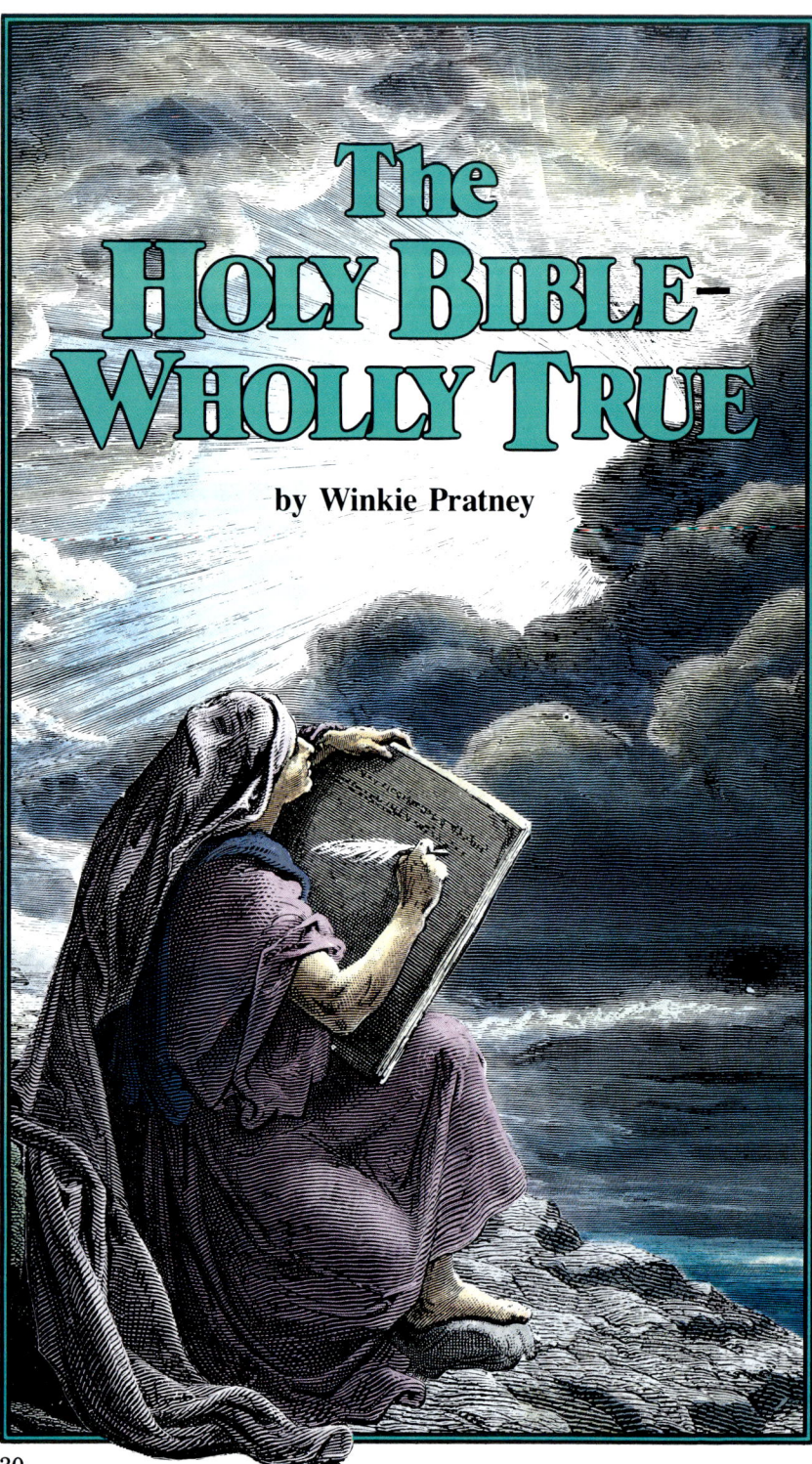

The Bible isn't like any other book that's ever been written. The claims of the Bible are unlike any other book–it's **not** a human book! God called His Word *living*. But unless you have a rock-solid commitment to truth, the Bible won't change your life–it will only be so many words in a sea of words.

Many of the Eastern thought forms use Scripture. They use it to capture people's hearts. That's because the Bible is so powerful you can't ignore it. God has built life into His Word, and all of the strong cults rip it off. They steal bites out of the Bible and use it. They use the truth of it to try to justify the lies they tell. Just the fact that pieces taken out of context are powerful enough to draw men's hearts should tell you what the **whole** Word, used under the inspiration of the Holy Spirit, can do!

Some Credentials

Here are some facts that will be valuable for anyone with an open heart. Now, you don't have to throw your mind away in order to believe these facts, but if you don't **want** to believe, **nothing** will convince you. Mark Twain said, "It's not the things I *don't* understand in the Bible that bother me, it's the things I *do* understand!" This accurate insight exposes the *real* reason most people are afraid to study the Scriptures. They're afraid they might meet the Author, and they know they're not ready to do that...

So what are this book's credentials? I could say to you, "I've just written a book and it's the Word of God. It's a great book...took me a whole year to write it." And you would have every right to say, **"Prove it!"** In the various world religions, there are 30 or 40 books, each one claiming to be a superior revelation. Jesus said, *"Heaven and earth will pass away, but My words shall not pass away." (Matt. 24:35)*

The Bible doesn't attempt to defend its inspiration. You won't find any verse that says, "This book is really true, so you **better** believe it!!" But here is an interesting thing: Genesis opens with the words, *"God said"* nine times in the first chapter. The statement, *"Thus says the Lord"* appears 23 times in the last Old Testament book–

Malachi. So you have *"God says"* from Genesis to Malachi. *"The Lord spoke"* appears 560 times in the first five books of the Bible and at least 3800 times in the whole of the Old Testament! Isaiah claims at least 40 times that his message came directly from the Lord; Ezekiel, 60 times; and Jeremiah, **100 times!** And the Lord Jesus quoted from at least 24 different Old Testament books–that's right, He just **quoted.**

In the mid-1700s Voltaire, one of the most influential writers of his day, held a copy of the Bible in his hand and stated that within 100 years from his time, Christianity would be swept from existence and would pass into history. What's hilarious is that merely 50 years after his death, the Geneva Bible Society used his house *and* press to print and distribute stacks of Bibles! They even made his house their headquarters! God has an incredible sense of humor!

Could *You* Write The Bible?

Say you were going to write a book, and this was how you had to write it: For a start find 40 different writers–**totally different** writers. Get some who are highly educated, even doctors–then get some farmers. Go dig a guy off a ranch somewhere and say, "I'd like you to help me write a book." Then find some fishermen. Go down to the wharf and find a couple of guys from San Francisco and say, "Hey! listen, help me write a book." And they say, "Sure, fine... we'll help you." And then you get all of them to write on the following things: religion, poetry, ethics, science, philosophy, the creation of the universe and where it's going–and ask them to throw in a few things about where they think it will all end.

Next, you need to collect all that information, and then... oh, by the way, you have to separate these people so they can't communicate by phone or telegraph... only possibly word of mouth, passed down over the years. Ah yes, years... you collect all this stuff over about one and a half thousand years, and compile the whole thing in one book. What would you have? I know what you'd have–you'd have the most

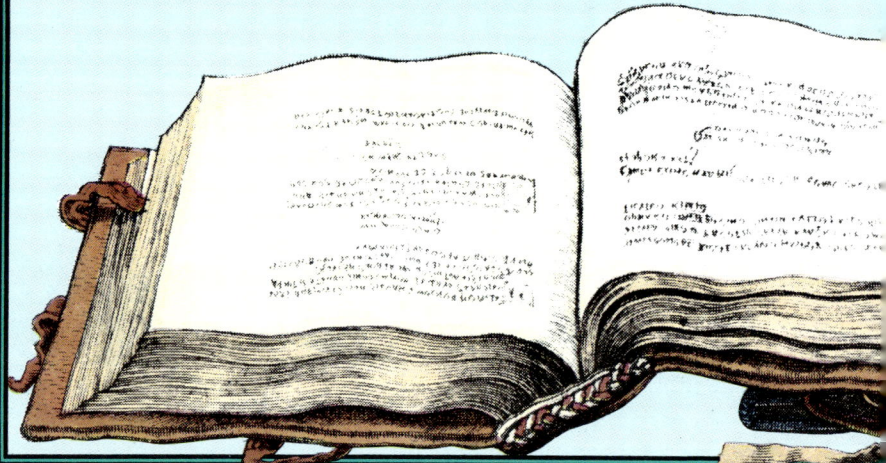

motley junk you've ever seen in your life, with people totally contradicting each other! I suggest you take a biology textbook from 60 years ago, and compare it with one today. And that's just **60 years!** But that's **not** what you have when you read your Bible. The more you read this book, the more you see the incredible unity of it. Because the more you get into it, the more incredibly detailed it is, and you find there are not 40 people who wrote it, but One Person.

The Bible: Your Science Book

The Bible is scientifically accurate. The God of the Bible is the God who created the universe. True science and Scripture will *always* agree–they both have the same Author! No statement in the Scriptures is scientifically incorrect. Science can tabulate the "what," analyze the "how," and probe for the "why," but it can't tell us the *"where from,"* nor the reason for which the universe exists. It can't say who you are or why you are here. It can tell us what we're *able* to do, but not what we *ought* to do.

At the same time the Bible was written, people thought the world was flat and held up by three elephants. **Big** elephants. Someone asked, "What holds the world up?" Another said, "Three elephants." Then someone ventured to ask, "And what holds up the elephants??" Someone answered, "A big tortoise." And so the early sciences grew.

Now, listen to what God said. Remember, this wasn't written in the last hundred years, or even the last thousand. This comes from over 2500 years ago... *"Have you not known? Have you not heard?...Have you not understood from the foundations of the earth? It is He that sits upon the **circle of the earth.**"* (Isaiah 40:21-22)

The word "circle" is the word "sphere" in Hebrew. Also, *"He stretches out the north over empty space, and hangs the earth on nothing." (Job 26:7)* Well, so much for elephants!

There are many other astounding scientific facts in Scripture, presented centuries before it became part of man's "knowledge."

Argument Melts Down

"But the day of the Lord will come like a thief, in which the heavens will pass away with a roar and the elements will be destroyed with intense heat, and the earth and its works will be burned up." (II Peter 3:10) This very verse was used nearly a century ago to prove that the Bible couldn't have been divinely inspired because, "How could there be a fire big enough to burn the whole world? Silly fisherman!" It took over two more generations for science to catch up to what God had spoken through Peter, that an atomic reaction could actually melt the basic building blocks of matter itself. God was prophesying how the world would end.

In fact, two verses later we find these words, *"...the heavens will be destroyed by burning, and the elements will melt with intense heat!" (vs. 12)* Do you know what the word "destroy" is? It's a Greek word that literally means to untie. That's an atomic physics statement from a 1st Century fisherman! These and countless other examples show us how the Lord has hidden unsurpassed knowledge and wisdom in His Word.

Lots Of Lucky Guesses?

If there's one thing the Bible dares to do, that *no other book in the world does,* it's to accurately predict the future. God can arrange the situations and circumstances of history to bring about patterns laid down before the foundation of the world. The outline of many of these patterns is revealed in the Bible.

There are about 3,856 verses directly or indirectly concerned with prophecy in Scripture–about one verse in six tells of future events! God's challenge to the world is *"Prove Me now–I am the **Lord**...I will speak, and the word that I speak shall come to pass." (See Jer. 28:9; Ezek. 12:25, 24:14)* Buddhists, Confucianists, and Muslims have their own sacred writings, but in them the element of prophecy is obviously absent. The destruction of Tyre, the invasion of Jerusalem, the fall of Babylon and Rome–each were accurately predicted in the Bible and fulfilled to the smallest details.

In the brief life of Jesus alone we see over **300 fulfilled prophecies.** The odds that these would *all* coincide by accident in *one* person are laughable. By the laws of chance, the *conservative* odds of even just 48 of those prophecies being fulfilled by one man are one in 10^{157}. (That's 1 followed by 157 zeros!!!) Let me try to give you an idea of how immense this number is.

We'll take a very small object, let's say an electron. (Electrons are so small that if you lined them up, it would take 2½ **quadrillion** of them to equal one inch.) Now let's go back to our figure of 10^{157}. If you tried to put this many electrons into a big pile, it would be 10,000,000,000 times larger than the universe as we know it–which scientists calculate to be 6,000,000,000 light-years across. (A light-year is the distance that light will travel **in one year,** moving at the speed of 186,000 miles **per second.**

Now, take just **one** electron out and color it red. Stir it back into this pile for a hundred thousand years with all the others. Then blindfold a man and send him in to pick it out–**first time!** Impossible? These would be the same odds that one man would live and die according to *only 48* of the prophecies about the Messiah, if it were only an accident. The Scriptures specifically predict events and happenings that are as modern as tomorrow's news release.

No Other Conclusion

You can put any test you like on this book and nothing is even in the same category, not even in the same class. It's not just a book–it is God who has spoken in history, and that's why He says that His Word is *"living and active and sharper than any two-edged sword"! (Heb. 4:12)* Only the 66 books of the Scriptures bear this divine seal. No other work of man in **any** language even faintly resembles the intricate structure and design of the Bible. The fact remains–only an **infinite mind** could have devised this **Book of books.**

The Bible is a book with a universal message for all men. It's the only volume that a child and scholar may find equal delight in. Its simple, life-related principles can work in any country, transcending barriers of culture and race to bring peace, love, joy, and forgiveness. Only the Bible can make bad men good **inside,** transforming the rebel into the saint.

The greatest proof of the Bible is the difference its message can make in **your** life. If you haven't done so–will you ask God the Holy Spirit to reveal the truth of His power to your heart through its pages? But pray *honestly,* "God, I don't know if this is Your Word or not, but if it is and You can help me, please show Yourself to me as I read," and God will meet you in a living demonstration of His reality.

This article is available in tract form as LD#5.

In Search of Mr. Right

by Keith Green

This is not meant to be a whole treatise on the subjects of dating and marriage. There have been more scholarly and complete articles, even whole books, written on these subjects. My purpose here is to point out some principles of the Word of God that are being neglected by the Church today.

*My desire is to tackle some future marital problems **before** they even happen. I would like to talk to those of you who are single. I want to talk you out of the idea that, "Someday, you are probably going to get married!"*

Single Christians

Today the "single Christian" is looked upon as some sort of an oddball. They are beseiged with such questions as, "Oh, you're **still** single?" or… "Are you married **yet?**" Out of the muck and mire of this "predestined-for-marriage" consciousness, comes a unique American phenomenon—it's called "the singles' group"—where anxious (sometimes even lusty) singles can "fellowship" in such spirit-led functions as "car-wash fund-raising drives" and "spaghetti-dinner and disco-parties!" Under the pretense of "meeting the single person's special needs," I have often seen singles' fellowships serve as nothing more than what a singles' bar does in the world. I'm not saying that all singles' groups are like this—or even most—I am just stating what the usual underlying reason is for their existence—to bring about the meeting and ultimate marriage of the single population of the Church.

Where Is Dating In The Bible?

The closest thing to dating in the Bible is found in the book of Ruth, chaper three. Ruth is told by her mother-in-law, Naomi, to seek Boaz as her husband. She gives her instructions, gets her all dolled-up, and

sends her off to seek her mate. In fact, dating (in the Bible) is really courting—seeking a husband or a wife. Today, dating by Christians has taken on all the aspects of the world. Many believers go in and out of relationships with as little thought or prayer as they would in choosing a restaurant for dinner.

We were never meant to try on people like shoes or clothes. Seeking a mate is to be done with much prayer and confirmation, and **only after** God's clear direction that we're called to marriage. But, since almost every church has a singles' group, and every single is unconsciously led to think he's weird if he doesn't get married—the "pressure is on" to date ... many get deeply hurt ... and many marriages occur that were never meant to be. I believe **this** is the cause of many unhappy and broken Christian homes.

Two Reasons For Marriage

According to the Bible, I can see two **basic reasons why God calls people** to marriage. The first is found in I Corinthians 7:9. This verse talks about those who have very little self-control—*"Let them marry,*

for it is better to marry than to burn." To someone like this, singleness is not only an emotional problem, but a physical trial as well. And God calls such a person to marry as His divinely ordained way of directing these feelings. (Don't get me wrong. I don't believe that marriage is an "out," or an escape for a Christian that finds himself with these hard-to-control feelings. I'm just saying with Paul that *"Each man has his own gift from God," (vs. 7)*–meaning that both marriage **and** singleness are gifts.)

The other reason that God calls two people to marry is for **His** sake. In other words, they can serve God better together than they can separately. Consider the example of such godly couples as Abraham and Sarah, Mary and Joseph, Zacharias and Elizabeth. Can you imagine how different their lives (not to mention history) would have been, if they would have remained single? You see, God directs people to marry mainly so they can please **Him** more–**and as they do, their own joy will be full.** But today, many are marrying out of selfishness, **not** obedience. They consider it their human right, something that eventually will happen, rather than a partnership for ministry, specially called for by the will of God.

A Close Look At
I Corinthians 7

My first impressions of I Corintians 7 were not too good. Paul's position on marriage seemed unromantic at best. When I first read this chapter, I thought that Paul had let his own private opinions creep into the

Word. I felt, "Well, Paul wants everyone to be just like him!" The Lord has since given me quite a respect for the Word of God; and as I studied this chapter, I started to see what Paul was saying. I realized that if God allowed Paul's views on marriage to get into His Word, then they were **God's** views on marriage.

Paul's Teaching

Paul says that if you marry, you *"will have trouble in this life, and I'm trying to spare you." (I Cor. 7:28)* By "trouble," Paul means in serving Jesus. He says *"I want you to be free from concern. One who is unmarried is concerned about the things of the Lord, how he may please the Lord." (vs. 32)* Paul is sharing the Lord's heart. Jesus desires His people to love Him with "**all** their heart." Paul doesn't mean that married people can't love and serve Jesus, he is just pointing out that it's usually only

partial devotion. *"But the one who is married is concerned about the things of the world, how he may please his wife, and his interests are divided." (vs. 33)* Paul seems to be of the opinion (which, by being in the Word, is **God's** opinion) that only a single person can give what he calls *"undistracted devotion to the Lord." (vs. 35)* Paul is in no way saying that marriage is wrong; for he says that the one who marries *"does well,"* but the one who remains unmarried *"does better." (vs. 38)*

Conclusion

My whole reason for writing this article is to point out that one of the highest callings a man or a woman of God can have is being married to Jesus and remaining single "unto the Lord." I have met a few people who have realized this, and are some of the happiest Christians I know. They don't have to bother wasting time dating or

looking for "the right one"—they've found Him! The only problem they have to deal with now is the opinion of the Church. They are looked upon as strange or even "latent homosexuals," and well-meaning friends are constantly putting pressure on them to date or trying to set them up. This is a tragedy, when God is looking for more full-time workers...people with complete "undistracted devotion." Even if the world looks upon a woman who remains unmarried as an "old maid," Jesus looks upon a godly one as a "young bride." Look, for example, at the witness and ministry of Corrie Ten Boom. Though she was never married on earth, she proved she had a Husband in Heaven.

Lastly, if you don't feel God is calling you to singleness, be patient. Don't "play the field" looking for the right one. But, *"Fix your eyes on Jesus, the author and finisher of our faith" (Heb. 12:2),* and He *"shall supply all your needs according to His riches in glory." (Phil. 4:19)*

Your wise Father says, *"Be still, and know that I am God." (Psalm 46:10)* Amen!

This article is available in tract form as LD#6.

GOSSIP!

by Melody Green

I think the main reason that God is letting me share a little bit with you about the problem of gossip is because I'm no stranger to it. I have not only listened to gossip...I've also spread it and been the victim of it...and let me say it's all equally as painful to the Lord.

When I told people things I shouldn't have, I usually justified it by saying, "We really need to pray for so and so, they're having this terrible problem..." But we usually didn't pray, we just "talked it through." Then, of course, it was great fun to listen to the latest tale about someone or some ministry. I again justified it by thinking, "Well, it's important to keep up with what's happening. Besides, I need to know how to pray..." which again, I hardly ever did. (In fact, if I had spent as much time on my knees talking to God as I did on my couch talking to friends, I would really be quite the woman of God by now.)

My awareness of the problem started early in our ministry when we first began our community. I realized that with so many close relationships forming, we had become a real breeding ground for gossip to grow and spread...infecting all who participated. I became very concerned about it, looked up a lot of Scriptures, and gave

a few very convicting Bible studies for the girls. But God didn't really open my eyes until I found myself and our ministry on the receiving end of some rumors and exaggerations that wounded me deeply. I was so stumbled! I started becoming very bitter, and wondered how people could **say** such things. But I think I was even more hurt over those who **listened** and just accepted the information as confirmed fact. I begged God to please make them stop! Well, it didn't take long for Jesus to take action, and boy, did He show me sin—but guess whose it was? Mine! He reminded me of all the times I had received and then spread rumors, not only about people I knew, but about many I'd never even met. Jesus showed me how I had planted poison in the body of Christ and done real damage to many reputations. At the time I didn't think I was hurting anyone...but now I knew differently. Jesus allowed me to see how it felt, and it was just awful. He also showed me that He was more grieved than anyone when His people were so unloving to each other. To say that I have totally conquered this sin through this experience would not be true. I am still tested almost daily, and sometimes I fail; but I can honestly say that there is a day-and-night difference in my life, and that I know Jesus is faithful to complete the work He started in me.

WHAT IS GOSSIP?

When we become Christians, we give up the "biggies" like lying, stealing, drinking, cheating, drugs, and fornication. We start spending time with our new-found friends, talking about the Lord, our lives, and what's going on around us in general. Harmless stuff...or so we think. But let's take a closer look. Many times these conversations are full of judgments, rumors, and hearsay...all tucked neatly away behind a concerned Christian smile.

Did you know the Bible talks a lot about gossip? It's not just a "little sin" as some of us like to rationalize. It says, *"The Lord hates a froward* [or perverted] *mouth" (Proverbs 8:13)*...and He commands us, *"You shall not go about as a talebearer among your* people." *(Lev. 19:16)* God also says, *"They go around from house to house; and not merely idle, but also gossips and busybodies, talking about things not proper to mention"* *(I Tim. 5:13),* and in Psalm 101:5 He says, *"Whoever secretly slanders his neighbor, him I will **destroy.**"* God also has the notion that those who gossip do not acknowledge Him and are given over to a depraved mind. He lists gossips together with those who are untrustworthy, unloving, unrighteous, full of envy, strife, and deceit, murderers and haters of God. Then He says those who practice such things know they are worthy of death, but it doesn't stop them from participating or encouraging others to do the same. *(Rom. 1:28-32)* These are pretty heavy Scriptures, and I cringe to think of their implications.

By the way, something doesn't have to be a lie to make it gossip. Many of us think, "Well, **it's true**...so I can tell anyone I want to." Not so! Telling the truth for the wrong motive can be even more destructive than telling a lie. In fact, here's a definition of gossip that's quite revealing: **Sharing anything about someone, when the act of sharing it is not part of the solution to that person's problem.**

MATTHEW 18

"And if your brother sins, go and reprove him in private; if he listens to you, you have won your brother. But if he does not listen to you, take one or two more with you, so that by the mouth of two or three witnesses every fact may be confirmed." (Matt. 18:15) I think the reason God put this in the Bible is because He knows how weak we are, and He knew we needed some real solid guidelines.

If we are offended or see someone in sin, we are to go to that person and **no one else!** Let me give you a few examples: If someone is in sin, what good does it do to go and tell someone else? What can **they** do about it? If we start running around talking about this "awful thing" we see in someone's life, and asking others if "they see it too," then we are causing them to form judgments and ultimately to be stumbled. Instead, let's restore that brother or sister to fellowship with God. You may be showing them a real blind spot that the Lord wants desperately to deal with. If he does not listen, then there are further steps to take. Be prepared for this, although it usually doesn't get to that point. Believe me, I have done my greatest growing when someone has come to me in genuine love and concern over an inconsistency they see in my life. I am thankful that they love me enough to confront me with it and give me a chance to change. *"Brethren, even if a man is caught in any trespass, you who are spiritual, restore such a one in a spirit of gentleness; looking to yourselves, lest you too be tempted." (Gal. 6:1)*

"TAKING UP AN OFFENSE"

Sharing our hurts and bitternesses, and listening to others share theirs, is another area where we need to be very careful. If someone is rude to your best friend, and your friend shares their hurt with you, then you're probably going to "take up the offense." This means **you get hurt** too, maybe even angry at the person who caused your friend pain. Later, they might make up and all may be forgiven and forgotten. But there's only one problem... **you're still bitter!** And the next time you see the person who hurt your friend, you realize that **you** haven't forgiven him. Unless you go right away and clear things up, you may carry around a subtle bitterness that comes to remembrance every time you see him or hear his name. Why? Because God did not give you the same amount of grace to forgive as He gave your friend. **You** were not the one offended. God gives grace to the humble and the afflicted *(James 4:6),* and you were neither. You just "happened" to become involved in something you shouldn't have been told about in the first place. The strife that one small incident can cause can be far-reaching and long-lasting, depending on how many people hear about it. So you see, it is totally irresponsible to involve others in your hurts and judgments. As far as I can see, we have no right to go to anyone except God and the offender, unless we are really at a loss as to what we should do. And then we need to go for counseling, not to our "most favorite person to talk to."

THE DIFFERENCE BETWEEN COUNSELING AND GOSSIP

Much gossip and slander goes on under the guise of "getting counseling." There is nothing wrong with counseling if you are indeed talking to a **counselor.** A counselor is someone who is mature in the Lord, exhorts you to godliness and reconciliation, points out **your** sin in the situation, will not repeat the matter or be stumbled by it, and is seeking God's will first and foremost–not yours. (A person like this is usually in a leadership position in a church or fellowship.) I'm afraid this leaves out 95 percent of the people we usually run to with the latest problem. If we really need counseling, we should get it. But most of the time when we share with someone, we are not really seeking a solution. We just want a sympathetic ear to agree with our point of view.

It seems we don't care how much division we bring, as long as we get people on "our side." We are too selfish to worry about the damage we are causing those we tell or those we tell on. *"There are six things that the Lord hates, yes, seven which are an abomination to Him: haughty eyes, a lying tongue, and hands that shed innocent blood, a heart that devises wicked plans, feet that run rapidly to evil, a false witness who utters lies, and one who spreads strife among brothers." (Proverbs 6:16-19)*

JUST LISTENING

Many of us like to believe that "just listening" to gossip is not really as bad as spreading it. This is not so. God says, *"An evildoer listens to wicked lips and a liar pays attention to a destructive tongue." (Proverbs 17:4)* In I Samuel 24:9, David exhorts Saul, *"Why*

do you listen to the words of men saying, 'Behold, David seeks to harm you'?" Well, why **do** we listen? Why are we so ready to believe the worst? The Bible says, *"Love hopes all things." (I Cor. 13:7)* Why don't we gently but firmly say, "I'm sorry, but you're telling me something I really don't think I should be listening to. You need to take this to the Lord, and those involved...not me." A few exhortations like that will stop most gossips in their tracks. At least it will stop them from coming to you with their treachery, and maybe give them something else to think about besides other people's business. The Bible warns us not to associate with gossips. *"He who goes about as a slanderer reveals secrets, therefore do not associate with a gossip."* (Proverbs 20:19)

"A MARK OF MATURITY"

"And I say to you, that every careless word that men shall speak, they shall render account for it in the day of judgment." (Matt. 12:36)

With every word we speak we are making a choice. We are either choosing to bless God or grieve Him by rebelling against His Word. *"Let no unwholesome word proceed from your mouth, but only such a word as is good for edification according to the need of the moment, that it may give grace to those who hear." (Eph. 4:29)* Again, sometimes we do not take seriously enough God's command for us to have control over our tongue. This is one of the true marks of a mature man or woman of God. James says, *"If anyone thinks himself to be religious, and yet does not bridle his tongue but deceives his own heart, this man's religion is worthless." (James 1:26)* We all know that the heart is deceitful above all things *(Jer. 17:9)*, and so it may seem easy to rationalize our behavior... but look how high the price is. I get convicted just writing this! I certainly don't want my walk with the Lord to become worthless because I'm not mature enough to control the words that come out of my own mouth.

ONE FINAL THOUGHT

Gossip and slander are Satan's tools. He knows that if he can get us to divide and fight each other, we'll be far too busy to unite and fight him! We need to stop and think before we speak, and purpose in our hearts to never receive or repeat gossip again. We can do it by the grace of God and a determination to make the right choices. You pray about it. There may be people you need to repent to and bitternesses that need to be confessed and healed. Go to God first and get your heart right. He will give you the power to do the rest. *"Let us rejoice and be glad, and give the glory to Him, for the marriage of the Lamb has come and His bride has made herself ready." (Rev. 19:7)* It may seem like a monumental task... but God is calling a holy bride and we need to do everything we possibly can to "make ourselves ready"!

This article is available in tract form as LD#7.

TOTAL COMMITMENT

COMMUNISM VS. CHRISTIANITY

by Keith Green

"These men who have upset the world have come here also!" (Acts 17:6)

When Jesus gave His final instructions to the disciples before He ascended to the Father, He made it clear that they had a job of mammoth proportions to accomplish. *"And you shall be my witnesses both in Jerusalem, and in all Judea and Samaria, and even to the remotest part of the earth." (Acts 1:8)* This was the first time the disciples were instructed to look beyond their little country. In fact, Jesus had commanded them on previous missionary journeys to *"not go in the way of the Gentiles* [people who were not Jews] *and do not enter any city of the Samaritans; but rather go to the lost sheep of the house of Israel." (Matt. 10:5-6)* All of a sudden their eyes were opened, their vision expanded. All prejudice, bigotry, nationalism, and cultural bounds had to snap at Jesus' words *"Samaria and the remotest part of the earth."* No self-respecting Jew would even step on Samaritan soil, let alone **speak** to one;

and *"the remotest part of the earth"* would mean preaching to the heathen Gentiles! "Surely," they must have thought, "He means we should preach to the scattered Jews in foreign lands!" It's almost funny, as you continue reading Acts, how one by one, God proved to each disciple that He meant just what He said... *"I have placed you as a light for the Gentiles, that you should bring salvation to the ends of the earth."* (Acts 13:47)

A Great Void

There's a great emptiness in the world, and in the hearts of all men. This is the void that Jesus is meant to fill, in every nation as King, and in every man's heart as Lord. If the void remains, then men and nations will seek desperately to fill it with something else that will fulfill them. Satan is always willing and ready to provide an alternate, a counterfeit peace. The greatest danger about a counterfeit is that it looks just like the real thing, but has no value whatsoever.

Christianity swept the world in the first century A.D. It is the force of truth that was meant to answer and quench the thirst in all mankind for a reason and purpose to life. The thing that made the good news so believable to those who heard it at that time was not the message itself... but the *messengers!* Charles Finney once wrote "Christians themselves are the greatest reason for accepting Christ. But they are also the greatest excuse for rejecting Him."

What made the early Christians so convincing? What was it that made 3,000 people convert in **one day** and be baptized in a city hostile to the Gospel... a city that had murdered their Lord only weeks before? *(Acts 2:41)* It was their **commitment.** It was their lifestyle. It was the Holy Spirit breathing the life and image of Jesus into a people who literally had left **everything,** were willing to suffer **anything,** and were ready to give **all** they had (possessions, time, even blood) to **anyone** to prove that their message was the **only** truth that could save men's souls from eternal suffering!

Communists' Zeal Surpasses Christians'

It is this same commitment, this same willingness to leave everything and anyone for the "cause," the "people," and the "Party"–this same desire to "save" the whole world from suffering injustice and social evils, that is causing individuals, nations, and even whole continents to turn to a godless counterfeit–one that promises to unite the world for the common good and establish a "world order" that will end all oppression of the "common people." Again, it isn't really the message, but the *messengers* who are convincing the masses. And it puts us as Christians to shame!

Many Christians felt strongly rebuked when Billy Graham first read the following letter, written by an American college student who had been converted to Communism in Mexico. The purpose of the letter was to explain to his fiancé why he must break off their engagement:

"We Communists have a high casualty rate. We're the ones who get slandered and ridiculed and fired from our jobs and in every other way made as uncomfortable as possible. A certain percentage of us get killed or imprisoned. We live in virtual poverty. We turn back to the Party every penny we make above what is absolutely necessary to keep us alive. We Communists don't have time or the money for many movies or concerts or T-bone steaks or decent homes and new cars. We've been described as fanatics. We **are** fanatics! Our lives are dominated by one great overshadowing factor–the struggle for World Communism.

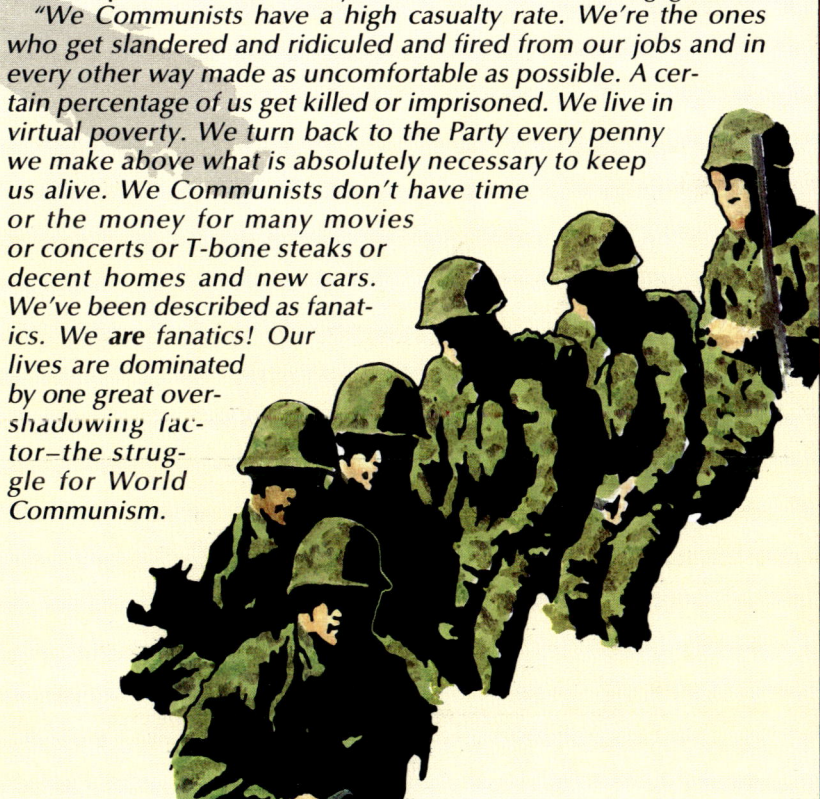

"We Communists have a philosophy of life which no amount of money could buy. We have a cause to fight for, a definite purpose in life. We subordinate our petty, personal selves into a great movement of humanity. And if our personal lives seem hard or our egos appear to suffer through subordination to the Party, then we are adequately compensated by the fact that each of us in his small way is contributing to something new and true and better for mankind. The Communist cause is my life, my business, my religion, my hobby, my sweetheart, my wife and mistress, my bread and meat. I work at it in the daytime and dream of it at night. Its hold on me grows, not lessens, as time goes on. Therefore, I cannot carry on a friendship, a love affair, or even a conversation without relating it to this force which both guides and drives my life. I evaluate people, books, ideas, and actions according to how they affect the Communist cause and by their attitude toward it. I've already been in jail because of my ideas, and if necessary, I'm ready to go before a firing squad."

If Communists can be as devoted as this, how much more should Christians pour themselves out in intense devotion for their glorious Lord!

The World Belongs To The Disciplined

One of the most alarming disclosures coming out of the communist world is that of the rugged training and discipline they are putting their youth through. In contrast, there has never before been such a mass pilgrimage to the altar of leisure in our country. At the end of the rainbow for every American is relaxation and recreation. The Western world loves to play. Americans average over eight hours a day of television per household!

In the 1920s, inter-collegiate debating drew large crowds. Now the debates are held in side rooms while crowds cheer at the basketball game. It takes discipline to learn a new art, or science, or skill; it takes no discipline to watch football or a wrestling match. The point must be made that the shift of excited, popular interest from debates to sports is a sign of cultural decline. As someone once said, "It is either discipline or decadence."

And the Church has not escaped. Never has there been such an interest in sports among "the saints." I've heard much more talk and excitement about the national ratings of college teams among Christians in churches and Sunday schools, than about how to conquer the land for God. As an almost unbelievable example, I recently heard about one large church in Texas who during the Superbowl (when the Dallas Cowboys were playing) feared that the Sunday evening service (not to mention the offering) would be poorly attended. So the pastor and elders came up with a wonderful idea! They brought a large-screen video projection system into the sanctuary and proceeded to "entertain" the parishoners with a nice, American, Christian display of "knockin' and hittin' 'em for Christ!" This might be a blatant example, but the spirit of "fun in the Son" is threatening to destroy what little hope we have left to avoid judgment, by having true cross-embracing revival. *"For it is time for judgment to begin with the household of God...and if it is with difficulty that the righteous is saved, what will become of the godless man and the sinner?" (I Peter 4:17-18)*

Communist Lenin once said: "With a handful of dedicated people who will give me their lives, I will control the world." This must have sounded like quite a rash statement to those who first heard it, but it did not prove an empty boast. In 1903, this one man, with 17 followers, began his attack on the world. By 1918, the number had increased to 40,000, and with that 40,000 he gained control of the 160 million people of Russia. And the movement has gone on and now controls over one-third of the population of the world. With this in mind, consider the warning of the American President, Theodore Roosevelt:

"The things that will destroy America are prosperity at any price, peace at any price, safety first instead of duty first, the love of soft living, and the get-rich-quick theory of life."

The Army Of God
(Eph. 6:10-18)

What's needed today is an army. A truly Christian force, armed to the teeth with love and the power of God, completely trusting God to meet their needs and lead them into battle and victory!

I have heard reports from missionaries visiting home that there is much division and contention between missionaries on the field. The same doctrinal differences that plague our denominations at home are bringing a bad name to our Lord in other lands. *"A house divided against itself will not be able to stand." (Mark 3:25)* What are we to do? A world starving for the truth will not wait for us to get our act together...it will pass us by and drink up the newest, nicest sounding philosophy or religion to come along. Mormons, Jehovah's Witnesses, and Moonies are not only making great gains in our country, but also in foreign fields as well. They seem determined, committed, and willing to sacrifice all the usual comforts to spread their "good tidings." Christians, by comparison, are lazy, apathetic, and mesmerized by the same materialism that is choking the very life out of both our nation and the whole of Western civilization.

God has commanded the Church to *"Go into all the world and preach the Gospel to all creation"! (Mark 16:15)* If we were really doing our job and living the lives Jesus has commanded us, then the people around the world would have the truth of Jesus and **His** holy promises to compare with the Marxist pipe-dreams.

Is Communism Really God's Worst Enemy?

"And you shall call His name Jesus, for He will save His people from their sins."   *(Matt. 1:21)*

I want to be extremely careful not to be misunderstood. I believe that Communism is a counterfeit that has its origins in hell. But all the pulpit-pounding and the sermon-screaming we have heard in recent years against the evils of Communism needs to be examined. Is God really as concerned about systems as much as He is about **sin?** Do you really believe in your heart that Communism breeds more sin than "the American dream"? Ask yourself this: do you think there is more adultery in Russia than in America? More fornication? More greed and lust? More stealing and murder? How about pornography and drugs, corruption and deceit? See what I mean? God is tremendously hurt, pained to His heart by the state of sin that the Western world has now accepted and pronounced **"socially normal."**

Of course, there cannot be a "Christian Communist." You cannot condone a system that denies the existence of God and share God's righteousness at the same time. But which is worse? Someone who denies that God exists, and acts accordingly? Or someone who believes there's a God and still lives a life that totally denies Him? *"For to whom much is given, much is required" (Luke 12:48),* and *"He who knows to do good, and does not do it, to him it is sin." (James 4:17)* **What do you really think grieves God more? A land that says "religion is the opiate of the masses," or a land whose money says "In God We Trust," yet is full of sin, violence, and immorality?**

Ezekiel 16

Remember, God's grief with His people Israel was far greater than His disappointment over Egypt or Babylon. He expected a land full of witchcraft and idolatry to act wickedly and perversely; but His heart was broken when He saw His bride, Israel, committing adulteries and harlotries with the heathen and their idols. Remember, God's enemy is sin, and the current revival which is being reported in the Church behind the Iron Curtain only shows that a godless system cannot keep God from moving among His own people. As long as the Church of the Western world flirts with the god of materialism, they will see no great move of God among them.

In a land of freedom, where believers have never had a greater opportunity to see the Lord's glory descend upon a nation, the cry of "Depart from Me, I never knew you!" awaits an unfaithful bride who loved her pleasures and programs, who delighted in her fundraising and building, more than the holy pleasure of delivering America and its spoil to a mighty God, through a true revival of prayer, repentance, and holiness. (See *Matt. 25:14-30*.)

The persecuted Church has little choice but to endure their tribulations to the end. *(Matt. 24:14)* But the fat, obnoxiously wealthy Church of our land "who has need of nothing" will be horrified when they see their temples were built of wood, hay, and stubble *(I Cor. 3:12-14),* and their gold, silver, and jewels (men's precious souls and the restored honor of God) were left lying on the ground, ignored, never having been put into the treasury of the Lord.

"So because you are lukewarm, and neither hot nor cold, I will spit you out of my mouth. Because you say 'I am rich, and have become wealthy, and have need of nothing' and you do not know that you are wretched and miserable and poor and blind and naked..." (Rev. 3:16-17)

We are in grave danger of being judged as the Church in Laodicea. Remember, there are two runners in the race–Revival and Judgment. Let us get on our knees and win!

This article is available in tract form as LD#8.

Do You Feel Like Giving Up?

by David Wilkerson

A growing number of ministers have been telling of their concern for those in their flock who are simply giving up. Today, more and more Christians are at the breaking point. None of the talk about giving up has to do with the Lord. Few Christians would even dare entertain thoughts of quitting on their love for Jesus. Most despairing Christians think only of giving up on themselves. You hear it so often now, "I can't go on anymore. I just can't make it. It's totally hopeless! Why try?"

I hear some ministers today who continually preach only a positive message. To hear them tell it, every Christian is receiving miracles—everybody is getting instant answers to prayer—everybody is feeling good, living good, and the whole world is bright and rosy. I really wish all those good and healthy things for God's people, but that's not the way things are for a great number of very honest and sincere Christians. How sad to hear such shallow theology being pushed from pulpits today. It's an insult to a lowly Jesus who became poor, who died a failure in the eyes of the world. It is this kind of materialistic preaching that has so ill-prepared an entire generation of Christians to endure any kind of pain. They have not learned to be content with such things as they have—to be abased and not always abounding. Serving God becomes a kind of Olympic race in which everyone must strive for gold medals.

No wonder our young people give up in defeat. They can't live up to the image created by the religion of a happy-go-lucky, rich, successful, always positive-thinking Christian. Their world is not that idealistic. They look in a mirror reflecting a face covered with ugly pimples. They live with heartbreaks, hour-by-hour crises, and horrible family problems. They look into the uncertain future, frightened and worried.

Positive thinking won't make their problems go away. Confessing that these problems don't really exist doesn't change a thing. These "apostles of the positive" should not exclude the Gethsemane experiences of life. The cup of pain, the hour of isolation, and the night of confusion were all part of the Master's lifestyle. Our great achievements, our successes, ought to take place at Gethsemane, not Fort Knox!

The sawdust trail for many has become the gold dust trail. The Bible has become a catalog, with unlimited order blanks for life's goodies. Anything having to do with Job-like pain and suffering is considered negative. God **is** good and one should always think on good and honest reports—but pain, poverty, and suffering have befallen some of the saintliest of God's people—just like righteous Job.

MARRIAGE

What do you say to that wife whose home is breaking up and she seems powerless to stop it? She's been advised by her friends, counseled by her pastor, and has been exhorted over and over again to "stay on your knees and believe God for a miracle." So she fasts, and she prays.

She bends over backwards, to the point of crawling on her knees to her husband. She exercises faith with every ability she possesses. But in spite of all her honest efforts, he grows hard and bitter, demanding a divorce.

Not all marriages are healed through prayer or good intentions. It takes two to make a marriage work, and even though prayer may bring down the power of Holy Ghost conviction upon a straying mate, that mate can resist all God's efforts and abort the solution.

Some may be wondering why I've spent so much time lately talking about marriage, divorce, and the home. The reason is simple enough. In my crusades, I talk to so many kids on the brink of suicide. An overwhelming majority tell me their depression stems from trouble at home. Their parents are having trouble, or they have already gotten a divorce.

Multitudes of husbands and wives are giving up on their marriages. A successful marriage counselor took me to lunch, and before the entree was served, he confessed his own marriage had been in jeopardy. "You just can't take any good marriage for granted anymore," he said. "I'm convinced Satan is determined to break up my marriage–and every good Christian marriage. It's a well-planned attack on the best of marriages. If Satan can get the strongest, most admired marriages broken up–then weaker ones will be tempted to quit struggling and give up."

The secret struggles in the Christian's personal life are just as critical. The inner battles of the average Christian today are staggering in intensity and proportion. Multitudes are involved in situations too hard to comprehend.

Paul said, *"For indeed while we are in this tent, we groan, being burdened."* *(II Cor. 5:4)* I doubt we could even count the great numbers of Christians who groan in secret because of the burdens they carry. Paul also talked about *"...affliction which came to us...we were burdened excessively, beyond our strength, so that we despaired even of life."* *(II Cor. 1:8)*

If you pulled back the facade from every great preacher and every admired personality, you would find moments of deep depression. You would find the same infirmities you find in any normal Christian. We all have seasons of despair accompanied by feelings of failure. At times, we have all thought of quitting. We have all had thoughts of giving up.

DOUBT

Why do we feel like giving up at times? Mostly because we act like God had forsaken the earth. We don't doubt His existence or His reality. But our prayers seem to go unanswered. We cry out for His help in such desperation, and He seems not to hear. We struggle along, making one mistake after another. We make promises to do better, we get into the Bible, we cry and pray, and stay busy helping others and doing good. But we are so often left with an empty,

> ...when everything seems to be coming apart, a voice deep within cries out, "Walk away from it all...Pack it in! Escape! Why put up with it? Run away...you don't have to take it. Do something drastic!"

unfulfilled sensation. The promises of God haunt us. We hold onto those promises–in what we believe is honest, childlike faith–but time after time we fail to receive what we ask for. In the hour of temptation–down we go!

Doubt creeps in and Satan whispers, "Nothing works. Faith in God doesn't produce results. In spite of your tears, prayers, and trust in God's Word–nothing really changes. Days, weeks, and even years go by, and your prayers, hopes, and dreams are still unanswered and unfulfilled. Quit! Give up!"

Every Christian on this planet reaches that crisis point at one time or another in life. And in that moment, when the walls seem to be caving in and the roof appears to be collapsing, when everything seems to be coming apart, a voice deep within cries out, "Walk away from it all...Pack it in! Escape! Why put up with it? Run away...you don't have to take it. Do something drastic!"

David, overwhelmed by the evil in his heart, cried out to God, "Awake, why do you sleep? Cast me not off...why do you hide? Why do you forget?" (Psalm 44:23-24)

Christian–does it amaze you that great men of old faced the same battles you and I face today? The Bible says, *"Beloved, do not be surprised at the fiery ordeal among you, which comes upon you for your testing, as though some strange thing were happening to you; but to the degree that you share the sufferings of Christ, keep on rejoicing, so that also at the revelation of His glory, you may rejoice with exultation."* (I Peter 4:12-13)

How can we learn to hold on and live one day at a time? You can begin by forgetting all short cuts and magic cures. The Christian doesn't need a supposed demon of despair cast out, as if his going would make life easier. Nor will God come down and do our living for us. The tempter will not be destroyed until that day God casts him into prison. Satan will always be here, deceiving, accusing, and trying to rob every believer of his faith.

The longer I live for Christ, the more difficult it is for me to accept easy, cure-all solutions. But in my own struggles, I've found great comfort and help in two wonderful absolutes.

The first absolute is: **God really loves me.** God is not in the business of condemning His children–failures or not. He yearns over us as a loving father, wanting only to lift us out of our weaknesses.

I caught a glimpse of that love recently while walking in the woods around our ranch. Suddenly, there on the ground just ahead flopped a crippled little bird. I stooped to pick it up. It was then a familiar Scripture came flashing through my mind. *"Are not two sparrows sold for a cent? And yet not one of them will fall to the ground apart from your Father." (Matt. 10:29)*

God is with us, even when we fall. He does not abandon us on our way down. Our Lord never gives up on any of us!

Have you also fallen? Do you relate to that crippled sparrow, flopping helplessly in the dust? Are you wounded, hurting, and feeling lost and lonely? Do you ever think to yourself, "How can God put up with someone like me? How can He still love me when I've failed Him so badly?"

Often, we can recognize His great love only when we have hit bottom. Don't panic. Deliverance will come. God answers us by showing His love. And when we have learned how weak we are and have learned to trust His love and forgiveness–He will stoop down and gently help us back to the nest.

The second absolute is: **It is my faith that pleases Him the most!** *"Without faith it is impossible to please Him." (Heb. 11:6)* God wants so much to be trusted. That trust He counts as righteousness. *(Rom. 4:3)*

What do I do when temptation rolls over me like a flood? When my inadequacies overwhelm me and I see the reality of my weaknesses? Give up? Quit? **Never!!** I bring to God all I've got left–**my faith in Him!** I may not understand why He seems to take such a long time to intervene, but I know He will. He will keep His word to me.

I am convinced Satan wants to rob me of only one thing–my faith. He really doesn't want my morals or good deeds or my dreams. He wants to destroy my faith and make me believe God has forsaken this earth.

A fall is never fatal to those who keep their faith intact. In spite of despair and pressures that bog the mind and sap the strength, I believe God. I believe He will *"keep you from stumbling, and to make you stand in the presence of His glory blameless with great joy." (Jude 24)*

Reprinted by permission from David Wilkerson Crusades; excerpted from Mr. Wilkerson's book, HAVE YOU FELT LIKE GIVING UP LATELY?, Fleming H. Revell, Publishers.

This article is available in tract form as LD#9.

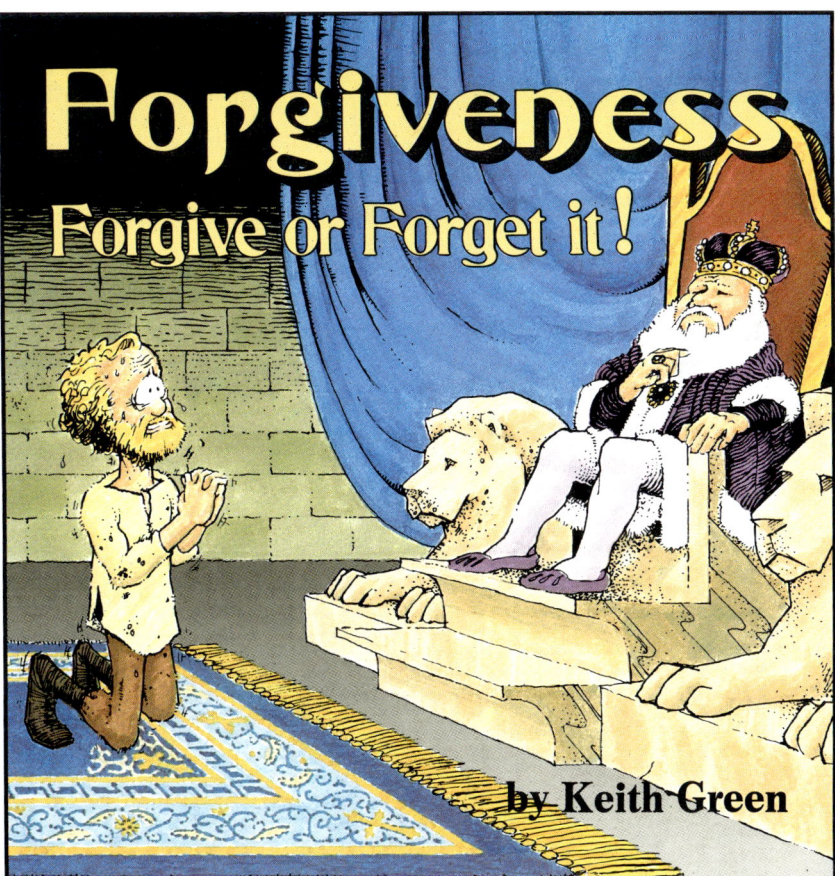

Forgiveness
Forgive or Forget it!

by Keith Green

There I was, seated in row 17, flying from Dallas to Los Angeles. I began to daydream, thinking about a friend of mine who had once treated me (what I thought was) unfairly in a financial dealing we'd had. As I turned the whole incident over in my mind, I remembered how I had originally consoled my bruised feelings by thinking to myself, "Well, that's okay, it's God's money anyway—God'll deal with him."

But flying on that jet through the night, I started to get an uneasy feeling inside, almost like vengeance. All of a sudden, it wasn't enough to put the whole thing in God's hands. I found myself thinking, "I sure hope the Lord brings that whole thing up when so-and-so stands before Him on the day of judgment."

And then, immediately, the Lord broke into my thoughts and said to me, "I'll be glad to bring it up—as long as you don't mind Me bringing up all the stupid things you've done!"

And the lord of that slave felt compassion and released him and forgave the debt. **MATTHEW 18:27**

I burst out laughing, right there in row 17. All at once I saw the sad hilarity of it all. I had never really forgiven him at all! Even with all my spiritualizing about the Judgment Seat, what I was really saying in my heart was, "He'll get his!" With one sentence, the Holy

A Root of Bitterness

Bitterness is a deadly thing—a real cancer. In Hebrews 12:15, it says, *"See to it that no one comes short of the grace of God; that no root of bitterness springing up causes trouble, and by it many be defiled."* According to this Scripture, bitterness cannot only hurt you, but it can spread like gangrene to others!

When you trace the life histories of men like Adolph Hitler, for example, you find that the great evils they engaged in later in life had their roots in deep-seated hurts from early in their childhood.

The mass-murders of the Charles Manson family stemmed from Manson's bitterness toward a record producer who didn't like his music. Outraged, Manson sent his "family" to the producer's house (not knowing that he had moved) and told them to kill anyone they found there. The appalling result was that all of

Spirit showed me gross unforgiveness in my heart—not only toward this brother, but toward many others who had hurt or offended me.

In an instant, I completely understood Jesus' words, *"If you do not forgive men, then your heavenly Father will not forgive your transgressions." (Matt. 6:15)*

The Unmerciful Slave

In the 18th chapter of Matthew (vs. 23-35), there's an incredible tale about this guy who owed the king a whole lot of money. *"And...there was brought to the king, one who owed him 10,000 talents"* (worth more than ten million dollars today). *"But since that slave did not have the means to repay, the king commanded him to be sold, along with his wife and children, with all that he had, and repayment to be made.*

*"The slave, therefore, falling down, prostrated himself before the king saying, 'Have patience with me, and I will repay you everything.' And the lord of that slave felt compassion and released him and **forgave him the debt.**"*

I think the most beautiful part of this story is the fact that the king forgave him the debt...*over ten million dollars worth!!* The main reason he canceled it was that, even though the slave

the victims ended up to be people who Manson had never even met, showing that when bitterness runs unchecked in our hearts, it can spill over into other people's lives, and *"by it, many be defiled."*

Cults can even develop when the leaders get bitter towards the main-line churches or denominations. The life stories of such men as Joseph Smith, Moses David (Children of God), John Todd, and Jim Jones all have one thing in common—their hatred for hypocrisy in the Church. But when their hatred turned to self-righteousness and intense resentment, it ruined the faith of many others—destroying whole families and even lives.

"For even though they knew God, they did not honor Him as God or give thanks; but they became futile in their speculations, and their foolish heart was darkened." (Rom. 1:21)

promised to eventually repay it, it was obviously an impossible amount of debt to ever work off in one's lifetime. Therefore, in his compassion, the king released him from it forever... or did he? Let's read on...

It says immediately in the very next verse (vs. 28), *"But that slave went out and found one of his fellow slaves who owed him a hundred denarii"* (a denarius was a day's wage–worth about 18 cents), *"and began to choke him, saying, 'Pay back what you owe!' So his fellow slave fell down and began begging him, saying, 'Have patience with me and I will repay you.' He was unwilling, however,* [to forgive him] *but threw him into prison until he should repay what was owed."*

Can you imagine the nerve? You've just been forgiven ten million dollars, and instead of going out and celebrating, you go and find some poor Joe who owes you 18 bucks! He's probably heard about your good fortune through the grapevine and thinks you're gonna invite him to the party, when all of a sudden you start strangling the daylights out of him. And when he asks you to be patient and give him a few days to repay you, you refuse and throw him in jail.

***B**ut that slave went out and found one of his fellow-slaves who owed him a hundred denarii; and he seized him and began to choke him, saying, "Pay back what you owe."*

MATTHEW 18:28

It might not sound like something you'd do, but I bet you've done it before. You see, if your sins have been forgiven by Jesus, you've had an incredible debt erased. Any bitterness or unforgiveness in your heart, after the total amnesty you've received, makes you as bad as the unmerciful slave. His unforgiveness was not only stupid, it also blew the whole deal with the king!

For... *"when his fellow slaves saw what had happened, they were deeply grieved and came and reported it to the king. Then, summoning the slave, the king said, 'You wicked slave! I forgave you all that debt because you begged me. Should you not also have had mercy on your fellow slave, even as I had mercy on you?'*

"And his lord, moved with anger, handed him over to the torturers until he should repay all that was owed him." Then Jesus adds the stinger... **"So shall My heavenly Father do to you, if each of you does not forgive his brother from your heart."**

And his lord, moved with anger, handed him over to the torturers until he should repay all that was owed him.   MATTHEW 18:34

Jesus certainly couldn't have made Himself any clearer about how upset our Father in heaven gets when, after forgiving us for an eternal debt of sin, we hold some little five-and-dime grudge against someone else "for whom Christ died."

I think it's also important to note that the debt the king had originally called off was now on again—**and in full!** This has many theological implications; but, since I'm no theologian (and the implicated subjects are perhaps some of the stickiest and most heavily debated in the Church today), I will safely say, "Whoever has ears, let him hear."

"If You Have Anything Against Your Brother..."

At any rate, all this goes to warn us that if we have **anything** in our hearts against **anyone,** we should go to that person quickly and get the whole thing totally cleared up. It might be our parents, or an employer, a teacher, or even a husband or wife. But in the light of this parable, we can see that however much anyone has hurt us, it doesn't even compare to the free gift of God's pardon for our sins. We must not put that forgiveness in danger of being made void by our refusal to "go and do likewise." For the Word of God says, *"If possible...be at peace with all men...for these things are from God, who reconciled us to Himself through Christ, and gave us* **the ministry of reconciliation.**" (Rom. 12:18; II Cor. 5:18)

This article is available in tract form as LD#12.

ZEAL-Love

Enoch had prophesied, saying, *"Behold, the Lord came with many thousands of His holy ones."* If Jesus had entered history like that, or had come on a dark night over Jerusalem in a blazing chariot of fire (like Elijah went up to heaven), then the clamoring crowds would have accepted and adored Him. But as the poet once said, "They were looking for a king, to bring salvation nigh, He came a little infant thing, that made a woman cry."

Cleansing The Temple

The local folk knew Jesus well, He was the best carpenter in the nation. But now He had stepped out of bounds, He accepted the nomination of that wild preacher John the Baptist as the Lamb of God. He had agreed to let the people mount Him on an ass and enter the city amid cries of "Hosanna." Now He had stirred the city by routing the moneychangers and cattle dealers from the temple. For almost thirty years He had watched men desecrate the place. He was outraged at their insolence and greed. He was disgusted that they had carpeted the temple courts with animal excrement, and polluted the place with the stench of urine.

ABLAZE!

by Leonard Ravenhill

Each of the Gospels tells of the whipping Christ. But Luke makes a very valuable difference as he records the events in the life of Jesus. He says that before Jesus had entered the temple, while He was still entering Jerusalem, He had stopped to weep over the great city. So we have the *weeping* Christ before we had the *whipping* Christ. Since He was about His Father's business at 12 years of age, Jesus had trod the temple courts and had always been grieved and outraged that they were defiled not just with animal dung, but with red-eyed extortioners, cheating moneychangers, and cattle dealers. For 30 years He had been growing in grace and in the knowledge of His Father—now He knew His mission! And His explanation for this one-man attack on the sacrilege and defilement of the house of God is summed up in these words: *"Zeal for Thy house will consume me."*

Zeal! What a baptism of this same zeal the weak and wilting Church of this day needs. Zeal in this context is *love ablaze*. Zeal without reason becomes fanaticism. *Jesus was not a fanatic*. Yes, His love was blind to all the possible dangers of His mission. This love ignores personal safety, disregards the odds against it, drops "sacrifice" from its vocabulary, requires no crutches, ignores all danger, is intolerant of sin, but not fanatical.

His was no sudden burst of anger; He had contemplated it all His life, but now the hour had come and men fled before His whip and holy anger.

Spiritual Ecology

"Pollution! Pollution!" cry the ecologists about our food, air, waters, and our auto emissions. But where, O where are the preachers crying out against the pollution in the churches? The heart of Jesus was broken over a nation that had the elect prophets of the Lord as its advisors. But who had heeded these prophets? They had not dined at kings' tables; they, like their Master, were despised and rejected of men. Some were men with scorching tongues, but they were also men with weeping eyes. Ah! but tell me if you can, where are the weeping preachers today?

The cattle dealers in the temple were more interested in selling sacrifices than in offering them. And so today there are Christians at this very hour fighting feverishly for some political cause, and yet they are never heated over the wretched filth in their own church.

Will we crusade against uncleanness in the "Church"? If not, better tell the sleepy saints again to eat, drink, and be merry, for tomorow we shall be raptured. *But Jesus will not rapture a ruptured Church!*

The Worst Thing In The World

There are some frightful tragedies in the world at this moment. When "wise" men swept aside the Bible, they told us that we would move into a new freedom for men. These wise men have proved that they are otherwise. Other smart men put their brains together to make a bomb so that we can turn a living city crisp in seconds. Then think of the implication of Afghanistan and Iran, the daily bleeding of millions in Kampuchea, and the masses waiting to leave Cuba. These are horrible things to contemplate, and yet I think there is one thing infinitely worse. It is a *sick Church in a dying world.*

Never has the great U.S. ever been more broken than today. Broken marriages, leaving millions of broken homes. Thousands and thousands of teenagers whose minds are broken with drugs. The people's confidence and trust in the government is broken. The economy is broken–the once-mighty dollar is broken. All is broken except the hearts of the believers.

We need broken hearts to face this colossal mess. Weeping is not only in order in the pulpit, it is commanded! *"Let the priests weep between the porch and the altar…let them howl." (Joel 2:17, 1:13)* Jeremiah wept over the sin of Israel. David wept. Paul wept. John wept. Shall we remain dry-eyed in the most crucial chapter in world history and in our own?

Counterfeit Zeal

The present lethargy in the Church is almost unpardonable. The Jehovah's Witnesses have zeal. The Mormons claim they are gaining more people from the evangelicals than we are gaining from them. The cultists zealously persist in getting a hearing in the streets.

Saul of Tarsus had fanatical zeal. He threw men and women in prison and broke up their families, persecuting them from city to city. Miraculously God cleansed him, baptized him with fire, and made him a model zealot for His Kingdom.

It is not enough in these days of such vast worldliness in the Church to say that we are fundamental or uncompromising in "doctrine." We must be ablaze with Holy Spirit-born anger. *("Be angry, and yet do not sin." Eph. 4:26)* We must feel the hurt of God over the devil's domination of this age. We must apologize to the Almighty that we have turned to our own way, and have been more loyal to a man-made theology than to the exceedingly sober words of our Master. Like Paul, we must be able to say in His holy presence, *"This **one** thing I do..."* I bear a broken heart over the coldness in the Church (including my own!). True, the zealous man of God lives for *one* thing only: to please God. He is impervious to the opinions of others about his zeal. He cares not what it costs him to burn out for God. In sickness or in health, in poverty or in wealth, whether he is esteemed or despised, flattered or flattened, considered a fool or a philosopher, through evil report or good report, kisses or curses, *he is set to do the will of God!*

This man sees the Church today fouled with showmanship, bingo and bake sales, dances, tinsel and trivia, *"holding to a form of godliness, although they have denied its power." (II Tim. 3:5)* He sees the ministers condoning divorce in high places. Maybe his minister is divorced and remarried himself.

Jesus today sees His Church unclean with disobedience *by a watered-down gospel.* We do not obey His commandments to *"love one another,"* or rejoice to act out Matthew 23:11 *"But the greatest among you shall be your servant."* If there comes a man into the assembly with a gold ring, we *do* give him honor *(James 2:2).* If he has great wealth but little spirituality, he is still welcomed as a member of the board. We do not insist that our young preacher boys tarry (until they get a seminary diploma? No!) until they are endued with power from on high!

The Pharisee's Prayer

The Pharisee who prayed in the temple said, *"God, I thank Thee that I am not like other people: **swindlers, unjust, adulterers.**"* **There are many so-called Spirit-filled men today, who cannot even pray that prayer! Unjust** they are for sure, they pay low wages and tell their workers that they are "doing this sacrifice for Jesus." **Adulterers**–there are famous preachers in this awful category. They, of course, have an explanation for their infidelity, yet many are accepted at conferences as keynote speakers. **Extortioners**–the radio preachers almost have this as a monopoly. A $25 Bible (God's Holy Word) is offered for a $100 gift! Other books are offered at five times their cost. "You are judging" someone will say. Correct, I am *told* to judge *(John 7:24)*. Jesus says, *"Judge with righteous judgment."* Also I, along with other true preachers of the Gospel, am a watchman and so have to warn others. Also, *"judgment must begin at the house of the Lord."* This *bait* to get money is an abomination. Preachers whine for money over the radio and television. "For this ministry" they say, and yet much of it is to sustain their extravagant lifestyle, costly airplanes, and fix up luxury Bible conference grounds. And now they have joined the Pharisees who *"rob widows' houses."* After emptying your pockets while you live, they ask for your house and estate after you die. *What next?*

Stealing The Glory

This is a day of the personality cult. Men on T.V. gospel shows are presented as having given up so much for the Lord. All they gave up with their retirement from stardom was hell and eternal punishment. Let it be shouted from the housetops that no man does God a favor. Elegant living, etc. for the rich evangelists proves nothing except that they have not left all to follow Him. The Spirit-filled need no status symbols.

The flattering introduction for gospel preachers is another great piece of blockage to revival. John 5:41 and 44 need soul-searching consideration. My heart is burdened and burning. God's house is polluted. The sinners scoff and say of the rich preachers, "Their creed is greed and their god is gold." We need a baptism of holy zeal to get us back to holy indignation that the money grabbers are back in the temple, and that God's heart is hurting.

The Church began in the Spirit, now She is operating in the flesh. There is no pillar of fire over the sanctuary. There are no preachers who can hold the hell-bound spell-bound. I am not sure that it can be proved that Nero fiddled while Rome burned. *It can be proved that the Church is fiddling while the world is burning!* The one reason that we do not have revival today is that we are content to live without it.

O for a generation of believers who can honestly say, "Zeal for Thy house will consume Me."

This article is available in tract form as LD#14.

Will You Be Bored In Heaven?

IT'S 8:00 AND HE'S MISSING OUT ON "MONDAY NIGHT FOOTBALL"

—by Keith Green

"But to this one will I look, to him who is humble and contrite of spirit, and who trembles at My Word." —Isaiah 66:2

Who today trembles at the Word of God? It seems to me that there are but few who really live with a passion for God—especially a passion just to be with Him. Today there is such a noise coming up before the throne of the Most High—the clamor of so-called praise, singing, and joyful shouting. But I wonder if the same people who love to sing and shout, loudly exclaiming the praises of God, really have

such an intense glory in their secret life with the Lord. When the meeting's over and there's no one there to listen except the only One who matters, do you still have that same passionate joy in your spirit, **just to be alone with the Living God?**

How Are You Ever Going To Enjoy Heaven?

The Lord made me realize recently that if I do not absolutely relish His company now, desiring to be with Him more than anyone in the whole world, then I would not really be comfortable in heaven at all—for it is there that we will spend all eternity in the company of the Holy One who made us.

I had always thought that even though now I might not desire with all my heart to be in the conscious presence of God, that somehow, mysteriously, I would not have that problem after I die. I had believed that salvation from a rotten devotional life would only finally come with death (and then naturally heaven!), but as a man of God said centuries ago, "There is no sanctification in the grave!" (See *Heb. 9:27*)

How many of us believe that even though we have some evil and sin in our hearts now, heaven will take care of all that? Why do we put our hope in some future redemption when God says, *"Behold, now is the acceptable time. Now is the day of salvation!" (II Cor. 6:2)* Do you think that even though you allow yourself pride and selfishness here, once you get to heaven everything will be all set because "it's impossible to sin in heaven"? Aren't you forgetting that Satan let pride, selfishness, and deceit rule his life, even though he had lived in heaven **since the day he was first made!** It must be seen that heaven can't take away our sins, only **Jesus** can take away our sins **and the power of sin over our life!**

The Gates Of Holiness

Don't get me wrong, I'm not trying to say that God will allow sin in heaven. On the contrary, He has prepared hell as the final dumping site for the devil—and **all** the sin in the universe! God will only allow what is holy to enter through the gates. *(Rev. 21:27)* That is why I implore you to see that it's not heaven that will finally purify us…only the blood of Jesus can cleanse and purify us, and that **must** take place here and now. For without holiness, *"no one shall see the Lord." (Heb. 12:14)*

If your heart takes more pleasure in reading novels, or watching TV, or going to the movies, or talking to friends, rather than just sitting alone with God and embracing Him, sharing His cares and His burdens, weeping and rejoicing with Him, then how are you going to handle forever and ever in His presence with no TV, movies, or singles' retreats? You'd be bored to tears in heaven, if you're not ecstatic about God now!

How could God invite you to heaven, where the most exciting thing to do all day is gaze upon His glorious face, if you're not in heaven right here on earth when you're alone with Him? Do you think that after you die, suddenly you'll be in heaven and "presto!" all at once you're not

Three Who Loved Not Their Own Lives

There was a converted Hindu Christian martyr whose skin was slashed and filled with salt and chili powder. He said to his tormentors, "Formerly Satan wounded me with his fiery darts. The blood of Jesus healed those wounds. The suffering caused by your wounds is not much." Enraged by these words, they started to skin him alive. "I thank you for this," he said, "tear off the old garment. I shall soon put on Christ's garment of righteousness." He was finally burned praying for his persecutors.
(*A Book Of Protestant Saints* by Ernest Gordon)

Then there was Alan Cameron, one of the "convenanters" of the great Scottish persecutions, who was shown the head and the hands of another covenanter, his own son Richard. They asked him the cruel question, "Do you know them?" He kissed them saying, "I know them …I know them. They are my son's, my own dear son's. It is the Lord. Good is the will of the Lord, who cannot wrong me nor mine, but has made goodness and mercy to follow us all our days."
(*Fair Sunshine* by Jock Purvis)

Thomas Haukes, after refusing to have his son baptized into the Roman Church, was ordered to a fiery death by the Bishop of London. During his agony, he stretched forth his burning hands and clapped them together three times, signifying to his friends that God was giving him grace in the fire. June 10, 1555.
(*Foxe's Book Of Martyrs* by John Foxe)

going to like worldly things anymore? All of a sudden you'll love more than anything else just to hang out with God, when you couldn't stand being alone with Him even 20 minutes a day?

The Excitement Of Death

"For to me to live is Christ, and to die is gain...I do not know which to choose, but I am hard-pressed from both directions, having the desire to depart and be with Christ, for that is very much better; yet to remain on in the flesh is more necessary for your sake. And convinced of this, I know that I shall remain and continue with you all for your progress and joy in the faith..."
—Phil. 1:21-25

What an amazing passage this is. But then again, what an amazing man Paul was! He speaks here as if he could snap his fingers and be in heaven any time he chose to leave the planet. He says that he'd really rather depart this life and be with Christ in heaven, but he was willing to stay **if** he really had to!

How different his attitude toward death is than ours. When we think of dying, many times it still holds the same dread for us as it does for unbelievers. Even worse, there are many believers who do not wish to "depart and be with Christ" any time too soon. When they think of going to be with the Lord, they hope it will be a long, long time in the future—in fact, going to heaven now would interrupt many of our plans (even "Christian" ones), cutting short a "long, productive life."

Be honest, would you be thrilled for the Lord to come back right before you get that college degree, or if you had your choice, would you prefer He wait until right after graduation day? Maybe you're engaged to be married. How would you like to go to heaven the day before your scheduled wedding? See what I mean? Paul really desired more than anything else to go to be with the Lord. We desire long, fulfilling "Christian" lives on earth—but we're willing to die and go to heaven... **when we really *have* to!**

Living Martyrs

What God seeks for today is a Church full of dead men and women. Dead to themselves, that is—and alive to their Beloved! Have you ever read *Foxe's Book Of Martyrs?* Such stories! Men and women tortured for a faith that seemed to the world (and the organized church of that day) to be in vain—because they chose to die for what they believed rather than accept the false, temporary peace of the so-called "religion" of the times.

The Bible still prophesies terrifying times ahead for the world, a time of horror and tribulation *"such as the world has never seen" (Matt. 24:21) "when men's hearts will fail them for fear." (Luke 21:26)* According to Jesus, these times will try believers' hearts and faith more than any other in all the history of civilization. We must prepare for these times in the same way the apostle Paul did. He openly shared his secret of enduring suffering, torments, and persecution with joy—"I die daily!" Paul was a living martyr. He had been to the cross and had been "crucified with Christ." He had laid down upon the altar and counted all his strengths, talents, and benefits from this life as garbage so that he might "gain Christ." *(I Cor. 15:31; Gal. 2:20; Phil. 3:7)* Paul shares experiences in II Corinthians 11 that would make most of today's fainthearted believers shrink away from the faith—because the crucified life is not taught, only the "victory of the believer." **But there is no victory without battle, and there is no resurrection without a cross.** Today, many people with "charismatic" experiences have been led into the "upper room" without first going to the cross!

The Rapture—The Great Escape?

"…then we which are alive and remain shall be caught up…in the clouds to meet the Lord in the air, and thus we shall always be with the Lord."
—I Thess. 4:17

Many believers (especially in America) are hoping this event—called the "rapture" by Bible teachers—will deliver them from the sufferings that the Bible says will torment the whole earth. In fact, there are many who are more excited about this "rapture" than they are about Jesus Himself. Do these same people believe that they are more worthy to escape tribulation than Paul, or James, who both were beheaded? Or Peter who was crucified upside down (because he thought himself not worthy to be crucified as his Lord had been)? Or Bartholomew who was actually skinned alive in Rome? What about the millions of saints through the ages who have suffered unspeakable fates as their reward on earth for their faithfulness, or those in prison even now in Communist lands—why has there been no rapture for them? And what makes us congratulate ourselves here in the West, to think that we deserve to go scot-free from suffering when *"men of whom the world was not worthy…did not accept their release, in order that they might obtain to a better resurrection"?* (Heb. 11:35,38)

"MAYBE IT'LL BE MID-TRIB…"

A Great Falling Away
(Matt. 24:10)

I think that one of the saddest stories I've ever heard was how the believers in China fared when the Communists took over their country in 1949. The Evangelical churches had been teaching that the Church would definitely be raptured before any "great tribulation" or suffering would befall the faithful. It had become such a central doctrine that all worry (and preparation) were abandoned, and praise for their absolute safety from harm and persecution was offered at every meeting.

Then the Communist government took over and a vicious attack was made upon the Church, including confiscation of property, beatings, imprisonment, and even the taking of children from parents. The unprepared Church was caught so off-guard that millions fell away and denied Christ, thinking they had been abandoned by a God who did not keep His promise. Ah, but that's just it! **God has promised tribulation—God has promised persecution!** *"In the world you shall have tribulation... he who desires to save his life shall lose it... all who desire to live godly in Christ Jesus will be persecuted."* (John 16:33; Matt. 16:25; II Tim. 3:12) But these promises from God (no less precious than His others) were neglected in the teachings of the Chinese Church... just as they are being neglected today in the West. How sad to think that so many have become mesmerized into believing that no physical harm or suffering can befall them because they are Christians. But Jesus said, *"Do not fear those who kill the body!"* (Matt. 10:28)

I'm not saying there won't be a rapture. I'm just not too sure about the timing. Yes, I believe that God **could** deliver all true believers from the great tribulation, but since He hasn't always gotten even faithful Christians off the hook from suffering (in the Bible **or** in Church history), there's no guarantee that He'll protect the many lazy, apathetic believers of today from something that might not only wake them up, but would certainly divide the true sheep from the "religious" goats.

When it comes to believing in either a pre-tribulation or post-tribulation rapture, my motto has always been: **pray for "pre" but prepare for "post."** That way we'll be ready for truly anything—which is exactly the way God wants us to be!

The thing that matters most to God is that His people will be found ready to rule as the Bride of Jesus when He returns. There are so many warnings about being unprepared *(Matt. 24:42-51; Luke 21:34-36; I Thess. 5:2-3)*, parables that tell the fate of those who are not faithful or do not keep watch *(Matt. 25:1-13; Luke 12:35-40, 19:11-27)*, and pleadings of a loving God who *"does not take pleasure in the death of the wicked."* (Ezek. 33:11) We should take heed the godly advice of the great apostle...

"Test yourselves to see if you are in the faith; examine yourselves! Or do you not recognize this about yourselves, that Jesus Christ is in you —unless indeed you fail the test?"   *—II Cor. 13:5*

This article is available in tract form as LD#15.

THE BACKSLIDER IN HEART

BY CHARLES G. FINNEY
Edited and paraphrased by Keith Green

This is an edited and paraphrased version of the 21st chapter from REVIVAL LECTURES by Charles Grandison Finney. This message is as much for the Church today as when it was first brought forth in a series of lectures in the 1830s. We earnestly pray that you'll "read it and weep!"

I cannot conclude any teaching on revival without warning converts against backsliding. In discussing this subject, I will show: 1) What backsliding in heart is not, 2) What backsliding in heart is, 3) What are the evidences of a backslidden heart, 4) What are the consequences of backsliding in heart, and 5) How to recover from this state.

What Backsliding In Heart Is Not

It does not consist of no longer having highly excited religious feelings. No longer having these great spiritual feelings may be an *evidence* of a backslidden heart, but it is not *the cause* of such a state.

What Backsliding In Heart Is

1) It consists in taking back that consecration to God and His service that constitutes true conversion.

2) It is the leaving by a Christian of his first love.

3) It consists in the Christian withdrawing himself from that state of entire and total surrender to God and coming again under the control of a self-pleasing spirit.

4) It also must be said that a person may have a backslidden heart even though he maintains an outward appearance of religion. We have all seen different men perform the same or similar outward acts from widely different (and often from opposite) motives. No doubt the most intense selfishness often takes on a religious form. And there are many considerations that might lead a backslider in heart to keep up this spiritual show, even though he has lost the power of godliness in his soul.

What Are The Evidences Of A Backslidden Heart

1) A lack of spiritual enjoyment is evidence of a backslidden heart. We always love saying and doing those things that please the one we love most. When the heart is not backslidden, real communion with God is kept up, and therefore all spiritual devotions are not only performed with pleasure, but the communion with God involved in them is a source of rich and continual blessing. If we do not *enjoy* the service of God, it is because we do not truly serve *Him*.

2) An outward formality in religious exercises. A stereotyped, formal way of saying and doing things that is clearly the result of habit rather than the out-gushing of a true spiritual life. In prayer or fellowship, this formality will be emotionless and as cold as ice, and will reveal a total lack of sincerity in the performance of all spiritual service. Such a state would be impossible where there existed a present, living faith and a true godly zeal.

3) An ungoverned temper. While the heart is full of love, the temper will naturally be patient and sweet. Or if at any time it should go so far as to escape from self-control, a truly loving heart will quickly confess and break down, repenting with true humility. Whenever, therefore, there is an irritable, uncontrolled temper, you may know that there's a backslidden heart.

4) The loss of interest in truly spiritual conversation. *"For the mouth speaks out of that which fills the heart." (Matt. 12:34)* No conversation is so sweet to a truly loving heart as that which relates to Christ and to our living Christian experience.

5) Searching for worldly amusements. The most grateful amusements possible to a truly spiritual mind are those that bring the soul into the most direct communion with God. A loving heart is jealous of everything that will break up or interfere with its union with God. When the soul does not find more delight in God than in all worldly things, the heart is sadly backslidden.

6) A lack of interest in foreign missions. If you lose your interest in these works and for reaching those in heathen lands, and do not delight in the conversion of souls everywhere, you may know that you are backslidden in heart.

7) The loss of interest in benevolent outreaches to the poor and needy. Surely if you were ever converted to Christ at all, you have had an interest in all charitable, Christian enterprises that came within your knowledge. Of course, a converted soul takes the deepest interest in all outreaches to reform, help, and save mankind–in the provision of the needs for the poor and needy–and in short, in *every good word and work*. Just in the proportion that you have lost your interest in these things, you have evidence that you are backslidden in heart.

8) The loss of interest in those newly converted. There is joy in the presence of the angels over one sinner that repents, and is there not joy among the saints on earth over those that come to Christ and are His newly born babes in the Kingdom? Show me a professing Christian who does not have a passionate interest in converts to Christ, and I will show you a backslider in heart and a hypocrite–he professes religion, but has none.

9) A fault-finding, critical spirit. The disposition to fasten blame, showing a lack of confidence in the good intentions and motives of others. It is a spirit of distrust of Christian character and what they say. It is a state of mind that reveals itself in harsh words and harsh judgments of individuals. This state is entirely incompatible with a true loving heart, and whenever a judgmental spirit is manifested by a professing Christian, you may know that there is a backslidden heart.

10) A self-indulgent spirit. By self-indulgence, I mean the inclination to gratify the appetites, passions, and to fulfill *"the desires of the flesh and of the mind." (Eph. 2:3)* The appetite for food is frequently, and perhaps more frequently than any other, the occasion for backsliding. Few Christians, I fear, sense any danger in this area. God's injunction is, *"Whether, then, you eat or drink or whatever you do, do all to the glory of God." (I Cor. 10:31)* Christians forget this and eat and drink to please themselves. More persons are ensnared by their tables than the Church is aware of. A great many people who avoid alcoholic drinks altogether will indulge in food that both in quantity and quality prove they follow no other law than that of their appetite. This indulging in gluttony threatens to ruin both body and soul together. Show me a gluttonous Christian, and I will show you a backslider.

11) Absence from scheduled prayer meetings for slight reasons is a sure indication of a backslidden heart. No meeting is more important to a Christian than the prayer meeting, and while they have any heart to pray, they will not be absent unless prevented by something urgent that God has impressed them to do. If a call from a friend at the hour of meeting can

prevent their attendance, it is strong evidence that they do not really *want* to go. That same person visiting at such a time would not prevent them from attending a wedding, a party, a picnic, or some other enjoyable event. The fact is, it is hypocrisy for them to pretend that they really want to go while they can be kept away by small excuses.

12) The same is true of the neglect of family prayer for slight reasons. While the heart is engaged in true religion, Christians will not readily omit a daily time of prayer and Bible reading with their family. And whenever they are ready to find an excuse to avoid these family devotions, it is a sure evidence that they're backslidden in heart.

13) When secret, private prayer is regarded more as a duty than as a privilege. It has always appeared to me most ridiculous to hear Christians speak of prayer as a duty. It is an infinite privilege to be allowed to come to God and ask for the supply of all our needs. But to pray because *we must* rather than because *we may* is a sad, sad thing, and a certain indication of a backslidden heart.

14) A lack of the spirit of prayer. While the love of Christ remains fresh in the soul, the indwelling Spirit of God will reveal Himself as the Spirit of grace and supplication (prayer). He will instill strong desire in the soul for the salvation of sinners and the sanctification of saints. He will often make intercession for them with great longings, strong crying and tears, and with groanings that cannot be uttered in words. *(Rom. 8:26-27)* If that Spirit of prayer departs, it is a sure indication of a backslidden heart. For while the first love of a Christian continues, he is sure to be drawn by the Holy Spirit to wrestle much in prayer.

15) A backslidden heart often reveals itself by the *manner* in which people pray. For example, praying as if in a state of condemnation, very much like an unconverted sinner, is an evidence of a backslidden heart. His confessions and self-accusations in prayer show to others what perhaps he does not well understand himself. Instead of being filled with faith and love, he is more or less convicted of sin and is conscious deep within that he is not in a state of acceptance by God.

It is often very striking and even shocking to attend a backsliders' prayer meeting, and I'm very sorry to say that many prayer meetings of the Church are little else. Their prayers are timid and hesitating, and reveal the fact that they have little or no faith. They will go round and round, one after the other, in reality praying for their own conversion. They could not make it any more obvious that they are backsliders in heart.

16) The loss of interest in the question of holiness. If you are a Christian, you have felt that sin was an abomination to your soul. You have had inexpressible longings to be rid of it forever, and everything that could throw light upon that question of agonizing importance was most desperately crucial to you. If this question has been dismissed and is no longer of any interest to you, it is because you are backslidden in heart.

17) A lack of interest in God's Word. Perhaps nothing more conclusively proves that a Christian has a backslidden heart than his losing his interest in the Bible. While the heart is full of love, no book in the world is so precious; but when that love is gone, the Bible becomes not only uninteresting, but often repulsive. There is no faith to accept its promises, but conviction enough left to dread its threatenings.

The Consequences
Of Backsliding In Heart

"The backslider in heart will have his fill of his own ways." –Proverbs 14:14

1) The backslider in heart will be filled with his own mistakes. He is not walking with God. He is not led by the Spirit, but is walking in spiritual darkness. In this state he is sure to fall into many terrible mistakes: mistakes in business, mistakes in relationships, mistakes in using his time, his tongue, his money. Indeed *all* will go wrong with him as long as he remains in a backslidden state.

2) He shall be filled with his own feelings. Instead of that sweet peace and rest in the Holy Spirit that he once had, he will find himself in a state of unrest, dissatisfied with himself and everyone else. It is sometimes very trying to live with a backslider. They are often touchy, faultfinding, and irritating in all their ways. They have forsaken God, and in their feelings there is more of hell than of heaven.

3) The backslider in heart will be filled with his own words. While in this state, he *will* not and *can* not control his tongue. It will prove itself to be an unruly member full of deadly poison. *(James 3:8)* By his words he will entangle himself in many difficulties and problems from which he can never free himself until he comes back to God.

4) The backslider in heart will be full of his own cares. He has turned back to selfishness. He counts himself and his possessions as his very own and tries to manage everything for himself in his own wisdom *and for his own sake*. Consequently, his cares will be multiplied and come upon him like a deluge.

5) The backslider in heart will be filled with his own lustings. His appetites and passions which had been kept under control have now resumed their full course, and having been kept down so long, they will seem to avenge themselves by becoming more demanding and unruly than ever. These animal appetites and passions will burst forth to the astonishment of the backslider, and he will probably find himself more under their control and enslaved by them than he ever was before.

6) The backslider in heart will be full of his own troubles. Instead of keeping out of temptation, he will run right into it. He will bring upon himself multitudes of trials. He is not at peace with God, with himself, the Church, *nor with the world*. But while he complains of being so tried by everything around him, he is constantly making things worse!

7) The backslider in heart will be filled with his own anxieties. He will be worried about himself–about his business, his reputation, *about everything!* He has taken all these things out of the hands of God. Hence, having faith in God no longer, and being unable to control events, he has to be filled with worry about the future. These anxieties are the inevitable result of his madness and folly in forsaking God.

8) The backslider in heart will be filled with his own prejudices. His willingness to know and do the truth is gone. He will very naturally oppose any principle or truth that comes down hard on a selfish spirit. He will endeavor to justify himself. He will not want to read or hear anything which would rebuke his backslidden state, and will become deeply prejudiced against anyone who shall reprove him or correct him. Considering that person as an enemy, he will hedge himself in and shut his eyes against the light, standing on the defensive and criticizing everything that might expose him.

9) The backslider in heart will be full of his own delusions. Having an evil eye, his whole body will become full of darkness. *(Matt. 6:23)* He will almost certainly fall into self-deception in regard to principles and doctrines. Wandering on in darkness as he does, he will very likely swallow the grossest delusions. Cults of every type and deceptions of every shade may be very likely to gain possession of him. Who has not observed this of many backsliders in heart?

10) The backslider in heart must be full of his own losses. He regards his possessions as his own, his time as his own, his influence as his own, his reputation as his own. The loss of any of these he accounts as *his own loss*. Having forsaken God, and being unable to control the events by which these things are maintained, he will find himself suffering losses on every side. He loses his peace. He loses his property. He loses much of his time. He loses his reputation. He loses his Christian witness, and if he continues...*he loses his soul*.

11) The backslider in heart is full of his own self-condemnation. Having once enjoyed the love of God, and then forsaking Him, he feels condemned for everything. If he attempts religious duty, he knows there is no heart in it, and hence condemns himself. If he *neglects* religious duty, he of course condemns himself. If he reads his Bible, it condemns him. If he does not read it, he feels condemned. If he goes to church meetings, the meetings condemn him. If he stays away, he feels condemned also. If he prays in secret, with his family, or at a meeting, he knows he is not sincere and is condemned. If he neglects or refuses to pray, he also feels condemned. *Everything condemns him!* His conscience is up in arms against him and the storms of condemnation follow him wherever he goes.

How To Recover From A State Of Backsliding

1) Remember from where you have fallen. Face the question at once and deliberately contrast your present state with that in which you once walked with God.

2) Take a good, honest look at your true position. Don't put off any longer dealing with the conflict between God and your soul and the differences between God and you.

3) Repent at once and do your first works over again. *(Rev. 2:5)*

4) Do not attempt to get back by merely changing what you do on the outside. Begin with your heart and immediately get right with God. Give yourself no rest until the question of your acceptance before Him is completely settled.

5) Do not act like a mere convicted sinner and think that you must "reform and make yourself better" before you can then come to Christ. But understand distinctly that *coming to Christ, alone,* can make you better! However much distress you may feel, know for certain that until you repent and accept His will *unconditionally,* you are no better and are constantly growing worse. Until you throw yourself upon His sovereign mercy, and thus return to God, He will accept nothing from you or from your hands.

6) Do not imagine yourself to be in a justified state, for you know in your heart that you are not. Your conscience condemns you, and you know that God ought to condemn you. *For if He justified you in your present state, your conscience could not justify Him.* Come then to Christ at once, like the guilty sinner that you are. Own up and take all the shame and responsibility upon yourself, and believe that in spite of all your wanderings from God, He loves you still. He has loved you with an everlasting love, and with lovingkindness is even now drawing you back to Himself.

This article is available in tract form as LD#16.

Uncovering the Truth about Modesty

by Melody Green

> "Likewise, I want women to adorn themselves with **proper** clothing, **modestly** and **discreetly,** not with braided hair and gold or pearls or costly garments; but rather by means of good works, as befits women **making a claim to godliness.**"
> (I Tim. 2:9-10)

This simple little Scripture certainly covers a lot of ground if we look at it closely. It especially becomes more clear when we consider the dictionary definitions of some of the key words that Paul uses. How many of us can say we are really living up to the light of this passage in I Timothy? The purpose of this article is to put a searchlight on our hearts and on our motives for the **way** that we choose to dress—**and why.** This is a subject that gets whispered or giggled about a lot, but rarely is

> **Modest**—Having a regard for decencies of behavior or dress; quiet and humble in appearance, style, etc.; not displaying one's body; not boastful or vain; unassuming; virtuous; shy or reserved; chaste.
> **Proper**—Specially adapted or suitable; appropriate; conforming to an accepted standard; correct; fitting; right; decent.
> **Discreet**—Lacking ostentation or pretension; "showing good judgment"; prudent; cautious; careful about what one says or does.

someone directly confronted about their lack of modesty. It is a very delicate subject… but that's all the more reason to talk about it openly and honestly.

Are You Making A Claim To Godliness?

Essentially, the Scripture in I Timothy says that it's all right to dress however you want unless you are **making a claim to godliness.** In that case, the way that you dress (along with the rest of your life) must be subject to the guidelines and control of the Holy Spirit.

Our bodies **are** precious because they are a gift from God. They are attractive because God made us in His image for His pleasure (and if we are married, to please our mates as well). But God never intended us to flaunt ourselves or exhibit our bodies in an immodest way. He wants our bodies consecrated to Him. *"I urge you therefore, brethren, by the mercies of God, to present your bodies a living and holy sacrifice, acceptable to God, which is your spiritual service of worship." (Rom. 12:1)* It surely must grieve the Lord to see the thoughtless way so many "modern" Christians dress. It's true that their bodies may be a living sacrifice–**but to which god?**

TRANSFORMED NOT CONFORMED

It might seem to many of us that modesty is a thing of the past. I know before I became a Christian I didn't have the slightest idea of what it meant to dress properly. Looking back, it's hard to believe I even left the house in some of the things I used to wear **(and not wear!)**, let alone that I wore them without even a blush! *(Jer. 6:15)*

The Bible in very clear terms tells us not to be conformed to the world, but instead, to be **transformed.** *(Rom. 12:2)* Webster's Dictionary tells us that to be transformed means a change of outward appearance or inner nature. I guess that's why it amazes me to see young Christian girls (and even more mature women) in church or at outdoor gatherings, hands uplifted in praise to God, while dressed in clothes that definitely do not give **Him** the glory.

In the summertime especially, we have our biggest opportunity to test our consecration to Jesus. Sheer blouses, halter-tops, **"short"** shorts, and skimpy bathing-suits are the norm for many careless Christian women. They use the rationalization that "it's hot" or "I'm swimming" to excuse their lack of modesty. Clothes that fit too tightly, tops that are cut too low, and skirts that are cut too short are not only a distraction to those around us–but the wearers show an unloving lack of concern for their responsibility as a representative of Jesus.

Unfortunately, it seems that many Christians are lost in their own selfish little world–either oblivious or uncaring about the affect they have on others. They may even appear to have a real excitement and love for the Lord–however, their body is sending out a totally different message. I know, because as I said before, I have done it–partly in ignorance, but mostly in rebellion. I can remember thinking, "Well, it's not **my** fault if they can't keep their eyes off of me and on the Lord. **They** just aren't spiritual enough. Why should **I** have to change just because **they** are weak?"

But the Lord showed me that it **was** my fault. I was responsible for causing my brother to stumble and it had to change. Once I really saw the damage my selfishness was doing to others and to the Lord, I was really ashamed of myself and embarrassed that I had been representing Jesus in such an unbecoming way. *"It is inevitable that stumbling blocks* should come, but woe to him through whom they come! It would be better for him if a millstone were hung around his neck and he were thrown into the sea, than that he should cause one of these little ones to stumble." (Luke 17:1-2)

THE FASHION QUEEN

Worldly dress is quite revealing. First and foremost it reveals a **worldly heart.** It also reveals wrong priorities and areas that are not yielded to God. Being dressed in a worldly manner does not always mean that you are dressed immodestly. It may simply mean that your style is flashy or overdone—generally speaking, just "too much." If your perfume arrives at church five minutes before you do, who are you trying to kid? Did you put it on for **Jesus?** If you are drawing attention to yourself, then you are drawing attention **away** from God and *stealing* **His glory.**

Here are some simple questions. Are you considered a trendsetter—usually the first to buy the latest style? Do you spend a lot of time and money shopping for new clothes? Are you always thinking about what you're going to wear? Do heads turn to see your newest outfit—and do you **enjoy** turning heads? If you can answer yes to even one of those questions, it's quite possible that you are seeking man's attention instead of God's. As a famous evangelist once said, "Be honest about it, would you take all this pain about your looks if every person were blind?"

Pretty... Not Painted

I believe that too many Christian women overdo it when it comes to putting on their make-up. They arrive to fellowship with the world's "come and get me" look painted on their face. They look like showgirls on their way to a nightclub, instead of someone coming in meekness and humility to meet their Lord. Their **faces** are prepared, but their **hearts** aren't! And if the Lord should really move in the meeting so as to bring some to tears of joy or repentance, they would have to fight back the tears for fear they would "ruin their face." How can you be open to a touch from God when you're so concerned about your outward appearance? It's very simple... **you can't be!**

"Charm is deceitful and beauty is vain, but the woman who fears the Lord, she shall be praised." (Proverbs 31:30)

Sheep In Wolves' Clothing

I would also like to include a brief word to the fellows in this article, for you are not always exempt from the sin of vanity and the desire to be noticed. Sadly enough, I have seen many of my Christian brothers drawing attention to themselves by wearing immodestly tight clothing and looking "just like the world." Many thoughtless Christian men unbutton their shirts halfway down their chest, surround themselves in a potent cloud of aftershave—and don't really care that they may be causing others to take their eyes off of Jesus. You too must be sensitive to others and give the Holy Spirit control of your life. You are responsible to surrender this whole area to Jesus and make sure that you are not causing those around you to stumble and fall.

Acting The Harlot?

God does not think beauty is evil—how could He, He invented it in the first place! But beauty corrupted becomes harlotry. In Ezekiel 16:14-15, God says, *"Then your fame went forth among the nations on account of your beauty, for it was perfect because of My splendor which I bestowed on you. But you trusted in your beauty and played the harlot because of your fame, and you poured out your harlotries on every passerby who might be willing."* Here God is speaking to Jerusalem about her abominations. He compares her to a harlot to make His point, since everyone is familiar with how a harlot acts. How many of you are acting like harlots—parading yourselves, seducing with your eyes and trusting in your looks to bring you love and acceptance instead of trusting in God and putting your confidence in Him? You have heard it said that "beauty is only skin deep"—and it's true. But God can see through to the inside, and the things that are beautiful to Him are not always apparent to the common eye.

Perfume, Powder, And Prayer
(A Challenge)

The world teaches us that in order to be loved we must be beautiful, sensual, and alluring. We are assaulted daily by billboards, books, television programs, movies, and magazines that teach us "a different gospel." Sure, everyone wants to be loved… but why and by whom? All that is supposed to change when we meet Jesus.

I think we will all agree that God is most concerned with the **inner man**…the heart. But I don't think we can say, "Well, I may **look** worldly, but Jesus knows that in my heart I'm not." It is true that Jesus knows our heart, but I believe in most instances our **outward appearance** reflects our **inward condition**.

God tells us to redeem the time because the days are evil *(Eph. 5:16)*, but many will spend more time in the morning preparing their "outward selves" than they do preparing themselves inwardly for the warfare of the day by seeking God in prayer and His Word. Sometimes we can spend so much time fixing up the outer man that the Spirit inside shrivels up and dies.

I want to present my brothers and sisters in the Lord with a challenge. Measure the time you spend "fixing yourself up" on a daily basis. Then give at least equal time to God in prayer and Bible reading **every day**. We all know He deserves so much more, but if you just start there, you can let it grow as you do.

The Other Extreme

I think it is important to make it clear that I don't think pretty clothes or a little bit of make-up is wrong. In fact, I don't necessarily think that the most godly way to dress is in a bland and unattractive manner. To be quite honest with you, I have seen many people go to the other extreme and try to draw attention to themselves by being untidy, unclean, and uncaring about themselves. They try to prove to others that they are spiritual because of their lack of concern about the way that they look. This too can be another form of pride and self-righteousness—and I believe it is all equally grievous to the Lord. He wants us to find a balance and seek to glorify Him in everything we do. Humility and moderation are principles that the Bible clearly teaches.

Marriage Is No Excuse!

There are many husbands and wives who encourage (and sometimes even demand) their mates to "look sexy." They feel that since they're already married, it won't really hurt to "turn each other on" in the way that they look and dress. I don't think there is anything wrong with dressing to please your husband or wife, in fact I think it's important that you do, but **not at the expense of others.** We must stay within the boundaries of the Holy Spirit, putting Jesus and **His** pleasure first in all we do.

One newlywed in our ministry held up a bare little summer dress to her husband, and shaking her head said, "This has got to go." He said, "But…that's one of my favorite dresses!" She said, "Yes, but **why** do you like it so much?" He slowly smiled and agreed—and out it went!

Closet Cleaning

Many of you may really feel convicted to change and wonder what you should do now, so I would like to give you a few words of simple advice before I close. First of all, go through your closets and drawers and pull out all of the clothing that obviously has to go—and get rid of it! Next, get in front of a full-length mirror, and try on the things that are questionable. Look at yourself from all angles using a hand-held mirror. Look at yourself close up and from far away and see what you "really look like" in the clothes you have been wearing. View yourself objectively, as if you were looking at someone else—and note what your first impressions are of "this person." Check for fit and transparency and get rid of **anything** that doesn't pass the test—this is no time to be sentimental! Finally, each day before you leave the house, do the "mirror check" on anything that hasn't previously been checked or if you have gained weight since last taking a look. You will be surprised to find that some of the things you were sure about won't pass the test. This will help you weed out your wardrobe as you go. Some of you may be afraid that if you do this, you'll end up with **nothing** left to wear! But just remember that the most important thing is to be obedient to God, even if it means having a very limited wardrobe. Besides, when you are all done with this project, you will become a much more careful shopper and end up being a better steward over God's money than you ever were before!

TRUE BEAUTY

True beauty is Jesus and Him alone. Letting that love flow through us to others is the beauty that is pleasing to God. Paul says we are to adorn ourselves with good works…as servants of the Lord, vessels through which others can feel His touch on their lives. Why would we want to substitute the world's counterfeit for the real thing?

True beauty radiates from the face of a godly man or woman. You won't notice much what they really look like because you are too busy noticing Jesus in them. Shouldn't that be our goal? Let's allow Jesus to so fully indwell us that we would never do or say anything that would bring shame to His name…yielding our whole lives to Him and serving Him in the inner courts of His holiness. Let's not forget that we are His Bride—and so dress accordingly as we fully divorce ourselves from the world and clothe ourselves with the righteousness of God! *(Isaiah 61:10)*

May God bless you as you seek Him about what all this might mean to you personally. Please take the whole matter to heart (and prayer) and then be obedient to change the things in your life that you find are displeasing to God.

"Give unto the Lord the glory due His name; bring an offering, and come before Him; worship the Lord in the **beauty of holiness**." *(I Chron. 16:29)*

This article is available in tract form as LD#17.

Christmas Mourning

by Keith Green

I'll never forget the incredible joy and expectation of Christmas. Our house smelled like a Douglas fir. The tinsel and ornaments sparkled in the colored lights. Friends and relatives came to visit...all with smiles and laughter...*and all with presents!!* The season was full of life, warmth, and giving. They are the very best memories of my childhood. The air outside was cold and crisp. And inside, always the smell of something baking. If anyone asked me to describe "joy" in one word, it would have been *Christmas.*

I remember taking a drive to an area of town where a whole street prided itself on their Christmas displays and lights. The whole neighborhood spent thousands of dollars to light up their front lawns with scenes of snow, Santas, reindeer, and mangers. I always used to wonder what the manger had to do with Santa, candy canes, and jingle bells, but it didn't bother me enough to ask.

When I was about 10 or 11, I noticed the word "Xmas." I wondered what the "X" was for. I concluded it meant "criss," as in "criss-cross." It never even entered my mind that it replaced "Christ"! Yes, there were school Christmas plays and other things that talked about the birth of Jesus having something to do with Christmas, but it never really was the main emphasis in my young mind. I only wished that it would be Christmas all year, and Jesus had *nothing* to do with it! But when I was 21, I met Jesus, and since then it *has* been Christmas all year...and Jesus has had *everything* to do with it!

The Origin Of Christmas

In the third century A.D., a wonderful thing happened. Constantine, the Roman emperor, became a Christian. For almost 300 years the Christians had been praying for their emperor's salvation. Nobody believed it was true! But then came the royal decree...Christianity was made the religion of the state. Everyone was strongly urged to accept Jesus Christ as their Lord and only deity. At the risk of seeming uncooperative (and believing that it would be safest politically and socially), almost everyone in the empire made "professions of faith" in the new religion. This, of course, delighted Constantine.

After a while there arose a great problem. What were they to do with all their other gods? And what about all the great feasts and celebrations, especially the winter solstice and the spring equinox? Before Constantine's conversion, the whole empire would lustily celebrate these festivals to their gods and goddesses. What would they do now? Constantine knew that, although almost everyone had outwardly confessed Christianity, they were in no way prepared to give up their cherished celebrations. What he had on his hands was a kingdom full of *"unconverted converts"!*

As the restlessness and dissatisfaction of his people grew, the emperor knew something had to be done. So, in desperation, he declared two major "religious" holidays. They would correspond exactly to the times of the old great celebrations. He declared December 25 (for centuries celebrated as Saturnalia, the birthday of the sun) as the celebration of the birthday of Christ. (Although historians say that Jesus was probably born sometime in October.) A great mass or religious service would be held in honor of Jesus' birth on that day (hence, Christ-mas). He also declared the old holiday of the spring equinox to be the celebration of Christ's resurrection. (The old emphasis of the festival was the worship of the goddess of fertility–which is where we get the Easter Bunny.) The grumbling masses were thus quieted when they realized that they could once again celebrate their great holidays. Oh yes, the festivals might be called something different, and they might have to go to some "religious ceremonies," but for the most part, things could get back to normal, and their old festivities could again be heartily resumed.

St. Nick

The history of the man Nicholas (who was later made a saint by the Roman Church) is vague and sketchy. But one thing stands out about his character–he loved the poor and needy, and at every Christmas he used to give gifts to the widows and orphans. He was loved by all, especially children. This is how the tradition and practice of gift-giving was started. The folklore fantasy called Santa Claus grew over the centuries and now is the central image of a secular Christmas, where an average of over $150 each is spent on gifts for every man, woman, and child in the United States alone!

The True Meaning Of Christmas

I've heard a lot of talk (especially by Christians) about the *true* meaning of Christmas. I've seen Christians go in for all the trappings and trimmings. They spend hours, even days, in department stores trying to figure out what to buy for friends and relatives who already have everything they need…sitting around the tree and watching nervously while someone opens up the present you got them, as they try to look surprised and squeal with delight...parents teaching their young what they call "a harmless fairy tale"—the story of Santa and how "he's gonna bring you lots of presents, so you better be good." And all the while, a world full of starving, deprived people are silently, invisibly looking in through your living room window begging for a scrap of food, a rag to keep them from shivering to death, and an answer to their misery, suffering, and oppression.

When we consider all the money spent by all of us, during a season that's greatest meaning is the Father giving us His only Son to come live and die for us, we must cry out against the injustice of an American, Christian people, who have *so much* and do *so little.* The *true* meaning of

this season should be to give ourselves to the work of spreading the Gospel. Proclaiming freedom to the captives! Giving them bread to eat, then pointing them to the Bread of Life, to fill their hungry souls.

Some Suggested Alternatives

As a part of your Christmas celebration this year we suggest taking your children to a ghetto, to a hospital, to an orphanage, to an old-age home. Teach them the meaning of giving. Teach them it is foolish for us to spend money on things we don't need, and on things that others don't need. Let them spread joy to those who are miserable! Let them give a smile to an old woman's face, whose own children have forgotten and abandoned her in a convalescent hospital. Let them empty their piggy banks and send the money to missions and the poor. Let there be giving! Costly giving! Let us give our Lord Jesus the whole world for His birthday! *The world and the Lord await our response…*

There's No Substitute For This Kind Of Experience…

This Christmas I went to Mexico to be a part of a Christian outreach distributing food and clothing to the poor. Each morning when we arrived at the arena there were hundreds of people waiting outside the locked gate in the bitter cold. We worked close to 12 hours a day in the freezing weather, but the Mexican people waited in the same cold with their small children, most without even a coat or hat. As they waited in the long lines, we ministered to them any way we could. Many of the children had sores on their faces caused by malnutrition. Many had no shoes, I could hardly believe it, it was **so cold!**

One day while working inside sorting clothes, a Mexican family knocked at the door and we invited them in. One of their children, a little girl about two years old looked up at me, her face and hands red from the bitter cold. She reached out her arms and I rushed over to her, taking one of her tiny hands at a time, and rubbing and blowing on them to warm her. My heart just broke. Others ran and got her a hat, coat, and pair of gloves, while her parents just stood there and cried. I had a new understanding of what Jesus must have felt when it says, "And seeing the multitudes He had compassion for them."

As the Gospel was preached and food and clothes given out, many of us and many of them were brought to tears. You might think there would be a communication problem for those of us who didn't speak Spanish, but I'll assure you, the love of Christ was shared and seen in more than words. What a rich time we had in Mexico. The more we tried to bless the Mexican people, the more God blessed us.

Was it hard not to be home during Christmas? Well, I only had time to think about it once or twice. There were too many needs to care for. I can say it was the richest Christmas in my life. What will I be doing next Christmas? Lord willing, I'll see you in Mexico, giving the Lord the best present I can–myself. I mean, whose birthday celebration is this anyway?!

–Keith Rinas, Lindale, TX

This article (excluding the letter) is available in tract form as LD#10.

WHERE ARE THE ELIJAHS OF GOD?

by Leonard Ravenhill

"...and he prayed again, and the sky poured rain, and the earth produced its fruit."   –James 5:18

It is our privilege to publish these excerpts from Leonard Ravenhill's powerful first book WHY REVIVAL TARRIES. Although the title of this article is also the title of chapter four of the book, we have taken some sections from other chapters as well. (We have also included most of the forward to the book written by Mr. Ravenhill's close friend, the late Dr. A. W. Tozer.) We thank God for how He has used this book in our lives, and in the lives of so many others, to reveal His burning heart of love towards His Church. We pray that you, too, will feel the flames...

Great industrial concerns have in their employ men who are needed only when there is a breakdown somewhere. When something goes wrong with the machinery, these men spring into action to locate and remove the trouble and get the machinery rolling again. For these men a smoothly operating system has no interest. They are specialists concerned with trouble and how to find and correct it.

In the Kingdom of God things are not too different. God has always had His specialists whose chief concern has been the moral breakdown, the decline in the spiritual health of the nation or the Church. Such men were Elijah, Jeremiah, Malachi, and others of their kind who appeared at critical moments in history to reprove, rebuke, and exhort in the name of God and righteousness.

A thousand or ten thousand ordinary priests or pastors or teachers could labor quietly on, almost unnoticed, while the spiritual life of Israel or the Church was normal. But let the people of God go astray from the paths of truth, and immediately the specialist appeared almost out of nowhere. His instinct for trouble brought him to the help of the Lord and of Israel.

Such a man was likely to be drastic, radical, possibly at times violent, and the curious crowd that gathered to watch him work soon branded him as extreme, fanatical, negative. And in a sense they were right. He was single-minded, severe, fearless, as these were the qualities the circumstances demanded. He shocked some, frightened others, and alienated not a few, but he knew Who had called him and what he was sent to do. His ministry was geared to the emergency, and that fact marked him out as different, a man apart.

To such men as this the Church owes a debt too heavy to pay. The curious thing is that She seldom tries to pay him while he lives, but the next generation builds his sepulcher and writes his biography, as if instinctively and awkwardly to discharge an obligation the previous generation to a large extent ignored.

Such a man as this is not an easy companion. The professional evangelist who leaves the wrought-up meeting as soon as it ends to hurry over to the most expensive restaurant to feast and crack jokes with his sponsors will find this man something of an embarrassment, for he cannot turn off the burden of the Holy Ghost as one would turn off a faucet. He insists upon being a Christian all the time, everywhere; and again, that marks him out as different.

Toward him it is impossible to be neutral. His acquaintances are divided pretty neatly into two classes, those who love him with all admiration, and those who hate him with perfect hatred!

—A. W. Tozer

(From the forward to WHY REVIVAL TARRIES)

"When we go to God by prayer, the devil knows we go to fetch strength against him, and therefore he opposeth us all he can." —R. Sibbes

To the question, "Where is the Lord God of Elijah?" we answer, "Where He has always been—on the throne!" But where are the Elijahs of God? We know Elijah was "a man of like passions as we are," but alas! we are not men of like prayer as he was. One praying man stands as a majority with God! Today God is bypassing men—not because they are too ignorant, but because they are too self-sufficient. Brethren, our abilities are our handicaps, and our talents our stumbling blocks!

Out of obscurity, Elijah came on to the Old Testament stage, a full-grown man. Queen Jezebel, that daughter of hell, had routed the priests of God and replaced them with groves to false deities. Darkness covered the land and gross darkness the people, and they were drinking iniquity like water. Every day the land, fouled with heathen temples and idolatrous rites, saw smoke curling from a thousand cruel altars.

Elijah lived with God. He thought about the nation's sin like God; he grieved over sin like God; he spoke against sin like God. He was all passion in his prayers and passionate in his denunciation of evil in the land. He had no smooth preaching. Passion fired his preaching, and his words were on the hearts of men as molten metal on their flesh.

Brethren, if we will do God's work in God's way, at God's time, with God's power, we shall have God's blessing and the devil's curses. When God opens the windows of heaven to bless us, the devil will open the doors of hell to blast us. God's smile means the devil's frown! Mere preachers may help anybody and hurt nobody; but prophets will stir everybody and madden somebody. The preacher may go with the crowd; the prophet goes against it. A man freed, fired, and filled with God will be branded unpatriotic because he speaks against his nation's sins; unkind because his tongue is a two-edged sword; unbalanced because the weight of preaching opinion is against him. Preachers make pulpits famous; prophets make prisons famous. The preacher will be heralded; the prophet hounded.

Ah! brother preachers, we love the old saints, missionaries, martyrs, reformers: our Luthers, Bunyans, Wesleys, Asburys, etc. We will write their biographies, reverence their memories, frame their epitaphs, and build their monuments. **We will do anything except imitate them.** We cherish the last drop of their blood, but watch carefully the first drop of our own!

We try to help God out of difficulties. Remember how Abraham tried to do this, and to this day the earth is cursed with his folly because of Ishmael. On the other hand, Elijah made it as difficult as he could for the Lord. He wanted fire, but yet he soaked the sacrifice with water! God loves such holy boldness in our prayers. *"Ask of Me, and I shall give thee the heathen for thine inheritance, and the uttermost parts of the earth for thy possession." (Psalm 2:8)*

Oh, my ministering brethren! Much of our praying is but giving God advice. Our praying is discolored with ambition, either for ourselves or for our denomination. Perish the thought! Our goal must be God alone. It is **His** honor that is defiled, **His** blessed Son who is ignored, **His** laws broken, **His** name profaned, **His** book forgotten, **His** house made a circus of social efforts.

> **"The man who can get believers to praying would, under God, usher in the greatest revival that the world has ever known."**

Does God ever need more patience with His people than when they are "praying"? We tell Him what to do and then how to do it. We pass judgments and make appreciations in our prayers. In short, we do everything **except pray!** No Bible school can teach us this art. What Bible school has "prayer" on its curriculum? The most important thing a man can study is the prayer part of the book. But where is this taught? Let us strip off the last bandage and declare that many of our presidents and teachers do not pray, shed no tears, know no travail. **Can they teach what they do not know?**

The man who can get believers to praying would, under God, usher in the greatest revival that the world has ever known. There is no fault in God. He is able. God *"is able to do according to the power that worketh in us."* God's problem today is not communism, nor yet Romanism, nor liberalism, nor modernism. God's problem is—**dead fundamentalism!**

> **"So because you are lukewarm, and neither hot nor cold, I will spew you out of my mouth."**
> —Rev. 3:16

This generation of preachers is responsible for this generation of sinners. At the very doors of our churches are the masses—unwon because they are unreached, unreached because they are unloved. Thank God for all that is being done for missions overseas. Yet it is strangely true that we can get more "apparent" concern for people across the world than for our perishing neighbors across the street! With all our mass-evangelism, souls are won only in hundreds. Let an atom bomb come and they will fall by the millions into hell.

Sin today is both glamorized and popularized, thrown into the ear by radio, thrown into the eye by television, and splashed on popular magazine covers. Church-goers, sermon-sick and teaching-tired, leave the meeting as they entered it—visionless and passionless! Oh God, give this perishing generation ten thousand John the Baptists!

Just as Moses could not mistake the sight of the burning bush, so a nation could not mistake the sight of a burning man! God meets fire with fire. John the Baptist was a new man with a new message. As a man accused of murder hears the dread cry of the judge, "Guilty!" and pales at it, so the crowd heard John's cry, "Repent!" until it rang down the corridors of their minds, stirred memory, bowed the conscience and brought them terror-stricken to repentance and baptism! After Pentecost, the onslaught of Peter, fresh from his fiery baptism of the Spirit, shook the crowd until as one man they cried out: "Men and brethren, what shall we do?" Imagine someone telling these sin-stricken men, "Just sign a card! Attend church regularly! Pay your tithes!" No! A thousand times no!

"Oh, my God! If in our cultivated unbelief and our theological twilight and our spiritual powerlessness, we have grieved and are continuing to grieve Thy Holy Spirit, then in mercy spew us out of Thy mouth! If Thou cannot do something with us and through us, then please God, do something without us! Bypass us, and take up a people who have not yet known Thee!"

As this is only a small part of the book, WHY REVIVAL TARRIES, we highly recommend reading it all, as well as the other books by Mr. Ravenhill.

This article is available in tract form as LD#19.

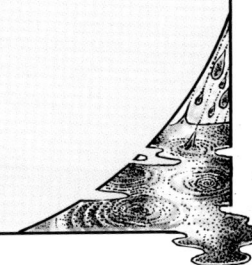

WHO CARES?

On one of my recent journeys, as I gazed from the coach window, I was led into a train of thought concerning the conditions of the multitudes around me. They were living carelessly in the most open and shameless rebellion against God, without a thought for their eternal welfare. As I looked out the window, I seemed to see them all... millions of people all around me given up to their drink and their pleasure, their dancing and their music, their business and their anxieties, their politics and their troubles. Ignorant—willfully ignorant in many cases—and in other instances knowing all about the truth and not caring at all. But all of them, the whole mass of them, sweeping on and up in their blasphemies and devilries to the throne of God. While my mind was thus engaged, I had a vision.

I saw a dark and stormy ocean. Over it the black clouds hung heavily; through them every now and then vivid lightning flashed and loud thunder rolled, while the winds moaned, and the waves rose and foamed, towered and broke, only to rise and foam, tower and break again.

by General William Booth
Founder of The Salvation Army
Put into modern English by Keith Green

In that ocean I thought I saw myriads of poor human beings plunging and floating, shouting and shrieking, cursing and struggling and drowning; and as they cursed and screamed, they rose and shrieked again, and then some sank to rise no more.

And I saw out of this dark, angry ocean, a mighty rock that rose up with its summit towering high above the black clouds that overhung the stormy sea. And all around the base of this rock I saw a vast platform. Onto this platform, I saw with delight a number of the poor struggling, drowning wretches continually climbing out of the angry ocean. And I saw that a few of those who were already safe on the platform were helping the poor creatures still in the angry waters to reach the place of safety.

On looking more closely, I found a number of those who had been rescued, industriously working and scheming by ladders, ropes, boats, and other means more effective, to deliver the poor strugglers out of this sea. Here and there were some who actually jumped into the water, regardless of all the consequences, in their passion to "rescue the perishing." And I hardly know which gladdened me most—the sight of the poor drowning people climbing onto the rocks, reaching the place of safety, or the devotion and self-sacrifice of those whose whole beings were wrapped up in the effort for their deliverance.

As I looked on, I saw that the occupants of that platform were quite a mixed company. That is, they were divided into different "sets" or classes, and they occupied themselves with different pleasures and employments. But only a very few of them seemed to make it their business to get the people out of the sea.

But what puzzled me most was the fact that though all of them had been rescued at one time or another from the ocean, nearly everyone seemed to have forgotten all about it. Anyway, it seemed the memory of its darkness and danger no longer troubled them at all. And what seemed equally strange and perplexing to me was that these people did not even seem to have any care—that is any agonizing care—about the poor perishing ones who were struggling and drowning right before their very eyes... many of whom were their own husbands and wives, brothers and sisters, and even their own children.

Now this astonishing unconcern could not have been the result of ignorance or lack of knowledge, because they lived right there in full sight of it all and even talked about it sometimes. Many even went regularly to hear lectures and sermons in which the awful state of these poor drowning creatures was described.

I have already said that the occupants of this platform were engaged in different pursuits and pastimes. Some of them were absorbed night and day in trading and business in order to make gain, storing up their savings in boxes, safes, and the like.

Many spent their time in amusing themselves with growing flowers on the side of the rock, others in painting pieces of cloth or in playing music or in dressing themselves up in different styles and walking about to be admired. Some occupied themselves chiefly in eating and drinking, others were taken up with arguing about the poor drowning creatures that had already been rescued.

But the thing to me that seemed the most amazing was that those on the platform to whom He called, who heard His voice and felt they ought to obey it—at least they said they did —those who confessed to love Him much and were in full sympathy with Him in the task He had undertaken—who worshipped Him or who professed to do so—were so taken up with their trades and professions, their money saving and pleasures, their families and circles, their religions and arguments about it, and their preparation for going to the mainland, that they did not listen to the cry that came to them from this Wonderful Being who had Himself gone down into the sea. Anyway, if they heard it they did not heed it. They did not care. And so the multitude went on right before them struggling and shrieking and drowning in the darkness.

And then I saw something that seemed to me even more strange than anything that had gone on before in this strange vision. I saw that some of these people on the platform whom this Wonderful Being had called to, wanting them to come and help Him in His difficult task of saving these perishing creatures, were always praying and crying out to Him **to come to them!**

Some wanted Him to come and stay with them, and spend His time and strength in making them happier. Others wanted Him to come and take away various doubts and misgivings they had concerning the truth of some letters which He had written them. Some wanted Him to come and make them feel more secure on the rock—so secure that they would be quite sure that they should never slip off again into the ocean. Numbers of others wanted Him to make them feel quite certain that they would really get off the rock and onto the mainland someday; because, as a matter of fact, it was well known that some had walked so carelessly as to lose their footing and had fallen back again into the stormy waters.

So these people used to meet and get up as high on the rock as they could, and looking toward the mainland (where they thought the Great Being was) they would cry out, "Come to us! Come, help us!" And all the while He was down (by His Spirit) among the poor struggling, drowning creatures in the angry deep, with His arms around them trying to drag them out, and looking up—oh! so longingly, but all in vain—to those on the rock, crying to them with His voice all hoarse from calling, "Come to **Me**! Come, and **help Me**!"

And then I understood it all. It was plain enough. That sea was the ocean of life—the sea of real, actual human existence. That lightning was the gleaming of piercing truth coming from Jehovah's throne. That thunder was the distant echoing of the wrath of God.

Those multitudes of people shrieking, struggling, and agonizing in the stormy sea, were the thousands and thousands of poor harlots and harlot-makers, of drunkards and drunkard-makers, of thieves, liars, blasphemers, and ungodly people of every kindred, tongue, and nation.

Oh, what a black sea it was! And oh, what multitudes of rich and poor, ignorant and educated were there. They were all so unalike in their outward circumstances and conditions, yet all alike in one thing—all sinners before God—all held by, and holding onto, some iniquity, fascinated by some idol, the slaves of some devilish lust, and ruled by the foul fiend from the bottomless pit!

"All alike in one thing?" No, all alike in **two things**—not only the same in their wickedness but, unless rescued, the same in their sinking, sinking...down, down, down...to the same terrible doom. That great sheltering rock represented Calvary, the place where Jesus had died for them. And the people on it were those who had been rescued. The way they used their energies, gifts, and time represented the occupations and amusements of those who professed to be saved from sin and hell—followers of the Lord Jesus Christ. The handful of fierce, determined ones, who were risking their own lives in saving the perishing, were true soldiers of the cross of Jesus. That Mighty Being who was calling to them from the midst of the angry waters was the Son of God, "the same yesterday, today, and forever," who is still struggling and interceding to save the dying multitudes about us from this terrible doom of damnation, and whose voice can be heard above the music, machinery, and noise of life, calling on the rescued to come and help Him save the world.

My friends in Christ, you are rescued from the waters, you are on the rock. He is in the dark sea calling on you to come to Him and help Him. Will you go? Look for yourselves. The surging sea of life crowded with perishing multitudes rolls up to the very spot on which you stand. Leaving the vision, I now come to speak of the fact—a fact that is as real as the Bible, as real as the Christ who hung upon the cross, as real as the judgment day will be, and as real as the heaven and hell that will follow it.

Look! Don't be deceived by appearances—men and things are not what they seem. **All who are not on the rock are in the sea!** Look at them from the standpoint of the great white throne, and what a sight you have! Jesus Christ, the Son of God is, through His

Spirit, in the midst of this dying mulitude, struggling to save them. And He is calling on **you** to jump into the sea—to go right away to His side and help Him in the holy strife. Will you jump? That is, will you go to His feet and place yourself absolutely at His disposal?

A young Christian once came to me and told me that for some time she had been giving the Lord her profession and prayers and money, but now she wanted to give Him her life. She wanted to go right into the fight. In other words, she wanted to go to His assistance in the sea. As when a man from the shore, seeing another struggling in the water, takes off those outer garments that would hinder his efforts, and leaps to the rescue, so will you who still linger on the bank, thinking and singing and praying about the poor perishing souls, lay aside your shame, your pride, your cares about other people's opinions, your love of ease and all the selfish loves that have kept you back for so long, and rush to the rescue of this multitude of dying men and women?

Does the surging sea look dark and dangerous? Unquestionably it is so. There is no doubt that the leap for you, as for everyone who takes it, means difficulty and scorn and suffering. For you it may mean more than this. It may mean death. He who beckons you from the sea however, knows what it will mean—and knowing, He still calls to you and bids you come.

You must do it! You cannot hold back. You have enjoyed yourself in Christianity long enough. You have had pleasant feelings, pleasant songs, pleasant meetings, pleasant prospects. There has been much of human happiness, much clapping of hands and shouting of praises—very much of heaven on earth.

Now then, go to God and tell Him you are prepared as much as necessary to turn your back upon it all, and that you are willing to spend the rest of your days struggling in the midst of these perishing multitudes, whatever it may cost you.

You **must** do it. With the light that is now broken in upon your mind, and the call that is now sounding in your ears, and the beckoning hands that are now before your eyes, you have no alternative. To go down among the perishing crowds is your duty. Your happiness from now on will consist in sharing their misery, your ease in sharing their pain, your crown in helping them to bear their cross, and your heaven in going into the very jaws of hell to rescue them. **Now, what will you do?**

This article is available in tract form as LD#20.

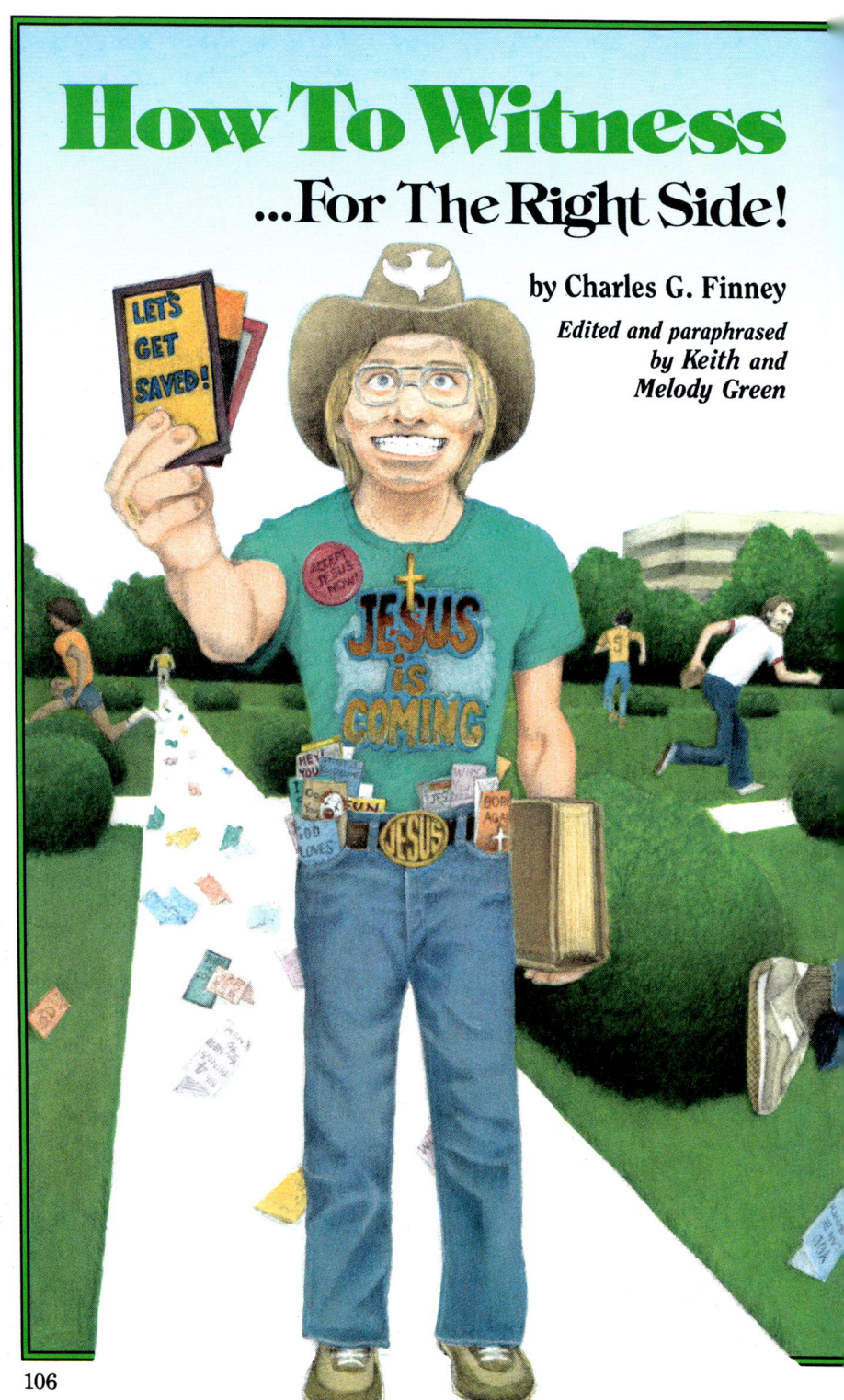

> *"'You are My witnesses,' declares the Lord,
> 'And My servant whom I have chosen.'"*
> —Isaiah 43:10

One great reason why God leaves Christians in the world after their conversion is so they may be **witnesses for God**—that they may call the attention of the thoughtless multitude to see the difference in the character and destiny of those who believe the Gospel and those who reject it. The very fact that most people never even think about their sins (or **any** eternal things) is the great difficulty that stands in the way of true Christianity.

Now the Spirit of God is always trying to awaken the attention of men to the subject of their sin and the plan of salvation. Miracles have sometimes been used to capture their attention, and in this way, miracles may become instrumental in conversion (although miracles in themselves never convert anybody). They may be the means of awakening, but are not always effective even as that, and if continued or made common, they would soon lose their power as an instrument of conversion. What is needed in the world is something that can be sort of an ever-present miracle, able not only to get the attention, but to keep it—something that will keep the sinner's mind in continual contact with the truth, until he yields to it.

Hence, we can see why God has scattered His children everywhere, in neighborhoods and among the nations—that they may be those continual, ever-present miracles.

On What Points Are Christians To Testify?

Generally, they are to testify to the truth of the Bible. They should be competent witnesses for this. Even the newest convert knows by his experience the truth of the Bible. He may hear arguments by atheists that he never thought of, and that he cannot answer, and all his reasoning may be confounded; but he cannot be driven from his ground. He will say, "I cannot answer you, but I know the Bible is true." It's as if a man should look in a mirror and say, "That is my face." Someone might ask him, "How do you know that's your face?" "Why," he replies, "by its looks." So when a Christian sees the truth pictured in the Bible, he knows what it is, **and he knows it is true!**

More specifically, Christians are to testify to:
1. The immortality of the soul. (The fact that conscious existence goes on forever—as this is clearly revealed in the Bible.)
2. The vanity and unsatisfying nature of all earthly good.
3. The fulfilling nature and glorious sufficiency of serving Jesus.
4. The guilt of sinners—and the reality of hell as a place of eternal punishment for them.

5. The love of Christ for sinners.
6. The necessity of a holy life, if we think of ever living for eternity in the presence of God. Without holiness, *"no one shall see the Lord."* (Heb. 12:14)
7. The necessity of self-denial and of living above the world.
8. The necessity of meekness, humility, and heavenly-mindedness.
9. The necessity of complete integrity and an entire renovation of character and life for all who would enter heaven. (Of course, it should be made clear that this, as well as the previous three, are only attainable by fully submitting by faith to Christ.)

In What Way Are They To Testify?

By word and example—on every proper occasion by their lips, but mainly by their lives. Christians have no right to be silent, they should *"reprove, rebuke, exhort, with great patience and instruction."* (II Tim. 4:2), but their strongest influence as witnesses is by their example. This is universally known, "Actions speak louder than words." But where words and living proof are both displayed, the greatest impact is made.

As to the manner in which they are to testify, **generally**—they should live in their daily walk and conversation as if they believe the Bible. But **more specifically:**

1. As if they believe the soul to be immortal, and as if they believe that death was not the termination of their existence, but the entrance into an unchanging eternal state. It is easy to see that words without example will do no good. All the arguments in the world will not convince mankind that you believe this, unless you live as if you really do. Your reasoning may be flawless, but if you do not live accordingly, your actions will defeat your arguments. They will say, "It's obvious that your reasoning is not true, and that you **know** it is all false because your life contradicts your theory." Or they will say that, "If it is true, **you** do not believe it at any rate!" And so all the influence of your testimony goes to the other side.

2. Against the vanity and unsatisfying nature of the things of this world. The failure to testify to this is the great stumbling block in the way of mankind's salvation. Here the testimony of God's children is needed more than anywhere else. Men are so struck with their senses (what they can see, hear, feel, etc.) and so constantly occupied with them, that they are most likely to shut out eternity from all their thoughts. A small object that is held close to the eye can shut out the whole ocean. So the things of this world that are near appear so magnified in their minds that they overlook everything else.

One important design in keeping Christians in the world is to prove this point to people, **practically.** Who could not see that it would be quite ridiculous for them to testify with their lips that this world is all vanity and all its joys are unsatisfying and empty, while their possessions, lifestyle, and daily conduct testify to everybody the very reverse? Who would believe what they said?

3. To the fulfilling nature of Christianity. Christians are called to show by their conduct that they are actually satisfied with the enjoyments of serving Jesus. They are to live like this world is not their home. Their professed belief is that heaven is a reality, and they expect to dwell there forever. But suppose they live in such a way as to prove that they cannot be happy unless they have a full share of the world, and as far as going to heaven, they would much rather remain here on earth than die and go there!

4. Regarding the guilt of sinners and the reality of hell. Christians are under solemn obligation to warn sinners of their awful condition, and exhort them to flee from the wrath to come and take hold of everlasting life. But who does not know that the way you say this is everything? Sinners are often struck under heavy conviction by the very way something is said.

Say you go to a sinner and talk to him about his guilt and danger, but in your manner you make an impression that does not correspond with your words. You may in effect bear witness the other way and tell him he is in no danger. A man may tell you that your house is on fire in such a way as to make exactly the opposite impression, and you will take it for granted that it is not **your** house that is on fire.

If you live in such a way as to show that you do not feel compassion for sinners around you, if your manner is not solemn and earnest, how can they believe you are sincere? Woman, suppose you were to tell your unconverted husband in an easy, laughing way, "My dear, I believe you are going to hell"—will he believe you? If your manner of life around him is light and gay, you show that you either do not believe there is a hell, or that you wish to have him go there!

5. To the love of Christ. You are to bear witness to the reality of the love of Christ, by the regard you show for His truth, His honor, His Kingdom. You should act as if you believe that He died for the sins of the **whole** world, and as if you put the blame on sinners for their rejection of His great salvation—and for the awful state they are in. This is the **only** legitimate way in which you can impress sinners with the love of Christ.

Christians, instead of this, often make the impression on sinners that Christ is **so** compassionate that they have very little to fear from Him. I've been amazed to see how a certain group of Christians want ministers to always preach about the **love** of Christ. But if a minister urges Christians to be holy and to labor for Christ, they call it "legalism." They say they want to hear "the Gospel."

6. The necessity of holiness in order to enter heaven. Just talking about this won't do—they must **live** holy. The idea has prevailed for so long that "we can't be perfect here" that many Christians do not even seriously aim at living a life without sin. They cannot honestly say that they really have tried to live without sin. They drift along before the tide in a loose, sinful, unhappy, and abominable manner, at which undoubtedly the devil laughs, because it is of all others the surest way to hell.

7. To the necessity of self-denial and living above the world. Christians ought to show by their own example what the Christian walk is. **That** is the most powerful preaching–the kind which shows sinners the great difference between themselves and Christians. Many believe they can best make people accept the truth by bringing religion down to the standards of men. As if the nearer you bring religion to the world, the more likely the world will be to embrace it. Now all this is as wide from the truth as the North Pole is from the South, but it is always the policy of carnal and worldly "Christians." And they think they are displaying such wonderful wisdom by taking so much pain not to scare people at the mighty strictness and holiness of the Gospel.

They argue that if you show people that such a great change is required in their life, why you will drive them all away! This seems reasonable at first, but it is not true. Let professing Christians live in this lax and easy way, and sinners will say, "Why I can see that I am about right, or at least so near right that it is impossible for God to send me to hell for the few differences between me and these Christians." No, the true way is to exhibit Christianity and the world in wide contrast, or you can never make sinners feel the necessity of a change. If Christians attempt to accommodate religion to the worldliness of men, they render the salvation of the world impossible.

8. They are to testify by meekness, humility, and heavenly-mindedness. The people of God should always show a temper like the Son of God, who *"while being reviled, He did not revile in return; while suffering, He uttered no threats."* (I Peter 2:23) If a professing Christian is irritable, ready to resent an injury, to fly into a rage, or to take the same measures as the world does to get even, how is he to make people believe there is any reality in a change of heart? Why, such a person contradicts the Gospel! But nothing makes such a great impression upon sinners or bears down with such tremendous weight on their consciences as to see a Christian, truly Christ-like, bearing injuries with the meekness of a lamb. It cuts like a two-edged sword!

9. Finally, they are to testify to the necessity of entire honesty in a Christian. This extends to every department of life. Christians need to show the strictest attention to integrity in every aspect of business and in all their dealings with their fellow man.

But unfortunately, the dishonesty of the Church is cursing the world. Now, I am not going to preach a political sermon, but I want to show you that if you mean to impress men favorably to your Christianity by your lives, you must be honest, strictly honest, in business, politics, and everything you do. What do you think those ungodly politicians, who know themselves to be playing a dishonest game in carrying on an election, think of your religion when they see you uniting with them? They **know** you are a hypocrite!

Some Important Remarks

1. It is unreasonable for Christians to be amazed that sinners are not concerned about their souls, nor think about eternal things. Everything considered, the thoughtlessness of sinners is not surprising. For sinners are so taken up with business, pleasure, and the things of the world, that they will not examine the Bible to find out what the truth is. Their feelings are only moved by worldly subjects, because these are the only ones brought into warm contact with their minds. But there is so little to make an impression on them in respect to eternity, or to bring the truth about God home to them, that they almost never have deep feelings about these things. If they were forced to examine the subject, they would be moved greatly—but they do not think about it, nor care anything about it—and they never will unless God's witnesses rise up and testify!

But considering the way the great body of Christians live, it seems they're testifying for the other side! God has left His cause here before the human race, and left His Church, **His** witnesses, to testify on His behalf. And behold! They turn around and testify the other way! Is it any wonder that sinners couldn't care less?

2. We see why it is that so much of our preaching does so little good, and why so many sinners seem to get "gospel-hardened." But if the Church were to live one week as if they believed the Bible, sinners would melt down right before them.

Suppose I were a lawyer and went into court and spread out my client's case. As the trial begins, I make my opening statements, tell what I expect to prove, and then call my witnesses. The first witness takes the stand, and then proceeds to contradict me to my face. What good will all further pleading do? I might address the jury for a month, and be as eloquent as Shakespeare, but as long as my witnesses contradict me, **all my pleading is in vain!** Just so it is with a minister who is preaching in the midst of a cold, stupid, and God-dishonoring church. In futility he holds up the great truths of the Bible, while every member of his church is ready to witness that he lies.

Yet there are ministers who will go on in this way for years, preaching to a people who by their lives contradict every word that he says. And these ministers think it is their duty to do so. Duty! For a minister to preach to a church that is undoing all his work, contradicting all his testimony, and refusing to change? No! Let him shake the dust off his feet as a protest, and go to the heathen or to a new place. The man is wasting his energies and wearing out his life, and just rocking the cradle for a sleepy church which is testifying to sinners that there is no real danger.

3. It is evident that the standard of Christian living must be raised or the world will never be converted. Many churches are depending on their minister to do everything. When he preaches they will say, "What a great sermon that was! He is an excellent minister. Such preaching **has** to do good. We shall have a revival soon no doubt!" I tell you, if they are depending on preaching alone to carry on the work, they must fail. Even if an apostle should rise from the dead, or an angel come down from heaven and preach, without the Church to witness for God, it would have no effect.

4. Every Christian makes an impression by his conduct and witness **either for one side or the other.** His looks, dress, and whole demeanor make a constant impression, one way or the other. He cannot help testifying **for** or **against** God. He's either gathering for Christ or scattering abroad. At every step, you tread on cords that will vibrate to all eternity. Every time you move, you touch keys whose sound will re-echo over all the hills of heaven and through all the dark caverns of hell. Every moment of your lives, you are exerting a tremendous influence that will affect the eternal destiny of souls all around you. You are *"letters, known and read by all men." (II Cor. 3:2)*

5. It is easy to see why revivals do not come and stay. How can they? Just look at God's witnesses and see what they are testifying to! Do you suppose I have such a vain imagination of my own ability as to think that I can bring a revival merely by my preaching, while you live on as you do? Do you not know that as far as your influence goes, many of you are standing right in the way of a revival? That your whole spirit and life produce an influence on the world which contradicts the truth? You contradict yourselves, you contradict one another, you contradict your minister. And the sum total of your whole testimony is: *there is no need of being holy!*

Do you believe the things I've been preaching are true, or are they just the ravings of a disturbed mind? If they are true, do you recognize the fact that they have reference to YOU? You say perhaps, "I wish some of the rich Christians could hear this!" But I am not preaching to them, I am preaching to **you!**

6. Finally, I remark that God and all moral beings have great reason to complain of this false testimony. God's chosen witnesses are turning and testifying pointblank against Him. They declare by their conduct that there is no truth to the Gospel. Heaven might weep and hell rejoice to see this. O how guilty! There you are, going to the judgment, red all over with blood. Sinners are to meet you there–those who have seen how you live, many of them already dead and many others whom you will never see again upon earth. What an influence you have exerted. Perhaps hundreds of souls will meet you on the Judgment Day and curse you (if they are allowed to speak) for leading them to hell by practically denying the truth of the Gospel. What will become of your city, and of the whole world, when the Church is united in practically calling God a liar? They testify by their lives that if they say a little prayer and live a good life, then that is religion enough. O what a doctrine of devils that is! **It is enough to ruin the whole human race!**

This article was edited and paraphrased from chapter nine of the book, *Revival Lectures,* by Charles Finney.

This article is available in tract form as LD#21.

WHAT'S WRONG WITH THE GOSPEL?

Section: 1
"The Missing Parts"
by Keith Green

I know that the title of this article will possibly raise some worried eyebrows. At first glance, some might say to themselves, "Oh no, Keith has gone too far **this** time!" But let me quickly put those possible reactions to rest. To the question, **"What's wrong with the Gospel?"** I can easily answer, **"Absolutely nothing!"** That is, of course, if you're talking about the Gospel of the Bible–the very message that Jesus preached–what the apostles Peter, Paul, John, and the others devoted their very lives (and deaths) to. *(Phil. 1:20-21)*

No, there's nothing at all wrong with this message from heaven. But what about the stuff that's being preached today? Is it truly "gospel-preaching"? Are the evangelists that preach in churches and arenas, on radio and television–are **they** preaching what Jesus called **the Gospel?**[1] And what about the mountains of modern "gospel literature"? You know, the tracts, pamphlets, comic books, newspapers, etc. Do they really contain the same message–the **whole** message–about the salvation that Jesus offered? How are we answering the awesome question that people are still asking the Church, as they asked on the day of Pentecost, **"Men and brethren, what shall we do to be saved?"**[2]

---

1) Matt. 4:23; Mark 1:14-15, 16:15; Luke 3:16-18.
2) Luke 3:10,12,14; Acts 2:37, 16:30.

Is Our Gospel The Gospel?

I believe with all my heart that Jesus would be ashamed of most of the "gospel" messages and sermons that are being preached today, mainly because they lack almost every major point He Himself preached on. *(Mark 8:38; Rom. 1:16; II Tim. 1:8)* How dare we try to change the Gospel. We remove most of its vital parts, and replace them with artificial limbs of our own. *(Gal. 1:6-7)*

Isn't Jesus the master evangelist? Shouldn't we judge **our** evangelism by **His** example?[3] Was His message anything like what we're hearing today? It is my intention to try to briefly cover in Section 1 each of the major parts of the Gospel that have been "surgically" removed in most of today's preaching. And in Section 2, we will go over each of the "new additions" that have become a very **part** of our modern gospel.

The Removed Parts Of The Gospel

The Blood of Jesus. It's a fact that the very word **blood** scares people. It's also a fact that the blood of Christ scares the devil, because it is the only cleansing agent for a sinsick soul.[4] Can you imagine what the preaching and writings of Paul would have been like, if he had been as squeamish in proclaiming the magnificent power and beauty of the blood of Jesus as our generation of preachers are? **What we have now is a bloodless gospel!**

Today, people are afraid to think and preachers are afraid to make them. The whole concept of Jesus being the Passover Lamb of the Old Testament[5] has been lost—"It takes too much time and thought to explain," you will hear some say. *(Heb. 5:11-14)* "We need to simplify the Gospel so that we can reach the masses." Oh, what logic! Remove **the blood** from the preaching of the Gospel, and you remove the power to conquer the devil for the souls of men!

The Cross of Jesus. Paul said, *"I determined to know nothing among you except Jesus Christ, and Him crucified." (I Cor. 2:2)* Nowadays it's "Jesus Christ and what He can do for **you!**" You cannot have more exact opposites than the Bible's **Christ-**centered Gospel,[6] and our modern, cross-less, **me-**centered gospel.

Today, if anyone preaches self-denial as a condition of discipleship, you can hear the comments afterwards: "old-fashioned," "harsh," "legalistic." I dare say that our Lord would have as much trouble finding acceptance among our preachers as He had among the religious leaders of His own day.

The Threats and Terrors of Hell, and the Guilt of Sinners. We often hear people say, "I'm tired of hell-fire and brimstone preaching!" "Well," I often reply, "when was the last time you heard any?" It **is** true, very few people preach on hell anymore—it is no longer in vogue. We shouldn't scare the poor sinners, no, that wouldn't do. They're just unfortunate,

---

3) Eph. 5:1; I Peter 2:21; I John 2:6.
4) Matt. 26:28; Acts 20:28; Rom. 3:25, 5:9; Eph. 1:7, 2:13; Col. 1:20; Heb. 9:14,22, 10:19, 13:12; I Peter 1:2; I John 1:7; Rev. 1:5, 5:9, 12:11, 19:13.
5) Exodus 12:23-24; Isaiah 53:7; Luke 22:15; John 1:29,36; I Cor. 5:7; I Peter 1:19; Rev. 5:6,12, 7:14, 22:1,3.
6) Matt. 10:38; Luke 14:27; I Cor. 1:17-18; Gal. 6:14; Eph. 2:16; Col. 1:20; I Peter 2:24.

> **Here's what A.W. Tozer says about the cross...**
>
> *"The cross is the most revolutionary thing ever to appear among men. The cross of Roman times knew no compromise, it never made concessions. It won all its arguments by killing its opponent and silencing him for good. It spared not Christ, but slew Him the same as the rest. He was alive when they hung Him on that cross, and completely dead when they took Him off of it. That was the cross the first time it appeared in Christian history.*
>
> *"With perfect knowledge of all this, Christ said, 'If any man will come after Me, let him deny himself, take up his cross and follow Me.' So the cross not only brought Christ's life to an end, it also ends the first life, the old life of every one of His true followers... this and nothing less is true Christianity. We must do something about the cross, and there's only one of two things we can do—**flee it or die upon it!**"*

misguided souls, right? Wrong! The Bible clearly shows that they are rebels who have robbed and dishonored the living God, infinitely offending Him.[7] They have no right to look at themselves in any other light.

But we, smart as we are, have decided to help God along. He doesn't understand our generation as well as **we** do. The things Jesus emphasized in His preaching were all right for the Jews, but **our** generation needs a more gentle, loving tone. **"Tell 'em about heaven!"** We talk about heaven, about the "rewards of being born-again," but we completely neglect the other side of the "two-edged sword." *(Heb. 4:12)* What right do we have to remove things from the Gospel that Jesus Himself gave great place to in His own preaching?[8]

The Law of God Preached to Convict One of Sin. Pages could be written on this subject, but there is room for only one brief example. When the rich young ruler came to Jesus, he asked a very direct question: "Good Master, what must I do to inherit eternal life?" Can you imagine what our preachers would answer him today? "Just admit you're a sinner, accept Jesus as your Personal Savior, go to church, pay your tithes, try to be good, and you're in!" But what was Jesus' answer? "You know the commandments... if you wish to enter into life, keep the commandments." (Matt. 19:17; Mark 10:19) **The commandments??** Why they went out with Cecil B. DeMille! Isn't this the "age of grace"?

Well, the truth is Jesus wasn't preaching the commandments to him as the way of salvation, He was using the commandments to specifically convict him of his particular sin—greed. That rich boy loved the bucks, and Jesus knew just how to flush him out of the bushes—**preach the Law!** And that's exactly what the Law is for—*"For through the Law comes the knowledge of sin"* (Rom. 3:20), that's what Paul said. The Law must be preached—not as the way of salvation, but as a searchlight put on the sinner's heart, so he can see how utterly rotten he is, compared to the way God requires him to be. *(Gal. 3:24)*

---

7) John 8:44; Acts. 13:9-11; I Cor. 6:9; Gal. 4:16; Eph. 2:1-3; James 4:4; II Peter 2:12-19.
8) Matt. 5:22, 8:12, 10:28, 13:41-42, 49-50, 22:11-14, 23:13,33, 24:48-51, 25:30,46; Luke 13:26-28.

But today again, we are wiser than God. Our preaching isn't filled with "dos and don'ts." No, we don't want to scare the "liberated generation" away. Why, if we said that fornication was wrong, or drugs, or abortion, or any other **specific** sin, people would feel all condemned and then how could they get saved? But that's just it, Jesus preached the Law to the rich young ruler so that, after feeling condemned about his greed, he could turn and obey Jesus and find true treasure in heaven. *"Go and sell all you possess and give it to the poor, and you shall have treasure in heaven, and come, follow Me." (Mark 10:21)* Unless people are truly convicted of sin, if they do not fully see that they are totally condemned by the requirements of God's Law, then it is virtually impossible to show them the need for a savior. Why, what would they need to be saved from? **Fun?**

That is why our modern gospel must dwell on "all the good things God'll do for you if you'd just accept Him!" We can't convince a sinner that he needs a savior by just getting him to admit that, "Well, generally, yes, I am a sinner." He must see how the Law of God totally condemns him as a sinner,[9] and then the beauty of the Gospel, the glory of the cross, the marvelous power of Christ's blood will be able to penetrate his anxious, waiting mind and heart. Only by the preaching of the Law can a man fully desire to be saved from his sin. For, *"I would not have come to know sin except through the Law." (Rom. 7:7)*

The Fear of God and the Judgment Seat of Christ. Instead of the awesome majesty of Jehovah, today the Lord is presented as a sort of "ice cream man–Santa Claus." And the Church is the "candy store" where you can get "every goodie your heart desires." Jesus Himself is portrayed as "a sweetie pie," **so** good, **so** loving, **so** forgiving, and **so** gentle, that you can almost hear the preacher whisper, "Aw, He wouldn't hurt a fly…" But what happened to *"It is a terrifying thing to fall into the hands of the living God" (Heb. 10:31),* or *"The fear of the Lord is the beginning of wisdom"? (Proverbs 9:10)*[10]

---

9) Rom. 2:12,20, 3:20-21, 4:15, 5:13,20, 10:4; I Cor. 15:56; Gal. 2:16,19, 3:10-11; James 2:9-11.
10) See also Duet. 5:29, 10:12; Joshua 24:14; II Kings 17:39; Psalm 2:11, 15:4, 19:9, 25:14, 31:19, 33:18, 34:7,9,11, 52:6, 60:4, 67:7, 72:5, 85:9, 86:11, 103:11,13,17, 111:5, 112:1, 147:11; Proverbs 8:13, 10:27, 13:13, 14:26-27, 15:16, 16:6, 19:23, 23:17, 28:14, 31:30; Isaiah 8:13; Jer. 32:39-40; Malachi 3:16, 4:2; Matt. 10:28; Luke 1:50; Acts 10:35, 13:26; II Cor. 7:1; Eph. 5:21; Phil. 2:12; Heb. 12:29; I Peter 1:17; Rev. 14:7.

The wise, new editors of modern preaching rhetoric have conveniently wiped out every reference to the Almighty's severity while emphasizing only His kindness. This they do, ignoring the balanced, biblical view of Paul, *"Behold then the kindness and severity of God." (Rom. 11:22)*

Repentance as Necessary for Forgiveness. It has always amazed me how the Church could have evolved to such a state as it is in now, with such clear, direct teaching from the Lord Jesus as to what is necessary to be right with God. Please read the first five verses of the 13th chapter of Luke. Here, Jesus is told the news about some Galileans who were executed by the Romans. He then says, *"Unless you repent, you will all likewise perish."* Using another example, He then repeats the same exact sentence.

I cannot conceive of conversion without repentance. The teachings of Jesus and the apostles are full of commands to *"repent and be saved!"*[11] Repentance is not just "being sorry"–that is only conviction. Repentance is not merely a change of heart and a change of mind, it is a change **of action!** God requires that if we are sincerely convinced that sin is wrong, then we will turn from it to God, and commit ourselves to not take part in sinful deeds any longer. God blesses such decisions and commitments with abundant grace. And it is by that grace that we can fulfill the desires of the Spirit within us.

But because there is so little real conviction of sin brought about by the preaching of our modern gospel, we cannot truly require repentance anymore. If we did, no one would "come forward" at all. For repentance is easy to him who sees how ugly and horrible sin is, but repentance is impossible where the Law does not convince the sinner of his wicked heart, compelling him to turn from his sin into the arms of a waiting, compassionate God. You see, all these removed parts of the Gospel are connected. In God's wisdom, every aspect of the appointed way of salvation is irreplaceable.

It is true that without God loving us first, we could not be saved. He made the first move, He always does. But **He** will not do what He requires of the sinner **himself** to do–and that is to **repent!**

"... God saw every rape committed today, He saw every murder, every person that starved to death, every pornographic film and book, every abused and battered child. How can anyone believe that He sees this and does not grieve?"

God's Sorrow and Broken Heart Over Sin. The picture of God as presented today by evangelists is that of an optimist–a positive-thinking good ole boy who lives in heaven, high above the trouble on earth, where

---

11) Psalm 7:12; Isaiah 30:15; Ezek. 18:32; Matt. 3:2; Mark 1:15, 6:7,12; Acts 2:38, 3:19, 8:22, 17:30, 26:19-20; Rev. 2:5,16, 3:3,19.

everything is rosey, "and the skies are not cloudy all day." Why, how could anything bother the living God? He isn't really troubled by all the mess down here, He has **everything under control!**

But again, the Bible paints a different picture of our King. Just look at Jesus weeping over Jerusalem *(Luke 19:41)*, or the pleadings of God with the nation of Israel through the prophets Isaiah or Ezekiel.[12] This God, the one in the Bible, is continually striving with men through His Spirit. It says in Proverbs, *"The eyes of the Lord are in every place, watching the evil and the good." (Proverbs 15:3)* That means that God saw every rape committed today, He saw every murder, every person that starved to death, every pornographic film and book, every abused and battered child. **How can anyone believe that He sees this and does not grieve?** Of course God can grieve. Doesn't the Bible implore us not to *"grieve the Holy Spirit of God"? (Eph. 4:30)*

You see, God is the most hurt and dishonored being in the universe. He could stop all this mess, all the perversion and crime and corruption any time He wishes, but He doesn't! Why? Because He waits for the souls of men and women. *"Regard the patience of our Lord to be salvation,"* Peter said. *(II Peter 3:15)* But the Church, which doesn't have one millionth of the compassion that God has, has turned around and created a god in its own image and likeness. A carefree, cheerful, above-it-all God. And then the Church has conveniently removed from the "gospel" it presents all reference to the pain and sorrow in God's heart. The Church doesn't want a God who's grieved with sin, because then this God would be grieved with them... (and He is!)[13]

The Necessity of Holiness to Please God. Hebrews says without holiness *"no one shall see the Lord." (12:14)* It is true that Jesus commands us to be perfect. *(Matt. 5:48)* It is also true that you most likely have never met a perfect person, nor do you probably ever expect to be perfect yourself. Nevertheless, we still have those uncomfortable words of the Lord, *"Be perfect as your heavenly Father is perfect"!*

Now, because of our dilemma in finding ourselves to be such numbskulls, and seeing the demands of Jesus, we have invented some pretty interesting and **caraazzeey** doctrines. Some Christians have said, "Well, when God looks at us, He doesn't really see us anymore, He sees Jesus instead. And when there's ever sin in our hearts, if God should happen to look at the wrong moment, He'll see a smiling face of Jesus there, instead of seeing our sin. So God sees me as holy –even though I'm not! But... I really am... er, well, you know what I mean!" (I don't happen to believe that God is that easily fooled, not even by Christians.)

Another stranger-than-truth doctrine is that blessed refuge of backsliders called "the carnal Christian." In this example of pretzel-logic, we are led to believe that any "believer" who isn't really "walking with the Lord" at the present time, and is indulging in the things of the world and the lusts of the flesh, can still be considered a "Christian," but not a Christian of the 1st class, no, a Christian of the 2nd class...a "**carnal**

---

12) Isaiah 1:18, 54:7; Ezek. 18:23,32, 33:11; Hosea 11:8.
13) Psalm 78:40-41; Mark 3:5.

Christian." Here we have a case of the "believer" who doesn't **believe.** Oh, he still "believes" that God is God, and that there is a heaven and hell, and so on (but don't forget, the devil believes all these things too!—*James 2:19*) He knows all the right things to say to convince granny, the pastor, and his Christian friends that he's still hanging in there. He even sort of believes it himself. Seems he's got everybody fooled—everybody that is, **except God!** The Bible is clear that *"If we say we have fellowship with Him, and yet walk in the darkness, we lie and do not practice the truth." (I John 1:6)*[14]

Today, possibly the greatest insult to the Gospel has been the almost total neglect of the preaching of holiness for the Christian. Jesus doesn't want to make believe that we're holy, He wants to **impart** His holiness to us by the Holy Spirit. But because people are not being driven to the cross, convicted by His Law to repentance and real rebirth, then we have to spend hours in our seminaries trying to find suitable, complicated ways to explain away the obvious meanings of scripture.

To all this you might be saying, "But what about all those people getting saved by the efforts of good men and ministries out there? They're not preaching the way you say they should, and **they** still have converts!" Well, the immediate answer to that question is, "The people are not getting saved

---

14) Here are only a few of the many scriptures that say this over and over again, in the clearest possible terms: Psalm 5:4,6; Matt. 7:22; John 3:20-21; II Cor. 6:14; I John 2:4,9-11, 3:10, 4:20.

because of their messages, they're getting saved **in spite** of them." But unfortunately, many of the people who make "decisions for Christ" through large evangelistic crusades, do not even attend church regularly in the years that follow. (And as you probably well know, "attending church regularly" does not guarantee that one is a true believer.) But let's take a closer look at what kind of "converts" today's gospel usually produces.

What's Specifically Wrong With Our Modern Gospel?

It's Me-Centered Instead of Christ-Centered. First and foremost, it is the gospel that appeals to the selfish. Instead of honoring God, it places the sinner at the center of God's love and plan. But the Bible places Jesus at the center of God's plan, **not** the sinner.

The sober, biblical truth that needs to be presented to the sinner's mind is "You have made yourself an enemy of God, and in your present state of rebellion there is absolutely no hope for you." In fact, God's "plan" for the sinner at this point in his life is to separate him forever from His presence in hell. However unpopular or unlovely that may sound, it is the **only** truth and reality about anyone who is an enemy of God through sin.

The whole line of reasoning in our modern gospel continues on and on in this mistaken way. "Sin has separated you from God, and the great things He has planned for you. Jesus came and died on the cross, so that you may experience all the blessings that are yours. You must accept Jesus now, so that you will not miss out on all the gifts God is waiting to give to you." **You, you, you, you!!! It's all for YOU!** I'm not sorry to say this, but Jesus did it all in obedience, for His **Father's** glory. *(Phil. 2:8-12)* Of course, it infinitely benefits those who love, serve, and honor Him, but that was a secondary consideration, not the primary one. (Please read *Ezek. 36:22-32.)* If people come to Jesus mainly to **get** a blessing, they will ultimately be disappointed. But if they come to repent and **give** Him their lives in honor and worship, then they will truly have forgiveness and joy–**more than they could ever imagine!** *(I Cor. 2:9)*

It's Shallow, Cheap, and Offered as a "Bargain." Our gospel reduces the good news to a "come and get it while you can" sale. We make every effort to take all the bones out–everything that might offend someone, might make them hesitate or put off their decision. Jesus didn't do this. He never lowered the requirements for anyone. One had to be completely sincere, totally humbled, having counted the cost, willing to leave everything, family and property, *"count all things loss"* so that they might *"gain Christ." (Phil. 3:7-8)* When that same rich young ruler *"went away sad, for he had many possessions" (Matt. 19:22),* Jesus didn't go running after him shouting, "Hey, wait a minute! Let's talk this thing over, it isn't as bad as it might sound. Maybe I was a little too harsh!"

Maybe we're so eager to "see the converts" that we'll do anything to rush someone into a "decision" before he's had a chance to really make one. The problem is, if you have to rush him into it, he probably will change his mind later anyway. For as a friend of mine says, "If somebody can talk them into it, somebody can talk them out of it!" *(I Cor. 1:17)*

Salvation is Shown as a Barter or Trade, Instead of the Result of Obedience by Faith. We offer forgiveness of sin like Monty Hall on "Let's Make a Deal." I've even heard, "You give Jesus your sin, and He'll give you salvation in return!" No one in the Bible ever thought so low of the grace of God to talk about the gift of eternal life like it was for trade. **It is a gift!** You can't earn it, or buy it, or give anything in return for it. How it must offend the Holy Spirit to hear people talk of His Jesus so. *(Acts 8:18-23)*

It Produces Selfish, "Blessed," and Feelings-Oriented "Converts." Anyone who is made to believe he becomes a Christian under such preaching will seldom bring forth the true fruits of a real convert. He will remain just as selfish as he always was, only now his selfishness will take on a religious form. If he wants something for himself, he will say he "has a burden" for something, or he will say, "It is the desire of my heart," or some other religious-sounding phrase like that. He will pray selfishly, desiring blessings for himself, and even if he does pray for others, it usually will be for selfish reasons. After all, when he "accepted the Lord," he was told how much Jesus wanted to bless him and how much God had stored up for his account, and how the Bible was like "a checkbook full of promises, just waiting to be cashed!"

Such a person always seeks to "feel" good about himself, his own church, his own pastor, etc. His whole world is built on **feeling blessed.** He was never shown how he was created to bless God...God was **not** created to bless him. *(Psalm 149:4; Phil. 2:13)*

As you can see, the "converts" described above are not like those pictured in the book of Acts, when the Church was new and the fire was hot. Take a look at *Acts 2:41-47* and *4:31-35,* and you will see the tender spirit of love, and the mighty spirit of power that prevailed among the brethren in those early days. I believe that one of the great reasons that *"everyone kept feeling a sense of awe" (Acts 2:43),* was because *"they were continually devoting themselves to the apostles' teaching and to prayer." (vs. 42)* I believe that Peter and the others made every effort to convey the **whole** message of the Gospel when they preached and taught, and that is why the Spirit of God could anoint and bless the new converts so powerfully—**God always anoints the truth!** *(Isaiah 55:11)*

We have looked in Section 1 at each of the aspects in the preaching of Jesus and the apostles that seem to be missing from today's gospel. In Section 2 we will see how the modern church has replaced these things with some *new* ideas of its own.

This article is available in tract form as LD#22.

What's Wrong With The

Section 2: "The Added Parts"

—by Keith Green

In each generation there have been various ways and means used to secure the attention of sinners so that they may be shown the truth and then led into a saving knowledge and true relationship with the Lord Jesus Christ.

It is a fact that man is a creature of habit. He loves form, doesn't like things to change "too quickly," and **he clings to tradition.** Unfortunately (for man), God is no such person. Though something has never been tried before, God simply does not care. His only concern is that it is the wisest and most direct way of accomplishing His desire.

This of course, threw the children of Israel into many a panic. "What's God doing now?" If there was a big sea in the way, no problem, He just split it. If there wasn't any water, snap! A drinking fountain from a rock. Food running low? Presto! It'll rain bread in the morning. And Jesus had the same way of dealing with things. When His disciples were far from shore, it didn't matter, Jesus just strolled over the waves. Problem with the weather? "Shut up wind!" And so it went...[1]

Now as you can see in the Bible, God had a lot of problems with man and his traditions. Just take a look at the Jews—how they loved their temple, their sacrifices, their Sabbath—too bad they didn't care much for their God. And Jesus ran up against the whole stubborn lot of them. "Did you see that? Why, He healed on the Sabbath!" *(Luke 13:14)* At every turn, Jesus tried to show them the truth, using the wisest reasoning and the best examples,

---
1) Exodus 14:21-22, 16:4, 17:6; Matt. 14:25; Mark 4:39.

but they kept getting hung up on His methods—**touching** lepers, raising the dead, hanging out with sinners, whipping moneychangers—it scared them to death![2] Their religion was basically peaceful, very solemn and quiet. But Jesus...why Jesus had the whole town in an uproar at least once a week! You can see why He bothered them; He disturbed their nice little religion...**with the truth!** *(John 8:44-45)*

It is obvious that God anoints men and women who are completely yielded to His Spirit. He also anoints methods and tools that we use—meetings, tracts, books, music, witnessing, preaching, etc.—when they are also fully submitted to Him in faithfulness. But there is a great danger when man (or even God) designs a tool to be used for God's glory, and then as time passes, people's attention starts to be fixed on the tool itself, rather than on the glory of God (which it was originally designed to promote).[3]

The following is a list of just some of the tools, methods, and concepts that I believe have become so much a part of presenting the modern gospel, that they have become just about inseparable from it. In fact, they are to such an extent considered necessary, that if many of them are left out of an evangelistic meeting, Christians can hardly believe that **anyone can be saved there.**

Some Inventions Of Man That Have Become Essential Parts Of The Modern Gospel

The Term and Concept of "Personal Savior." I find it very disturbing when something unnecessary is added to the Gospel. The use of the term "Personal Savior" isn't very harmful in itself, but it shows a kind of mindset that is willing to "invent" terms, and then allow these terms to be preached as if they were actually found in the Bible.

But why must we do this? Why must we add needless, almost meaningless things to the Gospel? It is because we've taken so much out that we have to replace it with "spiritual double talk." That's right, **double talk!** Would you ever introduce your sister like this: "This is Sheila, my **personal** sister"?! Or would you point to your navel and say, "This is my personal bellybutton"? Ridiculous! But nevertheless, people solemnly speak of Christ as their **personal** Savior, as if they've got Him right there in their shirt pocket—and as if when He returns, He will not have two, but **three** titles written across His thigh: **King of kings, Lord of lords, and PERSONAL SAVIOR!** (See *Rev. 19:16.*) This is only one example of how a non-biblical term can be elevated to reverence by the Church, as if to say, "Well even if it isn't in the Bible—it should be!"

The Altar Call. Imagine if you can, Jesus having people bow their heads after hearing the Sermon on the Mount, and then very slowly and softly (while Bartholemew plays "How Great Thou Art" on the accordian) saying to the crowd, "While your heads are bowed and your eyes are closed, if you really

---

2) Matt. 8:2-3, 9:11; John 2:15, 11:43-44.
3) See II Kings 18:4—Because it had now become an idol, King Hezekiah had to destroy the same bronze serpent that Moses had made in Numbers 21:8, which was used to stop the plague of death among the Israelites. This is the same bronze serpent referred to by Jesus in reference to Himself, in John 3:14!

want to be My disciple tonight, if you really want to show My Father and I that you truly mean to follow this sermon I have given, then I want you to slip your hand up slowly, so that I may see it. There now…yes…yes…I see that hand…and that one…and the one way back by the fig tree…yes! Now, please, while Bart plays another chorus, I'd like you to start moving down through the center of the crowd…yes, those who raised their hand. I want to know if you **really** mean business. I'd like to lead you in a prayer…"

I realize that there are some who will see such an illustration as sacrilegious. And that's just the point. They think that making fun of the "altar call" is making fun of God. But it isn't. Traditions die hard, because

they take so long to form. I once received a very intense letter from the pastor of a church who had sponsored me in a city-wide concert in his area. He was upset that I had "let several hundred souls go ungathered" because I had not given an altar call. He said, "It seems you have no burden for souls." (Nothing could be further from the truth.) But because I had not given the recognized "official invitation," this pastor could see no value in my presentation of the Gospel. Or as a minister I know once remarked, "If you don't give an altar call, they think you have committed the 'unpardonable sin!'"

The Gradual Altering Of The "Altar Call"

Believe it or not, the altar call was invented only about 150 years ago. It was first used by the American evangelist, Charles Finney, as a means of separating out those who wanted to talk further about the subject of salvation. Finney called the front pew "the anxious seat" (for those who were "anxious" about the state of their souls) or "the mourner's bench." Finney never "led them in a prayer," but he and a few others would spend a great deal of time praying with and giving specific instruction to each, one by one, until finally, everyone was sent home to pray and continue seeking God until "they had broken through and expressed hope in Christ," as Finney would say.

> **I believe that a true "sinner's prayer" will gush out of anyone who is truly seeking God and is tired of being enslaved to sin.**

The early Salvation Army, going a bit further on Finney's innovation, developed what they called "the penitent form" or "the mercy seat." After a rousing time of singing and preaching, they would invite any sinner present who wanted to confess his sins to God and repent, to come to the front, and they would be prayed for individually. I have met a few older Christians who used to attend some of these early meetings, and they said that sometimes people would stay there all night, and on a few occasions, even a few days, weeping and confessing their sins with broken hearts. There were always some who would stay right there to instruct them further, encouraging them to make a clean sweep of sin from their lives.

This is what the early "altar call" was like. But gradually, it began to become a fixed part of every meeting, and like all other traditions, it began to lose its original spirit. The "coming forward" part started to be more important than the "sorrow, confession, repentance, and instruction" parts. Eventually, anyone who would "come down the aisle" was excitedly proclaimed "a new believer in Christ!" No matter how they felt, they still were told, "Your sins are forgiven, brother! Rejoice in Christ!" How many a miserable, defeated, and confused person has come away from a meeting like this? *(Jer. 6:14)*

The Sinner's Prayer. Can you also try and imagine this scene where Jesus is leading some new "disciples" in the "sinner's prayer"?

"Wow! There are so many that came forward for salvation tonight!" (The multitude applauds.) "Now, it is very simple. You just repeat this little prayer after Me, and then you're a Christian! Now it doesn't really matter whether you fully understand the prayer...it works just the same. Now ready? Repeat after Me...'Dear Jesus...Come into my heart...'" and so on...

As you can see, when we try to picture Jesus Himself using our modern methods of evangelism, it seems completely foolish. I think this is a very good test for any method. "Could I see Jesus doing this?" or "Could I see Jesus preaching or teaching this?" Since the Bible tells us, *"Walk in the manner that He walked" (I John 2:6),* we should always try to compare our actions and message to the Master's.

It is obvious that there is no "set" **sinner's prayer.** There are many variations, with different lengths, different wordings, different endings, etc., but the contents are usually the same. The prayer usually includes phrases like, "Dear Jesus," "Come into my heart," "I admit I have sinned" (at least the **better** ones contain this last statement–there are some who do not even like to mention **sin** in their "sinner's prayer"), "Fill me with Your Spirit," "In Jesus' name. Amen." Extremely harmless...nothing wrong with a prayer like that, right? Wrong! It isn't the wording that's important, it's the state of heart of the one saying it.

I believe that a true "sinner's prayer" will gush out of anyone who is truly seeking God and is tired of being enslaved to sin. *(Matt. 5:6)* The very act of "leading someone in a prayer" is utterly ridiculous. You will find nothing even remotely like it in the Bible, or among the writings and biographies of those in Church history. It completely savors of crowd and peer pressure tactics, and (please forgive me) brainwashing techniques. I do not believe that Jesus wants to have His disciples "repeat after Me," I believe He wants them to **follow after Him!**[4]

Premature Birth

As with the altar call, the practice of having someone repeat a prayer with the minister probably originated from the best of intentions. And no doubt, there are those who have "followed through," continuing to pray and walk with God, entering into the path of righteousness through God's infinite grace. But also, like the altar call, the so-called "sinner's prayer" is one of those tools that make it alarmingly easy for someone to consider himself a Christian, when he has absolutely no understanding of what "counting the cost" *(Luke 14:28)* really means.

The greatest reason I believe that God can be grieved with the current use of such tools as the "altar call" and "sinner's prayer" is because they can take away the conviction of the Holy Spirit prematurely, before the Spirit has time to work repentance leading to salvation. With an emotional splash that usually doesn't last more than a few weeks, we believe we're leading people into the Kingdom, when really we're leading many to hell–by interfering with what the Spirit of God is trying to do in a person's life. **Do you hear?** Do you understand that this constitutes **"spiritual abortion"?** Can't you see the eternal consequences of jumping the gun, trying to bring to birth a baby that isn't ready?

---

4) Matt. 4:19, 8:22, 9:9, 16:24, 19:21; Luke 9:59; John 12:26, 21:19,22; I Peter 2:21; Rev. 14:4.

We are so afraid that we'll see a "big one that got away," that we'd rather rush someone into a shallow decision, and get the personal gratification of seeing him "go down the aisle," than take the time to fully explain things to him, even if it takes long hours **and** nights of travailing prayer for his soul. We just don't "have the time" to do things God's way anymore.[5]

But God would rather see **one true convert** than an ocean full of "decisions." Oh, can't you see what a mess we're in? What we've done to the Gospel? And when those "converts" no longer want to fellowship with us, when they want to go back to their old friends and their old way of life, we have the nerve to call it "backsliding," when we stood in the very way of them ever "front-sliding" toward the cross! Oh, it breaks my heart to think of that awesome day, when God will judge those who have "stumbled one of these little ones." *(Mark 9:42)*

Other Man-Made Methods That Have Made The Gospel Very Shallow, And Therefore Unbibical

Quick and Easy "1-2-3 Steps-To-Salvation" Booklets. Booklets like these usually mention a "sort-of" repentance like, "you must **turn** from your sins, to Jesus." But they rarely explain what "turning" really means.

---
5) In contrast to this, look at the amount of time and effort Jesus took to explain salvation to one mere Samaritan woman–John 4:3-42.

This is also true of such other vital terms such as "Lord"–they usually refer to Jesus as "Lord," but again, they seldom define "lordship"–and people go their merry way, believing they have the full right to continue running their own lives as long as they call Jesus "Lord." (See *Matt. 7:21; Luke 6:46.*)

I don't care how many letters I get saying how many have been "saved" through such and such a booklet. Jesus said, *"You will know them by their fruits" (Matt. 7:16)* and in another place He said that *"Your fruit should remain" (John 15:16),* which means **it should last!** I believe we shall see in that great day, when God spreads out the lives of men in judgment, just how many were **truly converted** by these booklets and how many were turned aside from the path of righteousness–being led to believe the pleasant half-truths contained therein.

With over a 100 million copies in circulation, these booklets are responsible for getting a certain amount of truth out to places and people that might not otherwise have heard anything about the Gospel. But this is no substitute for personal evangelism. These Gospel tracts cannot become our excuse to not *"preach the Gospel to every creature." (Mark 16:15)* We must not hide behind these tools or think that they can somehow do the job for us. Jesus dealt with each person on an individual basis, pointing out to each of them their particular sin (the woman at the well, the rich young ruler, etc.) and leaving them no place to hide. The content of these booklets is very limited, and they are, in most situations, inadequate to bring conviction of specific sin and break down the excuses that people have for not giving their lives to the Lord. Most people need more than the basic principles, they need to be confronted on their sin, deeply convicted, and exhorted to give up full control of their lives to God immediately.

The "Poor Jesus" Syndrome. This is the form of preaching that misuses the Scripture in Rev. 3:20, *"Behold, I stand at the door and knock…"* How many evangelists have used that Scripture to paint a pathetic picture of Jesus standing outside a door, waiting, knocking, knocking, waiting, for the sinner to open up and let Jesus in? Sometimes these preachers go on and on, until it starts to sound like, "Aw, poor Jesus is out there in the cold, shivering, waiting for someone to let Him in. Won't you go ahead and let poor Jesus into your heart?"

What a line of reasoning. First of all, this statement by the Lord in Revelation is not to the unsaved, it's to the Church in Laodicea (see *3:14*). The picture **is** truly pathetic. Jesus is standing outside of **His own church,** knocking for them to let **Him** in! (Sound familiar?) And if there's any doubt left as to who He's talking to, look at verse 22, *"He who has an ear, let him hear what the Spirit is saying **to the churches.**"*

Second of all, the truth of the matter for sinners is the exact opposite. Jesus is not outside of their world, knocking to come in–**they** are outside of **His Kingdom!** And they can knock all night like the five foolish virgins *(Matt. 25:11),* but Jesus will never let them in unless they meet the requirements: a humble and contrite heart, and a complete disgust for sin.

Then, and only then, will God deliver them from their slavery to sin—and transfer them by His grace to the Kingdom of His lovingkindness. God will never repent for someone—He will take every step possible to make the sinner see the folly of his ways, but the final move is up to the individual himself. Each person must make the final surrender, the desperate gasp of "I am a fool to run my own life! Lord, show me the way to **your** door, and I'll knock and knock, and beg forgiveness...I'll do anything, anything, ANYTHING YOU SAY!" Then, and only then, will God save a sinner.[6]

Bumper Stickers, Cheap Clichés, and "Christian" Slogans. It pains me to see the beautiful truths of Scripture being plastered about like beer advertisements. Many think it is wise to "get the word out" in this way, but I believe that we are really just innoculating the world with bits and pieces of truth—giving them their "gospel shots." (And we're making it hard for them to "catch" the real thing!) People become numb to the truth when we splash our gaudy sayings in their eyes at every opportunity. Do you really think this is "opening them up to the Gospel"? Or is it really just another way for us to get smiles, waves, and approval from others in the "born-again club" out in the supermarket parking lot, who blow their horns with glee when they see your "Honk if you love Jesus!" bumper sticker?

---

6) Psalm 34:18, 51:17; Isaiah 66:22; Luke 18:14; James 4:10.

What about those "other sayings"? You know, the quasi-biblical ones, like "Please be patient, God isn't finished with me yet," which can really be a horrible replacement for "I'm sorry." (And besides, it puts the blame on the wrong person–"The reason I'm such a creep is because **God** isn't finished with me yet.")

And if you really want to play "Stretch the Bible" there is that other fabulous excuse that absolutely ends all quests or expectations for holiness: **"Christians aren't perfect…just forgiven!"** Ah, how convenient. You might just as well say, "Christians aren't moral, just forgiven!" or what about "Christians aren't nice, just forgiven!" What we're saying by this glorious piece of prose is, "Madam, you cannot trust your teenage daughter with my Christian son, you'd better keep your eye on him…he's not safe…he's just forgiven!"

Maybe I've gone a little too far to make a point, but I think the world is completely sick to its stomach with our sayings and "witnessing tools." It's time for us to be expressing the truth with our lives, and then the **whole** truth of God with our lips!

"The Follow-Up Program." There is one last great mistake being committed in the name of evangelism. It is rightly called "follow-up." I say "rightly called" because it is following up the same miserable and incomplete gospel with a miserable, incomplete, and false replacement for what the Bible calls "discipleship."

Our "follow-up" usually consists of a "packet of literature," which almost always includes a complete list of all church services and functions. This "packet" also may include many "essential" items like a complete Bible study on "tithing." Also enclosed is usually at least one tithe envelope. (It's amazing that this is one "principle" that nearly every new believer learns right away!)

In my studies of the life of Jesus, it has amazed me that He never had "a follow-up program." It was usually His habit to let people "follow **Him** up." He never had to go door to door, looking for that fellow who He healed last week, wanting to share another parable or two. He always seemed to have the attitude of, "If they want life, then they'll have to come and follow Me."

Can't you see what fools we are? We preach a man-made, plastic gospel. We get people to come forward to "the altar" by bringing psychological pressures that have nothing to do with God. We "lead them" in a prayer that they are not yet convinced they need to say. And then to top it all off, we give them "counseling," telling them it is a sin to doubt that they're really saved!

Conclusion

And now we come to the end of this "Bible study." Yes, that's just what it has turned out to be. I hope you will take the time to look up each of the Scriptures given, and see for yourself what God has said in His Word about all these things. I realize that these articles will step on many toes, and some might even be deeply offended, but that is not my intention at all. My only prayer is that through this little effort, many will begin to take up the cross and preach the good news of our salvation with the same power and anointing that Jesus promised and gave to the early Church, and that when we ministers stand before Him on that great day, we will be able to say with Paul, *"I have fought the good fight, I have finished the course, I have kept the faith...I have fully preached the Gospel of Christ" (II Tim. 4:7; Rom. 15:19),* so that we may hear those sweet words from our King's lips, *"Well done, good and faithful servant!" (Matt. 25:21)*

Beloved family, the world around us is going to hell. Not because of communism, not because of television, not because of drugs, or sex, or alcohol, or the devil himself. **It is because of the Church! We are to blame!** We alone have the commission, the power, and the truth of God at our constant disposal to deliver sinner after sinner from eternal death. And even though some are willing to go...into the streets, the prisons, foreign lands, or even next door, they are taking a watered-down, distorted version of God's message which He has not promised to anoint. That is why we are **failing.** And unless we admit that we are failing, then I'm afraid there is no hope for us or the world around us. We have the choice between causing eternal tragedy for our whole generation, or bringing our beloved God a whole family full of "good and faithful servants."

Please pray over all of this. God is waiting to meet you in the closet. *(Matt. 6:6)*

The following is a list of books for further in-depth study on evangelism and the content of the Gospel:

Today's Gospel by Walter Chantry–The Banner of Truth Trust

Finney on Revival by Charles G. Finney–Fleming H. Revell Co.

Gems from Tozer by A.W. Tozer–Christian Publications, Inc.

That Incredible Christian by A.W. Tozer–Christian Publications, Inc.

This article is available in tract form as LD#23.

BEING A CHRISTIAN AT HOME

By Melody Green

"Dear Melody,

"You are a very real Christian source and authority for my 16-year-old daughter, and I am very grateful... but (here it comes) I feel there are areas in which parents (this parent anyway) need your support and help. You do well in many areas of teaching—and so does the local church. But in the area of **'practicing love in your own home,'** both the local church and the teen ministry aren't doing so well. The ministry to teens usually includes teaching on sex, dating, soul winning, honesty, problem parents, alcohol, etc. One really doesn't see many tracts called, 'Parents —Things We Throw Away?' or books titled, 'Do Yourself A Favor, Love Your Parents.'

"It seems that our 16-year-old likes to be responsible for either of our two cars, but not for washing the dishes or cleaning the tub or setting the table. Sure, if we pay her to clean the house, she will vacuum—but not very well. She feels she must love our neighbor, but not her nine-year-old sister. We find she speaks respectfully to those in church, but not to us. After all, dad isn't even a Christian—and all mom does is lecture! There seems to be an 11th commandment, 'Thou shalt work hard every place... except at home.'

"It is very difficult for me, as a parent, to get help at the local church when they see my daughter as 'perfect.' And it is also very difficult to even get prayer support when the reply is, 'Be thankful she's not on drugs, or out running around.' I **am** grateful she isn't doing these things, but it is hard to share the love of Jesus if we aren't proving it at home.

"Our daughter is a very good girl, but she isn't very loving to her family, and I feel **that** is where we really must practice the love Jesus has given us. I feel it is wrong to moan and groan over having to wash dishes or vacuum or hang up clothing. And I've noticed among Christian teens it is a sport to slander their parents' character, with tales of who's the most severe, unreasonable, and strict. I caught her in this sport. She admitted it, but never apologized. She will say the words, 'I'm sorry,' but not with her heart—and this is a very serious spiritual condition.

"Any attempt on my part to bring her to a repentant heart only brings the retort, 'Will you stop lecturing me!' But I hurt for my child and for myself. I want so much to get close to her and love her—but right now this doesn't seem possible. And until it is, I pray a lot for wisdom and courage, and for her eyes to be opened to the love this parent has for her.

"Thank you for hearing me out.

"I love you people,"
(Name kept anonymous)

> *"Do nothing from selfishness or empty conceit, but with humility of mind let each of you regard one another as more important than himself; do not merely look out for your own personal interests, but also for the interests of others."*   —Philippians 2:3-4

I responded to this letter shortly after receiving it, but the thought of answering it openly has always been in the back of my mind. I feel that the problem expressed by this mother is shared by many, and even goes beyond just "problem teenagers." I think it applies to all of us in one way or another—and that each of us can learn something from this mother's dilemma.

"You always hurt the ones you love," are the words to an old song. I used to nod my head in agreement...that is until I became a Christian. Now I know that those words are simply **not true.** They should be changed to, "You always hurt the ones you **love less** than you love **yourself!**" As I look back to all the times I've hurt those closest to me, I can honestly say that most of it was due to pure selfishness on my part. I wanted what **I** wanted—and I figured that those who loved me most were the most likely to continue loving me, no matter **how** I acted. They were committed to a relationship with me—they'd never say "get lost." Why, they understood my "moods" and knew "I really didn't **mean** to be such a jerk."

The hardest testing ground for our Christianity is right in our own homes—with our parents, our brothers and sisters, our husbands and wives, and our children. If we can't prove our Christianity there, we can't prove it anywhere! If we won't go the extra mile for those we literally share our lives with, who are we trying to kid when we knock ourselves out by being "super spiritual" at the Bible Study? You may be fooling your friends at church, but at home, in the eyes of those who know you best, you are nothing but a **religious hypocrite**–following in the footsteps of the Pharisees.[1] Real Christian love should start at home with those closest to you–and spread out to others from there. If on Judgment Day, God called your family as witnesses to your sincerity and example of serving Jesus–how do you think they would rate you?

Some Questions For Teens

You may be a teenager living at home like the girl described in this letter. Let me ask you a few simple questions: Do **you** cheerfully obey your parents in doing all they ask of you?[2] Do you respect them in your actions, attitudes, and manner of conversation? Can you receive a "no" as willingly as a "yes"? Do you do extra little things that you know will bring them joy, or do you fill their days with grief because of your selfish attitudes? Do you do your chores in a sloppy, half-hearted way, or do you "forget" them until mom gives up and does them herself?[3] Do you argue, pout, and throw yourself around when you can't have your own way?[4] Are you rude and sarcastic–refusing to be corrected?[5] Do you mock your parents behind their back?[6] Do you resent spending time with your younger brothers and sisters–helping mom with them, playing with them, teaching them? Do you sometimes lie–by telling only "part of the story"?[7] Do you raise your hands at your youth group to praise God before men[8]–but grumble and consider it a "supreme sacrifice" whenever you're asked to lift your hands to help around the house–or do you insist on being **paid** for it? Do you call yourself a Christian?

What About Mom And Dad?

I have unfortunately come across this problem with teenagers before, and it is a very sad one. However, as I see it, they are not the only ones who sometimes find it hard to be a Christian at home. I think this problem can extend out to every member of the family.

A very wise man who's been a Christian some 60-odd years once said to me, "I can always tell how spiritual a man is by the way he treats his wife." Husbands, are you kind, courteous, and patient–or do you growl and snap at the slightest provocation?[9] Do people at church see you as a real "spiritual giant"–while at home your family is starving for godly guidance, encouragement, and example?[10] Do you exasperate your children, causing them to lose heart, instead of bringing them up in the discipline and instruction of the Lord?[11] Do you share God's Word with others, but neglect to live it at home–ignoring family worship and Bible Study?[12]

---

1) Matt. 23:27-28
2) Col. 3:20
3) Col. 3:23-25
4) Phil. 2:14-15
5) Proverbs 15:5,10,31-32; 29:1; Psalm 50:16-17
6) Proverbs 30:17; Lev. 20:9; Mark 7:10
7) Rev. 22:15
8) Matt. 6:5
9) I Peter 3:7; Col. 3:19; I Cor. 13:4
10) Eph. 5:25-30
11) Eph. 6:4; Col. 3:21
12) Deut. 4:9-10; Isaiah 38:19

And what about us wives—do we whine, nag, and manipulate to get our own way?[13] Are we totally honest about everything, or do we keep things from our husbands—telling them "little white" lies?[14] Do we consider it more spiritual to serve on church committees than to serve our family—

"Do people at church see you as a real 'spiritual giant'—while at home your family is starving for godly guidance, encouragement, and example?"

cooking, cleaning, washing, and **caring**—making a real home for them?[15] Do we (even in "small" ways) show a lack of respect for our husband's authority to our children—teaching them rebellion and deceitfulness and thus invalidating the Word of God?[16]

Smile...You're On Candid Camera

If someone hid a secret camera in your home for a day, then showed the film the following Sunday at church, would you be ashamed for them to see the way you **really** treated each other when no one else was around? Do you go out of your way to serve or to **be served?**[17] Do you do the things you know will please, whether you are asked to or not? Do you quickly say you're sorry—and **really mean it**—when you are wrong?[18] Are you a godly example of Jesus to your children, showing them by your actions as well as your words what it means to love God—or do they see you at your worst...maybe even taking it out on them when you get in a bad mood?

Some Excuses

I think everyone has a tendency to rationalize their ungodly actions at home because—"They **know** I'm pressured by final exams" or "I had a terrible day at work" or "The washing machine broke down again!" We would never have the nerve to take our frustrations out on our friends the same way we do on our family. We know if we did, they probably wouldn't

---

13) I Peter 3:1-5
14) Rev. 21:27; Proverbs 28:13
15) Proverbs 31:10-31
16) Eph. 5:22-24; Col. 3:18; Titus 2:3-5
17) Mark 10:43-45
18) Proverbs 16:18; 26:12

stay our friends for long! It's really hard to understand how we can be so insensitive to the very people who have loved us and sacrificed the most for us. Why are we so quick to see their shortcomings—and so very slow to forgive, forget, and go on with them in tenderness and lovingkindness?[19]

Of course, when you live with others, their faults are more readily exposed—but then, so are **yours**. This just makes it all the more necessary to continually walk in the Spirit—with plenty of grace, forebearance, and mercy towards one another.[20] The home is a true testing ground and a real place of potential spiritual growth. We are constantly being sandpapered by those around us—the rough edges and snags becoming smoothed and polished. God uses us in this way with each other. If we see it in this light, we have a real opportunity to become more and more like Jesus. If we are self-righteous, stubborn, and constantly demanding our "rights"—we will not only be a grief to God, but a real source of misery to those who have to live with us.[21]

What Can Be Done?

If you have been falling short of the calling of God in your home—failing to be a constant example of Jesus—you need to fall on your knees before God and ask His forgiveness. Your home has been a refuge for your flesh far too long.[22] Do not take this matter lightly, for you have mocked God by living in such a disgraceful manner—bringing shame to the holy name of Jesus. **You must repent immediately!**[23]

Once you have ceased your rebellion and again become right with God, you need to go to the people you have offended and, with your whole heart, ask them to forgive you for the hurt you have caused them. Don't leave anyone out...from the youngest to the oldest. You must especially ask forgiveness of those who are **not** Christians—or how will they ever see in you the humble spirit and contrite heart of a true believer?[24] Perhaps you may want to call a family meeting and speak to everyone at once. However you decide to do it—do it quickly. Your rebellion toward God has been evident to all, and amends must be made. If you consider yourself a Christian, you must not delay in setting everything right. If you hesitate, you not only deceive yourself, but you make those around you see that serving God is a waste of time, since it has borne no real or lasting fruit in **your** life. You will remain a hypocrite in the eyes of your family, **and** in the eyes of God, unless you set your heart and mind to this matter immediately and determine to prove Jesus is real not only by the things you say, but by the way that you live![25]

"Those whom I love, I reprove and discipline; be zealous therefore, and repent."   —Rev. 3:19

---

19) Col. 3:12-14
20) Gal. 5:22-26
21) Eph. 4:30-32
22) Gal. 5:13,19-21
23) Rom. 2:5-8
24) Isaiah 66:2
25) James 1:22; 4:6-8; Rev. 2:5

A Word To Parents...

*"For I have told him that I am about to judge his house forever for the iniquity which **he knew**, because his sons brought a curse on themselves and he **did not rebuke them.**"*
–I Samuel 3:13

This word of the Lord was given to Eli the priest, who was an unfaithful father. Eli honored his sons above God *(I Samuel 2:29)* because he allowed them to openly sin–without taking any effective actions to correct them. We are commanded in the Bible to diligently discipline our children if we really love them. *(Proverbs 13:24)* To allow them to sin and walk in rebellion goes directly against everything the Bible teaches. Yet why is it so many Christian parents have such a hard time obeying God when it comes to this?

I think part of the problem is that parents tend to look at their children's sin–instead of their own. They throw up their hands in exasperation and say, "Well, if he wants to live that way, it's **his** choice." This is true to an extent–but I think many parents shun their biblical responsibilities with older children because the task sometimes seems impossible. *(Psalm 28:7)*

Some Guidelines

As long as a child is under his parents' roof, he should be expected to be an active member of the family. If he is allowed to treat his home like a "boarding house," coming and going as he pleases with no duties or chores, how will he ever learn godly discipline and responsibility?

He should also be expected to comply with the "rules of the house." If none are set up–**they should be!** They don't necessarily have to be written out, but they need to be communicated **and** understood. If these standards are not met, there should be consequences to be paid–which also need to be understood. Yelling and tirades of accusations are definitely out–instead, what is needed are swift and direct penalties in accordance to the disobedience. You must be fair and reasonable, **always** disciplining in love and remembering not to provoke your child to anger *(Eph. 6:4)*–but **you must be firm.** You have to let them know that their bad attitudes, rudeness, refusals to help, etc., simply cannot and **will not** be tolerated. *(Proverbs 29:15,17)* Remember, your son can't take the car unless **you** give him the keys...no matter how much he fusses. God will give you guidelines for the balance between love and discipline if you diligently seek Him–but whatever you do, don't neglect to discipline for fear that your children won't love you. *(Matt. 10:37)* Fear the Lord, **not** your kids. *(Deut. 8:5)* If you act obediently, your children will rise up and bless you–maybe not tomorrow, but in the end they will rejoice that you really loved them enough to care about their souls. *(Proverbs 31:28)*

The Right Balance

Many parents go to extremes–either they are too heavy-handed and oppressive or they let their kids sin without doing much about it. Both extremes are wrong–and they both show selfishness and lack of love on the part of the parents. It takes time and patience to discipline properly—this will mean discipline for the parents too! If you permit your kids to act in ways that violate their own consciences—in ways that they know are wrong—then you are allowing them to harden their hearts against God. Ignoring their sin is just programming them for apostasy! How will they ever obey God in the big things, if they won't even obey you in the small? Yes, there comes a time when they have to make their own choices, but as long as you have a hand in their life, it is utter rebellion on **your** part to allow such behavior to go on. *(I Samuel 15:22-23)* It is not merely a suggestion that you should raise up your children in the right way—but a command. *(Proverbs 22:6)* Why do so many parents see discipline as an **option?** Many times it's the parents' rebellion to God in this area that's inspiring their children's rebellion—both to God, and to **them.** The answer is not easy—but you have to start somewhere.

Sassy, rebellious teens should not be treated as if "nothing is wrong." Refusing to confront the issue may bring a momentary peace, but it will not uproot the sin from their heart. Immediate action is necessary. Sometimes previous plans need to be canceled or activities missed because of sin or lack of a repentant heart. Special privileges and allowances are also things that can be temporarily stopped or modified if necessary. Remember, the wages of sin is **death** *(Rom. 6:23),* and it's more loving for your children to experience a little chastisement now, than to suffer eternally because no one cared enough to see that they didn't become hardened to the voice of the Lord. Teenagers need a tremendous amount of prayer, love, and counsel, but they also need guidelines. In their hearts they are looking for someone to pull the reins in on them—their souls are crying out for it. They don't need you to be their "buddy" when they are in rebellion. They need the **parent** that God gave them to set up godly boundaries and to be diligent to see that they stay within them. *(Proverbs 22:15)*

Your Mission In Life

The most important job you have is raising your children in the ways of the Lord. You can't worry about what your children or others may say. You have to be obedient to God. You have to be right in His eyes. **True** love corrects, reproves, and disciplines. *(Proverbs 13:24)* Are you willing to stand by and let your kids go to hell because it's easier than trying to deal with them in a godly way? *(Proverbs 23:13-14)* You have to face it—they may not have years ahead to "sow their wild oats"—they may be in a fatal accident tomorrow. If that were to happen, would you have the peace of knowing that you did all you could towards the salvation of their souls?

Many Christian parents assume their kids are Christians because they "went forward" when they were five—or because they are involved with the church youth group. This can be very dangerous. If your child is not showing forth real fruit of salvation—there probably isn't any! Be sure you have a realistic view of your child's state with the Lord.

If you see that you have fallen short of your responsibility as a parent, you must seek God's forgiveness for your lack of obedience and determine to be the parent the **Bible** talks about. *(Deut. 32:46; I Chron. 28:9)* Do it now—while there is still time. *(Proverbs 19:18)*

This article is available in tract form as LD#25.

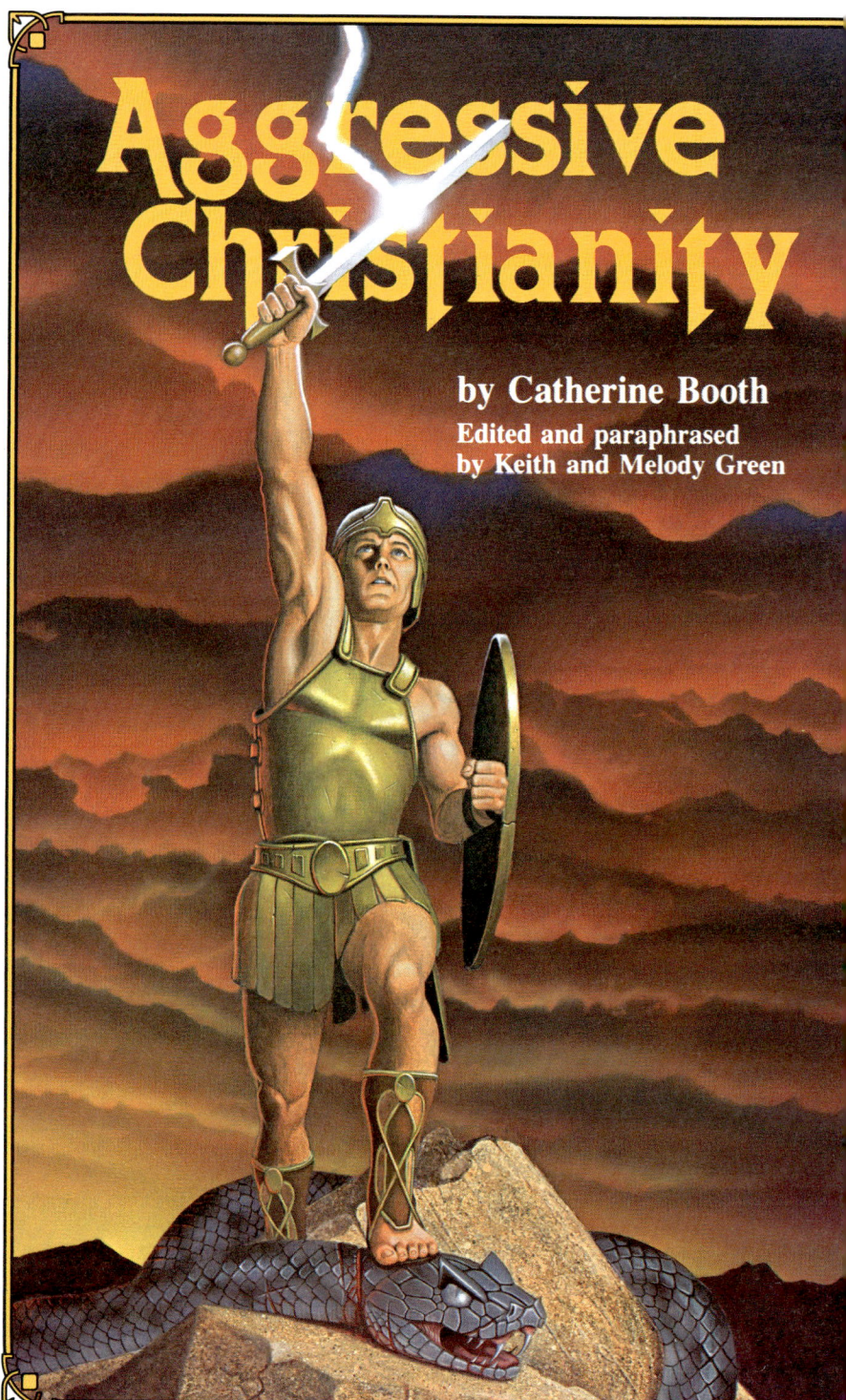

"And He said to them, 'Go into all the world and preach the Gospel to all creation.'"   *–Mark 16:15*

"And I said, 'Who art Thou, Lord?' And the Lord said, 'I am Jesus whom you are persecuting. But arise, and stand on your feet; for this purpose I have appeared to you, to appoint you a minister and a witness not only to the things which you have seen, but also to the things in which I will appear to you; delivering you from the Jewish people and from the Gentiles, to whom I am sending you, to open their eyes so that they may turn from darkness to light and from the dominion of Satan to God, in order that they may receive forgiveness of sins and an inheritance among those who have been sanctified by faith in Me.'"   *–Acts 26:15-18*

I was thinking, while I was reading these passages, what if we could erase from our minds all knowledge of the history of Christianity from the close of the period described in the book of Acts–and then looking at the book of Acts, sit down and try to calculate what was likely to happen in the world. We would most likely expect very different results–a radically changed world as the outcome of it all. A system which started with such power, under such promises and declarations on the part of its Author, and producing, as it did in its first century, such gigantic and monumentous results! We would have thought (if we knew nothing of what has intervened from then until now) that the whole world would have fallen long ago to the influence of that system, and would have been brought under the authority of its great Originator and Founder. I say from reading these Acts, and from observing the Spirit which moved the early disciples, that we should have anticipated ten thousand times greater results–and in my opinion, this anticipation would have been perfectly rational and just.

We Christians profess to have in the Gospel of Christ a mighty lever which, rightly and universally applied, would lift the entire burden of sin and misery from the shoulders (that is from the souls) of our fellow man–a total remedy for all the moral and spiritual woes of humanity. We all profess to believe this–Christians have professed to believe this for generations–and yet look at the world, look at so-called "Christian England and America." The great majority in these nations utterly ignore God, not even making a pretense of remembering Him even one day a week. And then look at the rest of the world. I have often become so depressed with this view of things that I have felt as if my heart would break. I don't know how other Christians feel, but I can truly say that *"My eyes shed streams of water, because they do not keep Thy law." (Psalm 119:136)* And because it seems to me that this dispensation[1] compared with what God intended it to be, has been, and still is, as great a failure as the one that preceded it.[2]

Now I ask, **how can this be?** I do not for one moment believe that this is in accordance with the purpose of God. Some people have a very convenient

---
1) The period of time from Jesus' death and resurrection until now–the new covenant.
2) God's dealings with Israel under the old covenant–the Mosaic Law.

way of hiding behind "God's purposes," and saying, "Oh! He will do His own will." **I wish He did!** They say, "You know, God's will is done after all." **I wish it were!** *He* says (in the Scriptures) it is **not** done, and over and over again laments the fact that it is not done. He wants it to be done... but it is NOT DONE! It is of no use to stand up and state theories and theologies that are in conflict with things as they really are. There has been far too much of this, and it has had a disasterous effect. We see the world is in this terrible condition... nearly 2,000 years have rolled by and here we are! How little has been done, comparatively. What little change has occurred in the habits, attitudes, and choices of the human race.

But some of you will say, "Well, but there *has* been a great deal done." Thank God for that! It would be sad if there were **nothing** done; but it looks like a drop in the ocean compared with what **should** have been done. Now I cannot accept any theory which so tarnishes the love and goodness of God in people's eyes, so as to make **Him** to blame for this lack of vitality and power in Christianity. And so far as **my** influence extends, I will not allow the responsibility and the blame for all of this to be rolled back upon God, Who so loved the world that He gave His only Son to suffering and death in order to redeem it. I do not believe it for a moment! I believe that the old arch enemy has succeeded in bringing about this state of things—in retarding the accomplishment of God's purposes and keeping the world largely under his own power and influence. And I believe he has succeeded in doing this, as he has *always* succeeded before—by ***deceiving God's own people.*** He has *always* done so. He has always conjured up a look-alike of God's real thing, and the closer he can get it to look like the original, the more succesful he is.

He has succeeded in deceiving God's people:

First, *as to the standard of their own religious life.*

And **secondly**—*he has succeeded in deceiving them as to their duties and obligations to the world.*

He has succeeded **first** in deceiving them as to the standard of their own religious life. He has gotten the church, nearly as a whole, to receive what I call an "Oh, wretched man that I am" religion! He has gotten them to lower the standard which Jesus Christ Himself established in His Book—a standard not only to be aimed at, but to be **attained**—a standard of victory over sin, the world, the flesh, and the devil—**real, living, reigning, triumphing Christianity!** Satan knew the secret of the great success of those early disciples. It was their wholehearted devotion, their all-encompassing love for Christ, their utter renunciation of the world. It was their entire absorption in the salvation of their fellow man and the glory of their God. It was an enthusiastic religion that swallowed them up and made them willing to become wanderers and vagabonds—for His sake to dwell in dens and caves, to be torn in two, and to endure persecution in every form to the ends of the earth.

It was **this** degree of devotion which Satan saw he had no chance against. Such people as these he knew would ultimately conquer the world! People could not resist that kind of spirit, that amount of love and zeal, and if Christians

"Many also of those who had believed kept coming, confessing and disclosing their practices. And many of those who practiced magic brought their books together and began burning them in the sight of all..."   —Acts 19:18-19

had only gone on as they began long ago, then the glorious prophecy would have **already been fulfilled**—the kingdoms of this world would have already *"become the kingdoms of our Lord and of His Christ."* (Rev. 11:15)

Lowering The Standard

Therefore the arch enemy said, "What must I do? I will be defeated after all. I will lose my supremacy as the god of this world. What can I do?" No use bringing in a gigantic system of error, which everyone will see to be error. Oh dear no! That has never been Satan's way. **His** plan has been to get ahold of a good man here and there who will, as the apostle says, creep in unaware and preach another doctrine, and who will *"mislead, if possible, even the elect."* (Matt. 24:24) **And he did it!** He accomplished his design. He gradually lowered the standard of Christian life and character. And although in every revival in church history God has raised it again to some extent, we have **never** gotten back completely to the simplicity, purity, and devotion set before us in these Acts of the apostles. For every time God was raising the temperature in the Church so that people were once again on fire with the Holy Spirit—in every age Satan has gotten someone to oppose and to show that **this** was too high a standard for human nature. It was altogether beyond us, and therefore Christians must sit down and just be content to be "Oh wretched man that I am" people, to the end of their days. He has gotten the Church into a condition that sometimes makes one positively ashamed to hear professing Christians talk. It is no wonder that thoughtful, intelligent men are being driven from such Christianity as this. It would have driven me off too, if I had not known the **power** of godliness. I believe **this** kind of religion has made more atheists than all the "atheistic books" ever written.

Yes, Satan knew that he must get Christians down from that high pinnacle of wholehearted consecration to God. He knew that he had no chance till he tempted them down from that blessed vantage point. And so he began to spread those false doctrines, to counteract what John wrote in his epistles–for before he died, John saw what was coming and sounded the alarm down the ages–*"Little children, let no one deceive you; the one who practices righteousness is righteous, just as He is righteous; the one who practices sin is of the devil; for the devil has sinned from the beginning. The Son of God appeared for this purpose, that He might destroy the works of the devil."* (I John 3:7-8) Oh Lord revive that doctrine! Help us afresh to put up the standard!

Oh! The great evil is that dishonest-hearted people, because they feel it condemns them, lower the standard to their miserable experience. I said when I was young (and I have repeated it many times in my maturer years) that **even if it sent me to hell** I would never pull the standard down. Oh, that God's people felt like that! There, in the Bible, the glorious standard is placed before us, the power is offered, the conditions laid down, and we **can** all attain it if we are willing. But even if **we** are not willing–for the sake of the children and for generations yet unborn, do not let us drag the standard down, trying to make it meet our weak and failing Christian experience. LET US KEEP IT UP! That is the way to get the world to look at it. Show the world a real, living, self-sacrificing, hardworking, toiling, triumphing Christianity, and the world will be influenced by it; but anything short of that, they will turn around and spit upon.

Duties And Obligations To The World

Secondly, Satan has deceived even those whom he could not succeed in getting to lower the standard of their own lives, concerning their duties and obligations to the world. I have been reading the New Testament lately with special reference to the aggressive spirit of original Christianity. And as far as I can see, we come infinitely short by comparison. ***"Go into all the world and preach the Gospel to all creation."*** Look at what is implied in this commission. I believe that no generation since that first century has yet fathomed the meaning of this divine commission. **Look at it!** Would it ever occur to you that it really meant, "Go and build chapels and churches, and invite the people to come in, but if they won't–leave them alone"? ***"GO!"*** To whom? *"To all creation."* Where am I to get at them? WHERE THEY ARE. *"All creation."* This is the extent of your commission. Seek them out, run after them, wherever you can get at them. ***"All creation"***–wherever you find a creature that has a soul–there go and preach My Gospel to him. If I understand it, **that** is the meaning and spirit of this commission.

In another commission to Paul, God says *"...I am sending you to open their eyes so that they may turn from darkness to light and from the dominion of Satan to God." (Acts 26:17-18)* They are asleep–go and wake them up. They do not see their danger. If they did, there would be no need for you to run after them. They are **preoccupied.** Open their eyes, and turn them around by your desperate earnestness, intense persuasion, and moral force. Oh! It makes me tremble when I think of how much one man can do for another! *"Turn from darkness to light, and from the dominion of Satan to God."* How did Paul understand this? He says, *"We persuade men." (II Cor. 5:11)* Do not be content with just putting it before them, giving them gentle invitations, and then leaving them alone. Paul ran after the poor souls, and pulled them out of the fire. Do the same! Take the blindfold off their eyes which Satan has bound them with; knock and hammer and burn your words into their poor, hardened, darkened hearts with the fire of the Holy Ghost, until they begin to realize that they are IN DANGER! Go after them. If I understand it, **that** is the spirit of the apostles and of the early Christians.

Sure it's okay to build churches and chapels; we **should** invite the people to them. But do you think it is consistent with these commissions to rest only in this, when three-fourths of the population utterly ignore our invitations and take no notice whatsoever of our buildings and of our services? **They will not come to us.** That is an established fact. Jesus Christ says, "Go after them." He says, *"Go out into the highways and along the hedges, and compel them to come in, that My house may be filled." (Luke 14:23)* I **will** have guests, and if you can't get them in by nice, civil measures, use military measures. Go and **compel** them to come in.

Oh! People say you must be **very** cautious. You must not push religion down people's throats. What! Should I wait until an unconverted, godless man **wants** to be saved before I try to save him? Am I to let my unconverted friends and acquaintances go quietly down to damnation, and never tell them about their souls until they ask, "If you please, I want you to preach to me!" Is this anything like the spirit of early Christianity? No! Therefore we must **make** them look, and if they run away from you in one place, meet them in another, and let them have no peace until they submit to God. This is what Christianity **ought** to be doing in this land, and there are plenty of Christians around to do it. Why, we might give the world such a time of it, that they would get saved in **self-defense**–if we were only aggressive enough and determined that they should have no peace in their sins.

An Example

I had been speaking in a town in the west of England on the subject of the **responsibility** of Christians for the salvation of people's souls. The gentleman with whom I was staying had winced a bit under the truth, but instead of taking it to heart in love and having it enable him to better serve God, he said, "I thought you were rather hard on us this morning." I said, "Did you? I should be very sorry to be harder on anyone than the Lord Jesus Christ would be." He said, "You can push things to extremes you know. You were talking about seeking souls, and making sacrifices. Now you know that we build the chapels and churches and pay the ministers—and if the people won't get saved, we can't help it!" I said, "It **is** very heartless and ungrateful of the people, I agree. But my dear sir, you would not reason this way in a serious physical matter. Suppose a plague were to break out in London, and the Board of Health appropriated all the hospitals and public buildings for the treatment of the disease. And suppose they were to issue proclamations saying that anyone who came to these buildings would be treated free of charge—and best of all, that the treatment was **guaranteed to cure them.** Now what if the people were so blind to their own well-being, so indifferent and uncaring, that they refused to come, and consequently the plague increased and thousands were dying. What would you say? 'Well, the Board of Health has done all they could, and if the people will not go to be healed, they deserve to perish —let them alone!' What? Let the whole land be depopulated? No! If the people will not come to them, **they must go to the people** and make sure that everyone had the necessary treatment to be saved from the plague."

I did not have to explain any further...he understood perfectly, and I believe, by the Spirit of God, he was able to see his mistake, to take it to heart, and determine to get to work for perishing souls.

What We Must Do

Men are preoccupied with many things, and we need to bring this subject of salvation powerfully to their attention. There is some **one soul** that you have more influence with than any other person on earth. Are you doing all you can for their salvation? Take them lovingly aside and say, "My dear friend, I have never spoken to you closely, carefully, and prayerfully about your soul." Let them see the tears in your eyes, or if you can't weep, let them **hear** the tears in your voice. Let them realize that you feel their danger, and are in distress for them. Then God will give His Holy Spirit so they **can be saved.**

It is a bad sign for the Christianity of this day that it provokes so little opposition. If there were no other evidence of it being wrong, I could tell from just that. When the Church and the world can jog comfortably along together, you can be sure there is something wrong. The world has not compromised—its spirit is exactly the same as it ever was. If Christians were equally as faithful to the Lord, separated from the world, and living so that their lives were a reproof to all ungodliness, the world would hate them as much as it ever did. It is the **Church** that has compromised, not the world. You say, "You're implying that we should be getting into endless conflict with the world!" Yes— *"Do not think that I came to bring peace on the earth; I did not come to bring peace, but a sword"* (Matt. 10:34) **There would be uproar, yes!** The Acts of the apostles are full of stories of uproars. One uproar was so great, that the Chief Captain had to get Paul over the shoulders of the people, otherwise he would have been torn to pieces. "What a commotion!" you say. Yes, and bless God, if it was like that now, we would have thousands of sinners saved.

The Dignity Of Love

"But," you say, "wouldn't that be inconsistent with the dignity of the Gospel?" It depends on what you mean by "dignity." It was a very undignified thing, humanly speaking, to die on a cross between two thieves. The Pharisees spat upon the humbled sufferer and shook their heads and said, "He saved others, He cannot save Himself." Ah! But He was intent on **saving others.** That was the dignity of everlasting, unquenchable love, baring its bosom to suffer in the place of its rebellious creature—man. It was incarnate God, standing in the place of condemned man—the dignity of LOVE!

Oh friends! Will you get this baptism of love! Then you will, like the apostles, be willing to stuff your body into a basket and be let down by the wall, if need be—or suffer shipwreck, hunger, peril, nakedness, fire, or sword, or even beheading *(II Cor. 11:23-33)*—if thereby you may enlarge His Kingdom and win souls for whom He shed His blood. Oh Lord, fill us with this love and baptize us with this fire! And then the Gospel will arise and become glorious in the earth, and men will believe in us, and in it. They will feel its power, and they will yield to it by the thousands, and by the grace of God, **THEY SHALL!**

This article is available in tract form as LD#26.

God Comes To New York

by **CHARLES G. FINNEY**

Edited and paraphrased
by **KEITH & MELODY GREEN**

This is an account of the Spirit of God's dealings with the people of Rome (a small village in sparsely populated upstate New York) in the 1820s. It is taken from Chapter XIII of Charles Finney's autobiography.[1] This chapter had a tremendous effect on my spiritual life and changed the very direction of our whole ministry. As you read, try to imagine yourself there. Ask yourself, "Have I ever seen anything like this in my life?" Remember this—the same God that moved like this a century and a half ago still desires to do the same today. He is ever waiting for the one who will take Him at His word.

–Keith

---

1) Still published in its entirety by Fleming H. Revel Company. There is also a somewhat condensed version published by Bethany Fellowship.

We were in the midst of revival—a tremendous moving of God's Spirit in the town of Western, New York. People from the nearby town of Rome began coming to the meetings in large numbers. I could see that the powerful effect the Word was having upon those coming from Rome clearly indicated that the work would soon be spreading to their town.

At this time a Reverend Moses Gillett, pastor of the Congregational Church in Rome, upon hearing what the Lord was doing in Western, came to see what was going on. He was greatly impressed by the work of God there. I could see that the Spirit of God was stirring him up to the deepest foundations of his heart. After a few days, Mr. Gillett came up again. On his second visit he said to me, "Brother Finney, it seems to me that I have a **new** Bible. I've never understood the promises like I do now; I've never gotten hold of them before. I cannot rest, my mind is full of the subject, and the promises are new to me!" The longer we talked, the clearer it became to me that the Lord was preparing him for a great work in his own church.

Soon after this, when the revival was in its full strength at Western, Mr. Gillett persuaded me to exchange Sundays with him.[2] I consented reluctantly.

The Work Begins

The day before our exchange, as I was traveling to Rome, I found myself regretting that I had consented to the exchange. I felt that it would greatly hinder the work in Western, because Mr. Gillett would probably preach some of his old sermons (which I believed would not be suited to the current state of revival there). However, the people were praying mightily, and although his preaching would not stop the work, it might set it back a bit. Nevertheless, I went to Rome and preached three times on the Sabbath—and the Word took **immediate effect.** I could see during the day that many heads were lowered, and a great number of people were bowed down with deep conviction over sin. I preached in the morning on the text, *"The mind set on the flesh is hostile toward God," (Rom. 8:7)* and followed it up with something to the same effect in the afternoon and evening.

I waited on Monday morning until Mr. Gillett returned from Western. I shared my impressions with him concerning the state of the people in his congregation. He did not seem to realize that the work was beginning with as much power as I believed it was. But he was at least willing to call a meeting for inquirers,[3] if there were any in his congregation, and he asked me to be present at the meeting. I told him I would, and that he should spread the news throughout the whole village that there was going to be a meeting of inquiry that evening.

---

2) Meaning that Finney would preach at Mr. Gillett's church, and Mr. Gillett would preach at the church Finney had been preaching at in Western.
3) People who were anxious to talk and pray about the salvation of their souls.

The First "Inquiry" Meeting

The meeting was called at the house of one of his deacons. When we arrived, we found the large living room crowded to its utmost capacity. Mr. Gillett looked around with surprise, obviously bothered—for he saw that the meeting was largely composed of the most intelligent and influential members of his church, including many of the prominent young men in the town. We spent a little while attempting to talk with them, but I soon saw that their feelings were so deeply aroused that there was great danger of an outburst of emotion that would be almost uncontrollable. I therefore said to Mr. Gillett privately, "It will not do to continue the meeting in this way. I will quickly share a few things they need to hear, and then dismiss them."

Nothing had been said or done to create any excitement in the meeting. The feelings were all spontaneous. The work had such power that even a few words of exhortation would make the strongest men writhe in their seats, as if a sword had been thrust into their hearts. It would probably be impossible for one who has never witnessed such a scene to realize what the force of the truth can be under the power of the Holy Ghost. It was indeed a sword, a **two-edged** sword.

Mr. Gillett became quite agitated. He turned pale, and with a good deal of excitement said, "What shall we do? What **shall** we do?" I put my hand on his shoulder and in a whisper said, "Keep quiet, keep quiet Brother Gillett." I then spoke to the people in as gentle but plain a manner as I could, calling their attention at once to their only remedy, and assuring them that it was a present and all-sufficient remedy. I pointed them to Christ, and kept on in this subject as long as they could endure it, which indeed was only but a few moments.

Southern view of

Mr. Gillett was becoming so shaken that I stepped up to him, took him by the arm, and said, "Let us pray." We knelt down right there in the middle of the room. I led in prayer, keeping my voice deliberately low and unimpassioned, but petitioned the Savior to intervene with His blood then and there, and to lead all those present to accept the salvation which He offered—and to believe so thoroughly, that their souls would be saved. The agitation deepened every moment, and as I could hear their sobs and sighs, I closed my prayer quickly and rose suddenly from my knees. They all arose and I said, "Now please go home without speaking a word to each other. Try to keep silent, and do not break out into any loud displays of feeling—but go without saying a word."

At that moment, a young man by the name of Walker so nearly fainted that he fell upon some young men that stood near him—and all of them began to faint and fall together. This had the effect of producing a loud shrieking from those around them—but I hushed them all down and said to the young men, "Please set that door wide open, and go out, and let everyone retire in silence." They did as I requested. They did not shriek, but they went out sobbing and sighing, and their sobs and sighs could be heard till they got out into the street.

This Mr. Walker, of whom I was just speaking, kept silent until he entered his front door, but then he could contain himself no longer. He shut the door, fell upon the floor, and burst out into a loud wailing—in view of his awful condition. This brought his whole family around him and scattered conviction among them all. I learned afterwards that similar scenes occurred in other families. But many, as I later found out, were converted at the meeting and went home so full of joy that they could hardly contain themselves.

The next morning, very soon after sunrise, people began coming to Mr. Gillett's home asking us to go and visit members of their families, whom they reported as being under great conviction. We took a hasty breakfast and started out. As soon as we were in the streets, people began running out of the houses, begging us to go into their homes. Every time we went into a house, the neighbors would rush in and fill the largest room. We would stay and give them instruction for a short time. Then when we'd go to another house, the people would all follow us.

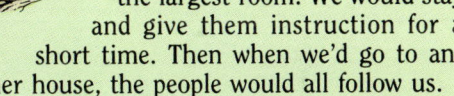
Rome, New York, 1830s.

We found a very extraordinary state of things. Convictions were so deep and felt by everyone that we would sometimes go into a house and find some in a kneeling position and others prostrate on the floor. We visited and conversed and prayed in this manner from house to house until about noon. And then I said to Mr. Gillett, "This will never do, we must hold another meeting of inquiry. We cannot go from house to house, for we are not meeting the needs of the people at all." He agreed with me, but the question arose—where shall we have the meeting?

Mr. Franklin's Dining Room

A Mr. Franklin, a religious man, ran a hotel at that time in the center of town. He had a large dining room, and Mr. Gillett said, "I will stop by and ask him if we can hold the meeting in his dining room." He easily gained approval, and we went immediately to the public schools and gave notice that at one o'clock there woud be a meeting of inquiry at Mr. Franklin's dining room. We went home, had our lunch and then started for the meeting. We saw people hurrying, some of them actually running to the meeting. They were coming from every direction. By the time we got there, the room, though a large one, was completely packed. Men, women, and children all crowded in.

This meeting was very much like the one we had the night before. The feeling was overwhelming. Some men of the strongest nerves were so cut down by the remarks which were made that they were unable to help themselves and had to be taken home by their friends. This meeting lasted nearly until sundown. It resulted in a great number of hopeful conversions, and was used to greatly expand the work on every side.

I preached that evening, and Mr. Gillett appointed a meeting for inquiry the next morning in the courthouse. This was a much larger room than the dining hall, though it was not so central. However, at the appointed hour, the courthouse was full. We spent a good part of the day in giving instruction, and the work went on with wonderful power. I preached again in the evening, and Mr. Gillett appointed another meeting of inquiry the next morning at the church (as no other room in the village was large enough to hold the inquirers).

The Work Continues

At evening we held a prayer and conference meeting in a large schoolhouse. But the meeting hardly began before the feeling deepened so much that, to prevent an undesirable outburst of overwhelming emotion, I proposed to Mr. Gillett that we should dismiss the meeting and request the

people to go in silence—asking Christians to spend the evening in private prayer, or in family prayer, as might seem right to them. Sinners were exhorted not to sleep until they gave their hearts to God. After this the work became so continual that I preached every night for about 20 nights in a row, and twice on the Sabbath. Every morning we held a prayer meeting in the church, then a meeting for inquiry in the afternoon, and I would preach in the evening. There was a spirit of solemnness throughout the whole place, and an awe that made everybody feel that God was there.

Ministers came in from neighboring towns and expressed great astonishment at what they saw and heard. Conversions multiplied so rapidly that we had no way of finding out who was being converted. Therefore, every evening at the close of my sermon, I requested all who had been converted that day to come forward and report themselves in front of the pulpit, that we might be able to talk with them a little while and give them some instruction. Every night we were surprised by the number and the social positions of the people that were coming forward.

"Unless Ye Become Like Little Children..."

A physician, a very likable man but a skeptic, had a little daughter and a praying wife. Little Heather, a girl perhaps eight or nine years old, was strongly convicted of sin, and her mother was excited about her state of mind. But her father was, at first, very indignant. He said to his wife, "The subject of religion is too high for **me**. I could never understand it. Are you telling me that this little child understands it enough to be intelligently convicted of sin? I do not believe it. I know better. I cannot endure it! It is fanaticism—it is madness!" Nevertheless, the mother of the child held fast in prayer. The doctor made these remarks, I learned later, with a good deal of anger, and immediately he saddled his horse and went riding several miles to see a patient. On his way, he later said, the subject of the salvation of his soul took possession of his mind in such a manner that it was completely open to his understanding—and the whole plan of salvation by Christ was so clear to him that he saw that even a child could understand it. He wondered why it had ever seemed so mysterious to him. He greatly regretted what he had said to his wife about little Heather, and felt he must hurry home so he could take it back. When he got home, he was another man—he told his wife what had gone through his mind, encouraged dear little Heather to come to Christ, and both father and daughter have since been earnest Christians and have lived long and done much good.

But in this revival, as in others that I have known, God did some terrible things in righteousness. On one Sabbath while I was there, as we were coming out of church, a man hurried up to Mr. Gillett and myself saying that he had just come from a place where a man had fallen down dead. We later found out that three men who had been opposing the work had met that Sabbath to spend the day drinking and ridiculing the revival. They went on in this way until one of them suddenly dropped dead. His companions were speechless! They could say nothing, for it was evident to them that their conduct had brought this awful stroke of divine indignation upon their friend.

The Spirit Of Prayer

I should say a few words regarding the spirit of prayer which prevailed at Rome during this time. Indeed the whole town was full of prayer. Go where you would, you heard the voice of prayer. If you were walking down the street and two or three Christians happened to be together, **they were praying.** Wherever they met, they prayed. Wherever there was a sinner unconverted, **especially if he showed any opposition,** you would find some two or three brothers or sisters agreeing to make him a special subject of prayer.

The state of things in the village and in the surrounding area was such that no one could come into the village without feeling awestricken with the impression that God was there in a peculiar and wonderful way. As an example of this I will relate a particular incident. The sheriff of the county resided in Utica. There were two courthouses in the county, one in Rome and the other at Utica. Consequently, the sheriff, Bryant by name, came to Rome quite frequently. He later told me that he had heard of the state of things at Rome, and he, together with many others in Utica, had laughed a great deal about it.

But one day it was necessary for him to come to Rome. He said that he was glad to have business there, for he wanted to see for himself what things were really like. He was driving in his one-horse sleigh, without any particular impression in his mind at all, until he crossed what was called the old canal, a place about a mile from the town. He said as soon as he crossed the canal, a strange impression came over him, an awe so deep that he could not shake it. He felt as if God permeated the whole atmosphere. He said that this feeling increased the whole way, until he came into the village. He stopped at Mr. Franklin's hotel, and the stable-man came out and took his horse. He observed, he said, that the stable-man looked just like he himself felt—as if he were afraid to speak. He went into the hotel and found the gentleman there with whom he had business. He said that they were both so obviously shaken that they could hardly attend to business. He reported that several times in the course of the short time he was there, he had to rise from the table abruptly and go to the window and look away, trying to divert his attention to keep from weeping. He saw that everyone else appeared to feel just as he did. Such an awe, such a solemnness, such a state of things he had never had any conception of before. He quickly concluded his business and returned to Utica—but (as he said later) never to speak lightly of the work at Rome again. And a few weeks later in Utica, he himself became converted.[4]

---

4) In the next chapter of Finney's autobiography, he describes how the revival moved from Rome to Utica, where this sheriff became converted.

The Effects And Results Of The Revival

As the work progressed, almost the whole population of the town became involved. Nearly every one of the lawyers, merchants, physicians, and almost all the principal men—indeed, nearly the whole adult population of the village, were saved, especially those who belonged to Mr. Gillett's congregation. He said to me before I left, "So far as my church is concerned, the millenium has come already. My people are all converted. From all my past labors, I don't even have one sermon that is suited at all to my congregation, for **they all are committed Christians.**" Mr. Gillett afterward reported that during the 20 days that I spent at Rome, there were 500 conversions in that town.[5]

The means that were used at Rome were the same as I had always used before, and no others—preaching, much prayer (secret and public), personal conversation and instruction, visitation from house to house—and when inquirers became large in number, I appointed special meetings for them. These were the means and the only means that I had used in attempting to secure the conversion of souls.

In this revival, the Spirit's work was so spontaneous, so powerful and so overwhelming, that it was necessary to exercise the greatest caution and wisdom in conducting all the meetings in order to prevent an undesirable outburst of feelings that would have quickly exhausted the emotions of the people. It is difficult to conceive of such a deep and universal state of religious feeling as was witnessed at Rome—with no instance of disorder, confusion, fanaticism, or anything that would be objectionable.

The moral state of the people was so greatly changed that Mr. Gillett often remarked that it did not seem like the same place. Whatever of sin that was left was forced to hide its face. No open immorality would be tolerated for even a moment. I have given only a very faint outline of what happened at Rome. A faithful description of all the moving incidents that were crowded into that revival would indeed take a whole book in itself.

But the Spirit's work did not stop there. Finney goes on to tell how it immediately spread to Utica (where Sheriff Bryant was converted). And then from village to village, city to city, the revival spread throughout the length and breadth of the land, until there were whole counties where there could hardly be found an unconverted soul. How grateful we are that Jesus Christ is able to change lives like this, and that He wants to enable His people, if they are willing, to be such vessels of His truth and power. "You shall find Me," He says, "when you seek for Me, with all your heart!"
—Jeremiah 29:13

This article is available in tract form as LD#27.

---

5) This number may not seem very great to you, but New York state was very sparsely populated in the 1820s when this revival took place.

Be Ye Angry And Sin Not

by Leonard Ravenhill

If you attend church at all, you will undoubtedly hear a thousand sermons on *"Be filled with the Spirit" (Eph. 5:18)* for every **one** sermon you hear preached on *"Be ye angry, and sin not" (Eph. 4:26).* This is a command! It is not a defense for a bad temper. It is not an excuse for an explosion of bitterness from your bruised ego for personal rejection. I am talking here of Holy Anger. God gets angry. *"The anger of the Lord was kindled against Moses" (Exodus 4:14), "God is angry with the wicked every day" (Psalm 7:11).* (If you must have a bumper sticker, try this last statement for a while—but be sure that you increase your insurance before you do so.)

The blessed preacher St. Paul walked down Main Street Athens, the intellectual capital of the world of his day. Acts 17:16 says in the sleepy Elizabethan English of the King James version, *"His spirit was stirred in him, when he saw the city wholly given to idolatry."* The Amplified says it this way, *"Now while Paul was awaiting them at Athens, his spirit was grieved and roused to anger as he saw the city was full of idols."* Such anger needs to come back to us today. I admit right here that I am downright angry. I am angry that Christ is wounded in the house of His friends.

Here Is An Example

Our home is less than 100 miles from Dallas—the "Athens" of the theologians. Therefore we are vulnerable to the students who come from the seminaries there, distressed, disgusted, and despondent over the low state of spirituality in their particular classes. A professor in one such seminary tells the preacher-boys, "Remember that preaching is now a profession, and not to be viewed or represented by a sweating evangelist in a sawdust-carpeted tent. Now the preacher has status like a doctor or a seasoned lawyer." Begone such idiocy! Preaching is not a profession—it is a **passion!** Paul sets the standard, *"Woe unto me if I preach not the Gospel!"* I am angry that these professors want

the world's smile on our holy calling. But no man called to the ministry needs a status symbol. He is, by the very nature of his calling, in the **highest** calling.

I am further angered by a statement by Bruce Cook—the former advertising agent for Coca Cola, who engineered the "I Found It" campaign. Here is his horrible comment, and it angers me: "Back in Jerusalem when the Church started, God performed a miracle there on the Day of Pentecost. They didn't have the benefit of buttons and media, so God had to do a little supernatural work there. But today, with our technology, we have available to us the opportunity to create the same kind of interest in a secular society."[1] This wretched interpretation makes me bristle. So buttons and modern media are as likely to start a Heaven-Born Holy Ghost Revival as was the Upper Room invasion from heaven? What is this but "Christian humanism"? WE are capable of producing the same thing as the Blessed Holy Spirit?

Homosexual "Christians"

I am angry when I read a letter from my friend and neighbor David Wilkerson announcing this near unbelievable perversion.

"*Homosexuals now claim more than 50,000 members in their 'all homosexual' churches. The Metropolitan Community Church is one of many homosexual denominations springing up across the nation. I sent an observer to one of their annual 'Holy Ghost' conventions in Dallas, Texas. What unbelievable blasphemy!*

"*Each delegate, as they registered, was given a packet which included, among other things, two 'boy' magazines of all nude men and a list of all the gay bars in Dallas—so that delegates could leave the evening service, go to their selected bar, and connect with a lover for the night. And those delegates call themselves 'ministers.' How they did sing! They praised the Lord with enthusiasm; but their evangelist corrupted the Gospel beyond comprehension. He said, 'Sure, Paul condemned men who changed the natural use and burned one toward another. But that's not us. We didn't change anything. We were born this way. So, come out of your closets.* **Be filled with the Holy Ghost, and enjoy your homosexuality!**'"[2]

My anger over this is intensified when I read that the cutback in federal spending will cause some old folks to miss meals. Yet the same federal folks on the 5th of May, 1981, gave the Metropolitan Community (homosexual) Church $380,000 of **our** tax money to operate four resettlement centers for Cuban refugee homosexuals.[3] (Just let the true Church of Jesus try to get the government to give us a dime to rescue men from an eternal hell!)

Clean Up America?

I am angry also when I hear preachers crying with great emotion, "Help me clean up America," when they dare not try to clean up the Church—riddled as it is with carnality and sensuality. I am

---

1) From "The Total Image," 1980, by Virginia Owens, Eerdmans Publishing Company.
2) "The Coming Purge," David Wilkerson Crusade.
3) "Your Newsletter," First Church of God, Fort Smith, AR.

angry and grieved when preachers weep over the TV that their income is decreasing, though I've never seen them weep on TV over the millions of lost souls they address every week. The God on TV is an inoffensive, undemanding God, wanting to give but requiring nothing in exchange. There is no need to take up your cross and follow Him.

"The Mush God"

Nicholas Van Hoffman has a penetrating column on the "Mush God" of today. Read it friend, read it twice and maybe you will weep as he speaks of the gross representation of the Holy Deity. Here is Van Hoffman:

"The Mush God has been known to appear to millionaires on golf courses. He appears to politicians at ribbon-cutting ceremonies and to clergymen speaking the invocation on national TV at either Democratic or Republican conventions. The Mush God's presence is felt during Brotherhood Week and when Rotarians come together. He is the lifeless deity President Carter was referring to when suggesting peace might come to the Middle East because the Egyptian president and Israeli prime minister both worshipped the Great Mushy One.

"The Mush God has no theology to speak of, being a Cream of Wheat divinity. The Mush God has no particular credo, no tenets of faith, nothing that would make it difficult for believer and non-believer alike to lower one's head when the temporary chairman tells us the Reverend, Rabbi, Father, Mufti, or So-and-So will lead us in an innocuous, harmless prayer, for this god of public occasions is not a jealous god. You can even invoke him to start a hookers' convention and he/she or it won't be offended.

"God of the Rotary, God of the Optimists Club, Protector of the Buddy System, the Mush God is the Lord of secular ritual, of the necessary but hypocritical forms and formalities that hush the divisive and the derisive. The Mush God is a serviceable god whose laws are not chiseled on tablets but written on sand, open to amendment, qualification, and erasure. This is a god that will compromise with you, make allowances and declare all wars holy, all peaces hallowed."[4]

More Anger

My Holy Anger and burning indignation is fueled by articles like this from the pen of a "Wiseman" from the East–the Bhagwan Shree Ragneesh, writing from the Meditation Center that bears his name.[5]

---
4) From "Sources And Resources."
5) "Time Magazine," July 20, 1981.

"SEX—never repress it. Never be against it—rather, go deep into it with great clarity, with great love. Go like an explorer. Search all the nooks and corners of your sexuality and you will be surprised and enriched and benefitted. Knowing your sexuality, one day you will stumble upon your spirituality [or get V.D.–LR] *then you will become free. The future will have a totally different vision of sex. It will be more fun, more joy, more friendship, more a play than a serious affair, as it has been in the past.* [The "serious affair" mentioned here must mean marriage–LR] *Sex is just the beginning, not the end. But if you miss the beginning, you will miss the end also."*

What logic and what warning! Why not miss the end which is torment here and hereafter? I wonder what folks who have tried this teacher's methods think about it. Does he have "revival crusades" with living, bright-faced "witnesses" telling of their rapturous emancipation from the "bondage of purity and a good conscience"?

Save Whose Children?

I am not angered that the Moral Majority boys campaign against abortion. I am angry when the same men who say, "Save OUR children" bellow "Build more and bigger bombers." That's right! Blast the children in other nations into eternity, or limbless misery as they lay crippled from "OUR" bombers! This does not jell.

I am angry that the pulpiteers can roar from their pulpits against political injustices, yet whisper about the wrong doings in their own fellowship—also that sin is called by other names. God has no mild views of sin, so let's get back to biblical language. The soothsayers in the world are dangerous, but the "smooth-sayers" in the pulpit are equally dangerous. We now call iniquity, infirmity. Wickedness is just weakness. Adultery and fornication, just "having an affair." Lust is called love. Sodomy is now being "GAY." The Harlot is not called a Whore anymore, she is inoffensively named a "Call Girl." These are not terms for every sermon, but they have some kind of intimidation and disgrace attached to them, which makes the preachers afraid to use them (and sinners afraid to hear them). **But the Bible uses them!**

I am angry when I hear preachers saying, "We had our best concert ever last week when the 'ZYX Singers' came to our church. The main auditorium was jammed with extra seats and we had to run extensions into the church hall for the overflow!" Yet, that same popular, prosperous church can comfortably seat its prayer meeting in just about the smallest room in the facility. What a slap in the face for a prayer-answering God! What a public declaration that the offering from the concert patrons is more important than prayer!

I am angry with people who withhold their own money from the Lord, but then turn His House into a Flea Market to raise church funds. And believe me, I am stirred, sick, and angry when I try to realize that 90% of Gospel preaching is to only 10% of the world's population.

Mormons Get "More Men"

"Newsweek" for April 27, 1981, states:
"This year the Mormons will field more missionaries—about 30,000 in all—than any other church in the United States...their single purpose is to labor 16 hours a day, 6 days a week, spreading the Gospel according to the Church of Jesus Christ of Latter-Day Saints. [Now notice the discipline attached to this effort.] *The discipline imposed on Mormon missionaries is as unique as their message: no movies, television, or popular music; no phone calls to parents or girlfriends; no dates—and no going anywhere alone. Under this quasi-military regimen the L.D.S. missionaries have carried the faith across the U.S. into six continents."*

I am angry at this false zeal, disturbed and deeply troubled that we have to make so many Christian Youth Camps a miniature Olympics to entice kids to so-called Bible study. Dare we try to get kids away from TV, sports, etc., for a week of solid concentration on eternal things? It seems more correct with the emphasis on sports and church programs, and church leagues of bowling, baseball, etc., that we should be singing: "Onward Christian Sportsmen—forget about the war—look at all the prizes—you're contending for!"6

I am angry when I think that the government will subsidize a science effort to find out where man came from, but will not give a dime to tell men where they are going. **God! baptize us with a Holy Anger that will set us on a course of hell-disturbing, heaven-enriching intercession!**

All these sad events I have mentioned would be taken care of by a heaven-born, sin-convicting visitation of the Spirit.

I am angry at the devil's monopoly of this age.

I am angry that the Church sleeps on.

I am angry that the Church, in many (and maybe most) cases, is an entertainment center. Lord have mercy! *"Wilt Thou not revive us again, that Thy people may rejoice in Thee?"* (Psalm 85:6)

This article is available in tract form as LD#28.

---

6) Sung to the tune of "Onward Christian Soldiers."

Creation or Evolution?
by Winkie Pratney

(The First of a Three-Part Series)

Earth. A unique blue-green planet, poised like a tiny jewel in the vast reaches of space. Somehow the race of Man lives, loves, and reaches out in a Universe so vast and desolate as to be frightening. How did we get here? Who is Man? Why are we here?

Over a century and a half ago, an academic controversy swept the world, as a liberal, materialistic philosophy collected data to give Man a new view of his origins. Strong religious reaction began; foolish and unfounded statements were made by uninformed church people. Science and faith quarrelled, and for the first time in a great many years, received a virtual divorce. Early viewpoints became clouded, ignored, or discarded; our century has thus inherited almost wholly humanistic thought. For over a hundred years we have accepted this philosophy and tried to live with it; till again, on the brink of nuclear disaster, we seem to have tried everything from drugs, sex, mysticism, and UFO-hunting to find a new future. Now the chips are down, the facts are coming in, and it's time we had a long, hard look at what an idea can do to a world.

The Origin Of Life—The Final Frontier

We've certainly come a long way since the day a researcher stood up to declare there was nothing significant left to discover. (Shortly before the invention of the **atomic bomb,** the **transistor,** and the **laser.**) Yet for all our advances, Life itself is the "final frontier" for a bewildering complex of sciences.

"Indeed, only two major questions remain shrouded in a cloak of not-quite fathomable mystery: (1) the ORIGIN OF LIFE (i.e. the events that first gave rise to the remarkable co-operative functioning of nucleic acids and proteins...) and (2) the MIND-BODY problem (i.e. the physical basis for self-awareness and personality). Great strides have been made in the approaches to both these problems... but the ultimate explanations are perceived very dimly indeed."[1]

Well, what ARE the options? Really only TWO. It all depends on your premises and presuppositions. Everything comes down to ONE OF TWO ALTERNATIVES, summed up like this:

(1) *"In the beginning, GOD CREATED the heavens and the earth..."* (Genesis 1:1) and *"By FAITH we understand that worlds were framed by the Word of God... so that which is seen does not owe its existence to that which is visible."* (Heb. 11:3 Weymouth Translation)

(2) "Once upon a time... perhaps two and a half billion years ago, under a deadly sun, in an ammoniated ocean topped by a poisonous atmosphere in the midst of a soup of organic molecules, a nucleic acid molecule came ACCIDENTLY INTO BEING that could SOMEHOW BRING ABOUT the existence of another like itself."[2]

Two choices. Pick the FIRST, and you see all natural history as divinely guided towards Man's coming; with it the conviction that man has special destiny and moral responsibility (with a probable

---
1) *Biology and the Future of Man*—Ed. Phillip Handler.
2) Isaac Asimov, science-fiction author: *The Well-Springs of Life.*

judgment on the horizon as well). Pick the SECOND, and you are left with no God, Heaven, Hell, or for that matter, any confidence in humanity and its future. The choice is really quite narrow. Of course both sides have their creeds, authorities, and prophets, and both in the final analysis are religious–are matters of **faith.** The only question is, which one has the **facts** going for it?

Six-Million Dollar Man?

"A man consists of some seven octillion (7x10 to the 27th) atoms grouped in about 10 trillion cells (10 to the 13th). This agglomeration of cells and atoms has some astounding properties. It is alive, feels joy and suffering, discriminates between beauty and ugliness, and distinguishes good from evil."[3]

How much ARE you worth? Old estimates (from the book *Time, Chance & Matter = Man & The Whole Universe*) put your value (with inflation) at around $7.50; the new reckonings are greatly revised. Your proteins, steroids, and hormones alone are terribly complex and costly, and as for LIVING ORGANS, how much is a replacement **heart** worth if you need a transplant? The point is, your value has been reappraised because we now appreciate much better the scarcity and sophistication of your molecules. Man IS marvellously complex, and complexity shows one of TWO THINGS: **incredible luck or intricate engineering.** The seven system-command computers on the Columbia space shuttle (cross-checking each other's facts and figures, and voting on the result) didn't mutate from some engineer's lost four-function calculator; yet Man's design leaves the computers' far behind!

Tackling The Evolutionary Obstacle Course

Naturally enough, since this theory was accepted by so many for such a long time, it takes some courage and conviction to change your position now, especially to the dismay or ridicule of professional

---
3) *Genetics of the Evolutionary Process*–Theodosius Dobzhansky.

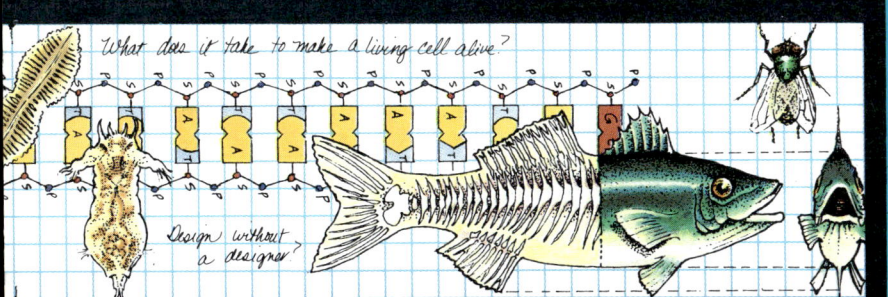

colleagues. Evolutionary theory still runs right through many, many sciences, and its collapses in one field are not always heard in others. People seeing real problems in their ONE area assume researchers in OTHER fields have the missing evidences; this forms a series of **interdependent "hurdles,"** making it difficult for honest researchers to see the situation clearly. Thus, "Expert Opinion" assumes "The **Specialist** is Always Right"–which dismays the poor specialist, who (as careful as he or she can be) is after all, only human. "Specialized **Biology**," for instance, may assume "the rocks are as old as the fossils"; while "Specialized **Geology**" assumes "the fossils are as old as the rocks." Hopefully, **geochronology** (dating-methods data) will unhesitatingly confirm the age of both! But if all else fails, won't a majority opinion prevail anyway? (I mean, that's right isn't it? How could **so many** be **so wrong!**... Lie still, and try not to think of Hitler.) Then again, if you are terribly committed to the premise that there "cannot possibly be a God" (Who will one day call us into account for all the funny ideas we had about His creation), you would no doubt always find some objections to what Creationists are saying.

"Now Just A Minute…!"

Pick up almost any magazine today to see how hot the Creation-Evolution debate has become. Creationists openly challenge Evolutionists to packed, public debates in university forums around the world. There is a growing body of creation-favoring research and literature, thousands of pro-creation scientists, and many Evolutionists willing to carefully and honestly consider both possibilities. Yet almost without exception, the secular media (accepting evolutionary theory uncritically for decades) has been deeply threatened; their "rebuttal" articles sound increasingly shrill, or are based on the idea, "say it often enough and people will keep on believing it–**despite the facts.**"

Many of the biased articles say:
 (1) Creationists "misuse the word 'theory' to convey the false impression that Evolutionists are 'covering up the rotten core' of

their premise." Translation: It is "not fair" to point out **well established rules** of science, especially if according to these rules evolution doesn't even qualify as a scientific THEORY much less as proven FACT. (The key to the scientific method is to SEE it and REPEAT it; with macro-evolution you can do **neither**.)[4]

(2) Creationists "misuse a popular philosophy of science to argue they are behaving scientifically in attacking evolution." (Really? Improper to criticize an idea in the light of DIRECT SCIENTIFIC EVIDENCE–such as the fossil record, laws of probability, thermodynamics, and laws of genetics?) Current media tactics also repeatedly CALL evolution "a fact" then discuss how it is BOTH fact AND theory, getting fact and theory hopelessly (purposely?) confused.[5] Stanley Weinberg recommends that Evolutionists do not publically debate, as they will not win. He says this is mainly because Creationists use "selective quotations"; "They put them together in such a way as to make an argument which the writer had no intention of making."[6] Creationist authors usually do two things: quote directly from evolutionist sources **and** document everything, so the quotes can be checked out in context.

"Watch Them Sneaky Creationists!"

Gould says the Evolutionists' best approach is to say: (a) "creation isn't 'science' as it is universally defined today"; (b) "tearing down a scientific theory doesn't make that critics' program scientific"; and (c) "a scientific argument against evolution is not automatically an argument for creation."[7]

Is creation really not "science" as it is "universally defined today"? The whole world of research is undergoing tremendous change; once again it appears science is rapidly moving AWAY from materialistic world-views as new discoveries break down our

---

4) As opposed to micro-evolution, which means changes within kind, or "species"–as in the development over the centuries of different breeds of dogs, cattle, etc. which of course, obviously occurs. Macro-evolution would involve one species evolving into another–like a lizard evolving into a bird.
5) S.J. Gould: *DISCOVER* Magazine, "Evolution As Fact & Theory," pp. 34-37, May 1981.
6) Stanley Weinberg: *Science Council of New York*, Dec. 1980.
7) Jim Adams: *St. Louis Post Dispatch*–"Evolution–An Old Debate With A New Twist," May 17, 1981.

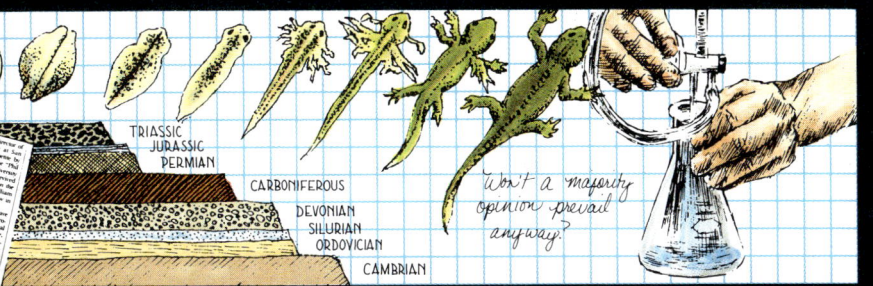

last century's limited and totally inadequate picture of reality. Much of the life-sciences, locked into a century of old physics, are now under intense scrutiny and challenge. What is significant about all this is one fact— the cutting edge of research today points DIRECTLY TOWARDS THE SPIRITUAL.

On Mollusks To Monoliths In Media...

Some magazines' editorial policies seem peculiarly devoted to evolutionary thought, like *Time/Life, Science Digest,* and of course, *Scientific American*. Evolution is a basic idea in popular movies of the past like "King Kong," "Planet of the Apes," and its sequels. More recently in the sci-fi field, the theme develops still further: Man may eventually reach a "God-like" state, as in the conclusion of what A.C. Clarke called "the first ten and a half million dollar religious film"–the classic "2001: A Space Odessy," and more recently, "Star Trek–The Motion Picture."

On T.V. we had "Battlestar Galactica" with its city of lights, and Carl Sagan's multi-million dollar "Cosmos" T.V. series. It seems there is too much evidence for **design** on Earth, but since we can't go on talking about **God,** we might as well come up with a novel solution to the design problem: "There IS intellect and personality behind Man's creation all right–super-beings from space!" Bring on Eric VonDanniken and his *Chariots of the Gods* or *Gods from Outer Space*. (And let's not talk about how THEY got there, shall we? Perhaps "long, long ago, in a galaxy far, far away..." If we move the problem back far enough and long ago enough, maybe it'll go away.)

Premises, Premises...

Do Christian researchers "bring in God" just to explain what cannot currently be explained? Is He invoked to "fill gaps" for faulty theories, perhaps to be squeezed out by the next scientific advance? No way. We honor Him as Creator God, evident in His

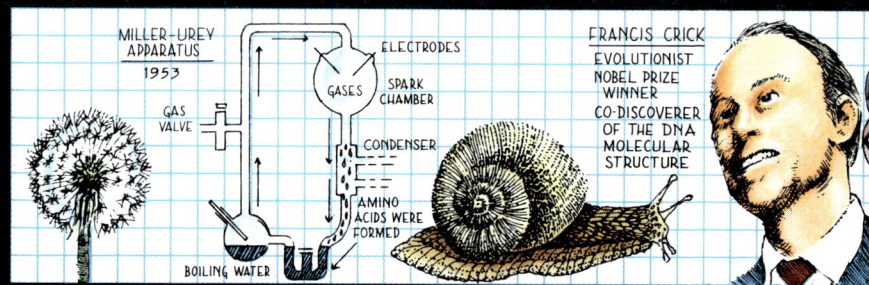

Universe NOT because other explanations fail, but becaus studies point to His mind, His purpose, and His planning. Can there be "gaps" about **origins?** To acknowledge God as Creator is to honor Him where science reaches its limits and cannot ever expound.

A lot depends on your PREMISES. A "premise" is an idea you **start** with (a "presupposition") before you collect facts to try to answer questions. Very often it is not the facts that cause arguments; conflicts come because two people start with very different BASES by which they interpret what they see.

For instance, a **fish** and a **submarine** are alike in some ways; they both have tails, move underwater, and so on. The FACTS are: they are SIMILAR in many ways. Now assume the PREMISE: **"Similarity equals COMMON ANCESTRY."** With all the right FACTS (the noted similarities), we decide therefore that "the fish is a highly-advanced, miniaturized great-nephew of the submarine." This is no doubt offensive to fishes as well as common sense, but "facts are facts!" **CHANGE your PREMISE** to **"Similarity equals common DESIGN,"** and with the SAME SET OF FACTS you see something very different: "Both fish and submarines were DESIGNED TO WORK UNDERWATER" (one by Man, one by Man's Creator). **With the right FACTS but a wrong PREMISE, you can come up with the WRONG answer for all the RIGHT reasons.**

Some Of The Facts

Great fussing is going on today about "the origins of life." We had **Miller** and **Ureys'** experiments, shooting little sparks through organic gases in concentrations carefully picked to favor the formation of some of life's building blocks. Not surprisingly, some were formed. Never mind that Earth's original atmosphere couldn't hold HEAVY gases like xenon and krypton (shades of Superman!) let alone the LIGHTER ones used in the experiments (like methane and ammonia), or that a REAL lightning bolt would effectively FRY a darling little amoeba-in-the-making. It is bothersome also that ultra-violet light from our sun knocks out ammonia

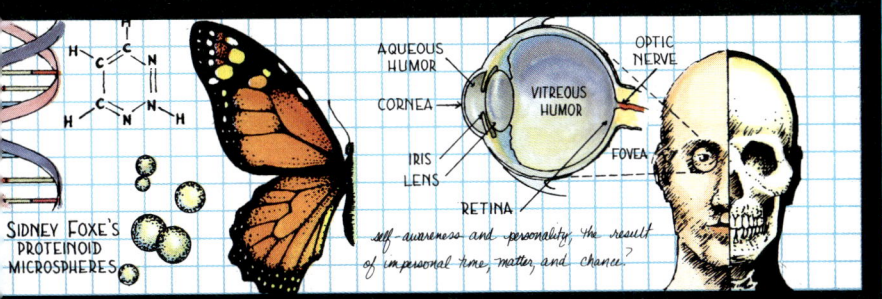

faster that it can form, and old sedimentary rocks ought to show significant amounts of organic stuff in them if this is the way it was, but they don't.[8]

A Left-Handed Creation?

Add to that what **Louis Pasteur, Linus Pauling,** and **Francis Crick** (evolutionist co-discoverer of the DNA structure) all pointed out: The amino acids of life, from mold up to Man, are all of ONE SPECIAL FORM. John Maddox, English biologist, calls this **"an intellectual thunderbolt"**: Randomized experiments always give a "racemic" mixture,[9] approximately EQUAL proportions of D- and L-, right-handed and left-handed amino acids (chemically identical, but "mirror images" of each other)—whereas life proteins consist of LEFT-HANDED MOLECULES ONLY![10]

Now why in the world should that be so ACCIDENTAL? It's enough to drive poor scientists batty trying to dig up some exotic catalyst that might shift the yield in some tiny way (to date always less than 10%) in the "right" direction (left!).[11] What is even more disappointing is that NO high-order, information-carrying molecules like those life uses EVER arrive in the soup, let alone anything remotely looking as if it could move, eat, or reproduce itself.

Foxy Microspheres

Then there is **Sidney Foxes'** ingenious "microsphere" idea. "Perhaps," he thinks, "volcanoes did it." Cook a dry mix of L-amino acids and you get a "thermal pan-polymer" or "proteinoid." Drop these amino acid chains into water and they clump into little groups he calls "microspheres." Since these little shapes look and

---

8) P. Abelson: "Some Aspects of Paleobiochemistry," *Annuals of New York Academy of Science,* 69:275, 1957; "Chemical Events on the Primitive Earth," *Proceedings of the National Academy of Science,* 55:1365, 1966.
9) A mixture of both right and left-handed molecules.
10) Francis H.C. Crick: *Molecules and Men,* Seattle, University of Washington Press, 1966, p. 60; John Maddox: *Revolution in Biology,* New York, Macmillan Company, p. 59.
11) James F. Coppedge: "The Mystery of Left-Handed Molecules in Proteins"; *Evolution–Possible or Impossible?,* pp. 55-79.

act physically in many ways like living things, Mr. Foxe believes this is the way it happened. Top marks for ingenuity, but proteinoids resemble life like a junkyard resembles a Ferrari, and they grow like a wet toilet roll, not like an orange. Real life proteins are unique because of their structure and information-carrying sequence. "ProteiNOID" is not at all protEIN; the name looks the same to the innocent, but they lack tertiary[12] form, their structural mix of amino acids is hopelessly different, and they are essentially random, too fragile, and too simple. Other than superficial, physical similarities, they have nothing complex enough going for them inside or outside to ever grow up to be real proteins.[13]

Life In A Test-Tube?

"But didn't scientists make life in a test-tube somewhere?" No Virginia, they did NOT. (Some have TRANSPLANTED little lives—the "test-tube babies"—but that is another story.) Neither DNA nor protein is a molecule that can duplicate itself; DNA is the servant of the cell. Likewise the **virus** is absolutely dependent on the cell for its survival, and either came AFTER the cell or was created WITH it.[14] Gary Parker, an ex-evolutionary biologist and geologist (whose excellent little book *Creation—The Facts of Life*, along with Wysong's detailed volume was one of the best resources for this article), has written *DNA: The Key to Life*,[15] a programmed textbook on the subject. He asks, "What does it take to make a living cell alive? The answer is something every scientist recognizes and uses in his laboratory, something every scientist can infer from his observations of DNA and protein... CREATIVE DESIGN and ORGANIZATION. What we know about the DNA-protein relationship suggests that living cells have the CREATED KIND of design."[16]

Frankenstein Had A Better Idea:

People have shot long-suffering pools of chemicals with everything they can think of—sound, light, heat, gamma-rays, even bullets, but naturally enough, they stay dead.[17] All this with the express and intelligent PURPOSE of creating life by ACCIDENT.

We could save a lot of trouble and revisit Dr. Frankenstein who had a better idea. All the material we need is in the morgue. Why bother battering around poor old amino acids when there are all

---

12) A technical term involving a three-fold arrangement of molecules.
13) S.L. Miller & H.C. Urey: "Organic Compounds Synthesis on the Primitive Earth," *Science*, 130:247, 1959; Fox, Harada, Woods, & Windsor: *Archives of Biochemistry & Biophysics*, 102:439, 1963; H. Holter: "How Things Get Into Cells," *Scientific American*, 205:167-180, 1961; M. & L. Hokin: "The Chemistry of Cell Membranes," op. cit. 213:78-86, 1965.
14) R.L. Wysong: "Is Life Definable?," *The Creation-Evolution Controversy*, Inquiry Press, 1978, pp. 190-220.
15) Educational Methods Inc., Chicago.
16) Parker: *Creation—The Facts of Life*, pp. 14-15.
17) J. Keosian: *The Origin of Life*, N.Y. Reinhold 28, 68, 1968.

the cells, DNA, enzymes, and proteins you need ready assembled in the proper order in your local cemetery (or even the supermarket)? Save the taxpayers millions; hit, burn, and shoot sparks into corpses or chicken gizzards. When all is said and done, there's a great deal more said than actually done. "Chemistry is not then our **ancestor,** it's our **problem.** When cells lose their biological order and start reacting in chemical ways, we die...what's lost at death is balance and biological order that otherwise uses food to put us together faster than chemistry can tear us apart!"[18] If the ultimate computer/researcher interface successfully synthesizes an egg, no self-respecting hen will touch it. Life is not merely chemical complexity, but a gift from the Living God.

Dust Or Destiny

Take your pick. We are either (1) the product of a cosmic crap-game; or (2) imagineered by Wisdom, Love, and Power beyond comprehension. Those are the options; accident or design, chance or creation. You either have three impersonals: Time, Chance, and Matter, adding up to Impersonal Man and an Impersonal Universe; or you have Pre-existent Personality imposing order on creation, giving meaning to love, truth, and dignity. These options have profound implications for the way you feel about yourself and others in this world. What, for instance, do you do when overwhelmed by the beauty and awesome, orderly arrangement of a flower? Vote scenario two and say "Thank You God!" Vote scenario one and be stuck with "Praise and honor be to Gases, Geology, and Genes." And did you ever think it odd that a brilliant man could spend fifty years of his life in a lab trying to duplicate life to show NO INTELLIGENCE WAS NECESSARY to form it in the beginning?

This article is available in tract form as LD#29.

Photo on page 162 courtesy NASA.

18) Parker, op. cit. pp. 8-10.

Creation or Evolution?
Part II—The Historical Record

by Winkie Pratney

The Men of Science Who Believed In Creation

The idea that "creation halts human inquiry," and that a picture of reality starting with God "finishes off any ideas of research," is a modern fiction. Once again, life-sciences have many Christian researchers like those in the past, such as **Linnaeus,** the great Swedish botanist, and his predecessor **John Ray** (whose book *The Wisdom of God Manifested in the Works of Creation* blocked evolutionary thought in science for 200 years). History is filled with the genius of men like **Kepler, Galileo, Bacon,** the brilliant **Isaac Newton, Pascal,** and **Leibnitz,** who (despite the strange silence on this aspect of their lives from the secular researcher) all outspokenly and unashamedly loved God and studied His world with joy. Darwin's time was no exception.[1]

Faraday's Electricity

In 1831, when Darwin was a backslidden, 22-year-old ministerial student starting out his five-year voyage on the "Beagle," Michael Faraday, then 40, began a series of experiments that demonstrated the principle of electromagnetic induction. "Very few men," said Sir William Bragg, "have changed the face of the world as Faraday has done. He was one of the greatest experimental philosophers that ever appeared in this country or indeed in all the world. The whole world of **electricity** started with a simple experiment carried out in the Royal Institute by one of the greatest scientists of all time."

Born the year John Wesley died (1791), at 44 recognized as the leading man of science and honored with a doctorate by Oxford University, he became an elder at 50 in the Chapel Meeting House in Pauls Alley, London, preaching there every Sunday, often to fellow scientists. Near his death in 1867, and holding no less than **97** unsought distinctions from international academies of science, he said, "My worldly faculties are slipping away day by day. Happy it is for all of us that the true good does not lie in them. As they ebb, may they leave us as little children trusting in the Father of Mercies and accepting His unspeakable gift. I bow before Him who is Lord of all." Significantly, the principal men to follow him in constructing the electrical age all owned the same Christ as their Lord—**Lord Kelvin** (William Thompson), **James Clerk Maxwell,** and **Sir John Ambrose Fleming.**

Lord Kelvin's Second Law

The **Absolute Temperature Scale** still bears Lord Kelvin's name, but other exploits in his day, like the **submarine cable,** revolutionary **ships compass** and 69 other patented brainwaves, made him a household word. He died in 1907 with over **600** published scientific papers to his credit, **70** patented inventions and **21 honorary degrees.** Elected unanimously at 22 as Glasgow University's youngest professor ever, he opened every lecture with prayer. "A firm believer in creation for his entire life...he often insisted that the power to analyze, to look for causes, was itself a creation of God. He never ceased to look for causes, causes of causes, and for causes of these in return. Seeking a cause for the escape of heat from the Earth, he became in the end a founder of geophysics and the **joint discoverer** of the Second Law of Thermodynamics." He was 35 in 1859, when Darwin published his "Origin of the Species."

Could he have dreamed then that the Law he helped co-discover would today be one of the biggest headaches to Darwin's theory? "The sheer venturesomeness of Kelvin's speculations were possible

---

1) R.E.D. Clark: *Creator God or Cosmic Magician? Symposium on Creation,* vol. IV, pp. 117-118; Peter Masters: *Men of Purpose,* pp. 9-20, 93-101, 114-121.

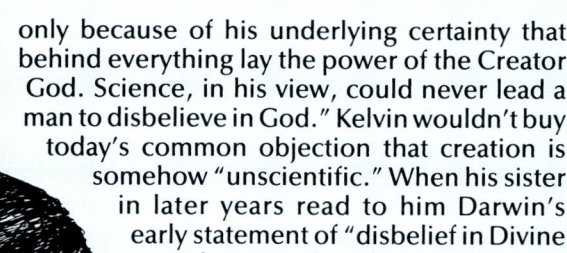
Michael Faraday

only because of his underlying certainty that behind everything lay the power of the Creator God. Science, in his view, could never lead a man to disbelieve in God." Kelvin wouldn't buy today's common objection that creation is somehow "unscientific." When his sister in later years read to him Darwin's early statement of "disbelief in Divine revelation and evidence of creative design in the Universe," Lord Kelvin "unhesitatingly denounced it as utterly unscientific."

Darwin apparently published his theory with much apprehension, fearing the scorn of fellow scientists; in the first edition of his "Origin," he prepared a line of retreat along Lamark's ideas in case his theory of natural selection was found indefensible.[2] Professor C.D. Darlington was of the opinion that Darwinism began "as a theory that could be explained by natural selection; it ended as a theory that evolution could be explained just as you would like it to be explained."[3]

John Fleming's "Valve"

John Ambrose Fleming (inventor of the vacuum tube) was 11 when Darwin published "The Origin." Charles Williams' YMCA and William Booth of the soon-to-be-founded Salvation Army, had both been ministering in England 15 years; John's father was a pastor. A great spiritual awakening took place that year with many people in his father's church becoming Christians. Although his early life was financially difficult, John grew up to contribute some of the greatest discoveries of his day in physics and electrical engineering. "Busy though he was at scientific affairs, he had another loyalty to the Friend he had found as a young man. He began to be less quiet as a Christian believer and to use his remarkable powers as a lecturer in speaking about the Bible. He loved the Bible and studied it as the Word of God. 'It contains,' he said, 'the record of events quite out of line with normal human experience and predictions—some of which have already been remarkably fulfilled... it is, and always has been, revered as the communication to us from the Creator of the Universe, the Supreme and Everlasting God.'"

---

2) *Life & Letters of Charles Darwin*–Ed. Francis Darwin, D. Appleton & Company, 1888, vol. 2, pp. 12-15.
3) Darlington: "The Origin of Darwinism," *Scientific American*, 200, 5:60; May 1959, pp. 60-61.

Few other men could equal his skill in completely enthralling an audience. He was a brilliant speaker, getting popular scientific lectures across to non-scientific audiences; copies of his published works kept in University College fill five volumes. He was an outspoken opponent of Evolution theory, and could not bear to look on quietly while an "unproven and unscientific theory was blatantly taught as fact to the ordinary public." From 1904, under the title *Evidence of Things Not Seen,* he lectured on the unadorned facts about Evolution.

When J.W. Swan of Newcastle made a carbon-filament lamp, it was further improved by Edison, who appointed Fleming to be his chief electrician. Fleming was later also called in by Marconi to help get his wireless telegraph to work; progress was held up without an essential technology that Fleming finally designed in 1904–the **"valve"** as he called it, or the vacuum tube.

Son Of Darwin Meets Multiprocessor
(A Science-Fact Horror Movie For An Old Theory)

Darwin had been dead 33 years. He had no idea that his theories could ever be practically tested. Charles Babbage's "analytical engine" had failed to get off the ground 70 years before, awaiting the very technology that Fleming launched. It was left to John Mauchly and J. Presper Eckert in 1946 to build the first nail for the coffin of Darwin's time-protected theory in **ENIAC**, a clanking, hard-wired monstrosity weighing 30 tons that used 19,000 of these vacuum-tubes, prototypes of the modern microchip.

Some of us forget **how long ago** Darwin lived. Born the same year as Abe Lincoln (1809), nine years after Volta re-invented the electric battery, it would have really blown his circuits to see a home micro-computer, let alone to run a CRAY-1 or a S1 Mark IIA Multiprocessor with the capacity of eight BILLION operations a second. In Darwin's day, the great salvation of his theory was that no one could **live** long enough to disprove it. For over a century the standard argument ran like this: "Just because you can't see it working today doesn't mean it **didn't;** you haven't **looked** long enough, so there! Given enough time and chance, anything can happen–**and probably did.**"

Lord Kelvin

Enter digital logic, integrated circuitry, the programmable computer: and with it a whole new ball game. You see it is now possible to duplicate millions of years and billions of random variations, simulate original conditions, accelerate any possible spontaneous process–to practically shrink awesome numbers into time slots of months, weeks, sometimes days or hours. Darwin's theory **can** be tested, today, NOW.

And it has been. With embarrassing results. Put simply, it doesn't work. Put bluntly, nothing else outside of INTELLIGENT DIRECTED CONTROL does anything more than jam test programs into **chaos.** This has led to interesting shouting matches between the cyberneticists (those who ran the tests on the computers), and the neo-Darwinists, and some mad scrambles for some exotic new catalyst or concept to account for the disappointing facts. Leave a system to itself and all you have at the end of a long time is a **bigger mess** than you started with. And new discoveries on the complexity of molecules and the conditions necessary to create them only seem to make the problem worse.[4]

The Master-Law Of Nature–Entropy

Remember Lord Kelvin and his co-discovery of the Second Law of Thermodynamics?

The Second Law defines that all things run down, not up. Complex things break down; life becomes more disorganized (look at your desk or bed). Time and Chance make things WORSE, not better. A field, a room, a person, left alone and unattended, fall apart. "Entropy,"[5] says **Jeremy Rifkin,** in applying the law in his radical book to both economics and politics, "is the universal master-law, an unbroken reality written all around you."

When you think about it, there are only **two basic ways** to get order out of disorder:

(1) **Chance and Time.** These two factors form one alternative. Say we start with these, nothing and no one else. Does it help? Not a lot. A chance garden is called a jungle. Time passing makes things fall apart, not fall together. Both only tend to make things worse, so that really seems to rule them both out.

(2) An **Agent** and a **degradable Energy supply.** That is to say: Someone deliberately acting on the disorder with the power to use in fixing it up. Of course, the Agent must pre-exist the system, and must be at least as complex as the order you want in the system.

---

[4] *Mathematical Challenges to the Neo-Darwinian Interpretation of Evolution*–Ed. Moorhead & Kaplan, Philadelphia: Wistar Institute, 1967; Murray Eden: *Inadequacies of Neo-Darwinian Evolution as a Scientific Theory*, p. 11; M.P. Shutzenberger, pp. 73-75; A.E. Wilder-Smith: *The Creation of Life–A Cybernetic Approach to Evolution*, Baker; James F. Coppedge: *Evolution–Possible or Impossible?* Zondervan, 1973.
[5] The tendency of an energy system to run down–*Webster's New World Dictionary*.

Putting all this more simply, if you want to dig ditches, you have to BE THERE first—with the energy and the tools to do it. You also have to be smarter than the ditch!

Refrigerators make water (less complex) into ice (more complex) because an AGENT of GREATER WISDOM than the ice blocks (Frigidaire design team?) put together a MACHINE (on special at Sears) that uses DEGRADABLE ENERGY (your astonishing power bill!). The "randomness" was transferred out of the water into heating air behind your fridge, and you finally got something to put into your lemonade—paying only for a fridge, electricity, sales tax and commission, and your service contract when the whole thing succumbs to the Second Law again on Tuesday and breaks down.

That is why some have made an open challenge for anyone to prove that MACRO-evolution is scientifically possible. Like R.G. Elmendorf, who offers a $5,000 cash reward for anyone who can find a natural process in which available energy, structure, and information INCREASE with time—WITHOUT requiring PRIOR and HIGHER energy, structure, and information:

"**Evolution** is here defined as a real, natural, self-caused, continuing, uphill process —involving energy, structure, and information—which goes from disorganized to organized, from random to ordered, from lower to higher, from simple to complex, from atom to amoeba, from molecules to man. All uphill processes (photosynthesis, growth, etc.) are local and temporary, and all require a creative trio of prerequisites in order to operate:

(1) **ENERGY**—an appropriate outside source of energy.

(2) ENERGY **CONVERSION MACHINE**—a fit structure or mechanism to use and transform the above energy.

(3) **INTELLIGENCE**—an intelligent information and control system to direct the machine (found only in life)."[6]

Are YOU "Breaking Down"?

Do not put off getting right with God. Do not say to yourself, "Give me **time** and I'll be okay." Entropy contradicts you. Time will never make you better; time only INCREASES disorder. Are you going to take the awful chance that you are right and the Word of God is wrong? Some things are not a gamble—they are **suicide**. The testimony of the Universe is against you. Chance offers no safety. Her deck is stacked in favor of the house. **All that can bring order out of disorder is greater Power and higher Intelligence.** Such is the Second Law—in physics **or in life.**

This article is available in tract form as LD#30.

---

6) R.G. Elmendorf–"$5,000 Reward," September 1, 1976; Bible-Science Association Western Penn., Bairdford, PA 15006.

Creation or Evolution?

Part III
The Fossil Record

by Winkie Pratney

Strange as it may seem, Darwin himself said that the fossil record is "one of the most obvious and serious objections which could be urged against the theory," and "the absence of transitional forms between species... presses hardly on my theory."

He realized what many people today do not realize: the record of the rocks is more a testimony to EXTINCTION than to evolution. We see CHANGE all right between fossil and modern forms, but only of the "variation within kind" accepted by Creationists. Fossil forms on the whole are MORE COMPLEX and VARIED than their counterparts today, except from those creatures like the Coelacanth, the Tuatara, cockroaches, ants, and dragonflies. Like other "living fossils," they have not changed significantly at all—a real problem in a theory that assumes life-forms tend to change![1]

Darwin hoped that further research by the science of paleontology (then still in its infant stages) would SUPPORT his theory; he thought he just didn't yet have enough data. "He who rejects this view of the imperfection of the geological record will rightly reject the whole theory. For he may ask in vain where are the numberless transitional (missing) links which must formerly have connected the closely allied or representative species..."[2]

"Missing Links" *Still* Missing

Few scientists are still looking for "missing links"; it looks as if they will STAY missing. The most famous, **"Archaeopteryx,"** once considered the link between reptiles and birds, is now generally acknowledged as one of the first birds; the discovery of another bird femur in the same strata has ruled her out as being the ancestor of birds, because they ALREADY EXISTED in her time.[3]

"The fossil record," says Douglas Dewar, a British naturalist and once an ardent evolutionist, "cannot be regarded as other than a HOSTILE witness against evolution; the earliest known fossils of each class and order are not half-developed but have all the essential characteristics of their class and order."[4]

"As we look at the main groups of fossil flora, we find there that at definite intervals they are all at once and quite suddenly there, in full bloom in all their manifold forms. Any change is entirely lacking. This all stands as crass a contradiction to the evolution theory as could possibly be imagined... all my investigations have led to incredible contradictions... on account of which the theory of evolution ought to be entirely abandoned... it is a serious

---

1) James Millot, *Scientific American*, Dec. 1955, p. 37; Charles M. Bogert, *Scientific Monthly*, 1953, p. 167; "Insects in Amber," *Scientific American*, Nov. 1951, pp. 57-58, 60-61; "The Dragon-Fly – Fossil on Wings," *Science Digest*, May 1961, p. 6.
2) **Darwin**, op. cit. 179.
3) Gary Parker: **Creation—The Facts of Life**, pp. 101-102.
4) **Why We Believe in Creation**, p. 312.

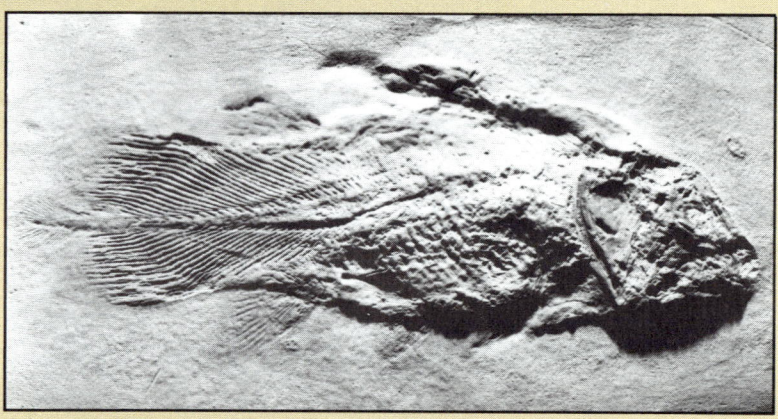

A fossilized coelacanth. A fish thought to have been extinct for at least 70 million years.

The cast of a modern coelacanth. A specimen was caught off the coast of South Africa in 1938 (very much alive).

obstruction to biological research. My attempts to demonstrate evolution by experiments carried out for over 40 years **have completely failed.**"[5]

"Hopeful Monsters?"

More recently some, like **Stephen Gould** of Harvard, have returned to the "hopeful monster" theory ("saltatory" [jumping] evolution, or the "punctuated equilibrium") of **Richard Goldschmidt** in the 1930s;

---

[5] Dr. Herbert Nilsson, Professor of Botany, Univ. of Lund, Sweden, after a LIFETIME STUDY of genetics and the fossil record.

the idea that **radical change** in genes or chromosomes made a lizard, for instance, give birth to a bird–a "hopeful" idea indeed. Gould himself points out problems with this. (How VERY lucky can you get? And if you think **people** have problems finding a mate, how about our hopeful monster?)[6]

Illogical Geological Conclusions

There are some big (and I do mean BIG) problems getting the facts to fit in Sir Charles Lyell's geology. The neat "geological ages" chart you see on school walls is a MYTH–it never exists like that anywhere on earth or it would be a hundred miles high. Then there are the many examples of totally REVERSED "strata layers" that no known force could have produced that way–some are THOUSANDS of square miles (the **Lewis overthrust** for instance, weighs in at around 800,000 BILLION TONS, but shows no signs of grinding or sliding that a true "overthrust" would produce).[7]

Other embarrassing discoveries of modern times include: human skulls, gold chains, and an iron pot in coal; human skulls in the Pliocene strata; pollen and anthropods in Pre-Cambrian layers; even pictographs of a dinosaur among other animals on ancient canyon walls, which would knock some 70 million years out of the geologic column![8] Only two explanations are possible: (1) Modern man lived in the earliest years of evolutionary history; (2) History must be shrunk to the time of man. Neither of these is acceptable to a geology based on uniformist principles. Albert C. Ingalls said, "If man...existed as far back as the Carboniferous period in any shape, then the whole science of geology is completely wrong."[9]

How About Dating Methods?

A brief word on radioactive and other dating methods. We do not have space to go into the problems of some of the different methods used to establish the "long ages" of Earth's fossil records in a short treatment like this; suffice to say that although these systems have value in confirming the age of more recent creatures or artifacts, much is based on ASSUMPTIONS that no radical changes have taken place in Earth's atmosphere or radiation decay rates.[10]

---

6) Stephen Gould: "The Return of Hopeful Monsters," *Natural History*, June-July 1977.
7) William G. Pierce: *Bulletin of Amer. Association of Petroleum Geologists*, Vol. 41, 1958, p. 596; John G. Read: **Experiences in Overthrust Areas**, Bible-Science Association, op. cit. pp. 1-6.
8) Otto Stutzer: **Geology of Coal**, Chicago, Univ. of Chicago, 1940, p. 271; R.L. Wysong, op. cit. pp. 370-383; E. Scoyen: *Arizona Highways*, 27, July 1951, pp. 36-39.
9) "The Carboniferous Mystery," *Scientific Monthly*, Vol. 162, January 1940, p. 14.
10) W.F. Libby: **Radiocarbon Dating**, Chicago, Univ. of Chicago, 1952; F.B. Juneman: *Industrial Research*, 14, 1972, p. 15; Anderson & Spangler: "Radiometric Dating: Is The 'Decay Constant' Constant?" **Pensee**, 4, Fall 1974, p. 34.

Twenty-Three Century Snails

This may lead, for instance, to numerous ridiculous findings, like LIVING snails being dated (C-14 method) at 2,300 years old, NEW wood from growing trees at 10,000 years, and Hawaiian lava flows KNOWN to be less than two centuries dated by the potassium-argon method at up to 3 BILLION years old![11] Wysong and others give a large list of factors that point to a **young** Earth, like Gentry's "pleochroic halos," oil gusher pressure, decay of Earth's magnetic movement and its slowing spin rate, the shallow dust layer of the moon, and much more.[12]

For nearly a century and a quarter, people have attempted to improve this "imperfection of the geologic record." Darwin would have been sick if he had seen what has been collected. The Curator of the Field Museum For Natural History in Chicago (housing 20% of all known fossil species) says, "... Ironically we have even FEWER examples of evolutionary transition than in Darwin's time. By this I mean that some of the classic cases of Darwinian change in the fossil record, such as the evolution of the horse in North America, have had to be discarded or modified as a result of more detailed information."[13] "Famous paleontologists at Harvard, the American and even the British Museum say we have NOT A SINGLE EXAMPLE of evolutionary transition at all."[14]

Am I My Keeper's Brother?

How about fossil men classed as pre-humanoid? How about all the pictures of beetle-browed, club-lugging Neanderthal muggers? How about them, indeed! Although some textbooks and magazines don't seem to have caught up with recent research, it seems as if "ape-men" are largely figments of the artistic "reconstructor's" IMAGINATION. The vast majority of fossil finds (which include thousands of apes and a great many skeletons of MODERN man) have been shown to be either **fictitious** or **mistaken classification.** We shall not mention in detail embarrassing cases from the past like the elephant's knee-cap assigned to **"Pithecanthropus"** in 1926, or the **"Hesperopithecus"** tooth of 1922 introduced as evidence in the famous Scopes trial, but which turned out to be that of a pig! Others like the DuBois **"Java Man"** and **"Peking Man"** (whose remains "mysteriously disappeared") have been quietly removed from the textbooks,

11) Keith & Anderson: "Radiocarbon Dating: Fictitious Results with Mollusk Shells," *Science,* 141, 1963, p. 634; Funkhouser & Naughton: *Journal of Geophysical Research,* 73, 1968, p. 4606; Laghlin: **Excess Radiogenic Argon in Pegmatite Minerals,** op. cit. 74, 1969, p. 6684; R.L. Wysong: "Youth Or Antiquity?" op. cit. pp. 145-179.
12) op. cit. pp. 158-178.
13) David Raup: "Conflicts Between Darwin and Paleontology," *Field Museum Bulletin,* January 1979.
14) Parker, op. cit. 95.

along with **"Piltdown Man,"** the clever but shameful hoax of Charles Dawson that fooled specialists and men of science for nearly 40 years.

More recently, **"Australopithecus"** ("southern ape") was news; that is now quite probably all Donald Johanson's **"Lucy"** is.[15] Louis Leaky found tools at the site, and assumed Australopithecus made them; his son found "bones virtually indistinguishable from modern man" (the toolmaker?) underneath them 13 years later, and said then his discovery "shattered standard beliefs in evolution."[16] Many fossilized skeletons of MODERN man have been unearthed at locations as OLD or OLDER than the supposedly less advanced humanoids found.[17] The "Cro-Magnon" men of Europe have superior size and brain capacity than modern man; a number of men of great age, but truly human, of gigantic size have been unearthed in the Far East, especially in Java. All these findings add to the principle that developmental evolution is not the universal law of biology, but rather DETERIORATION or degeneration.

The World That Then Was Perished

How did the fossils form? James Hutton introduced to geology **"uniformitarianism,"** an idea popularized by Sir Charles Lyell and deeply influencing Darwin's work—that **"the present is the key to the past."** Sometimes it is indeed. Erosion, sedimentation, and the occasional island formation or flood, give us pictures of what has happened in some places. Of course, this all takes TIME and lots of it. And fossils do not form like that. Creatures that die today quickly vanish from decay or scavengers. Fossils are the children of CATASTROPHE—a living thing is buried suddenly by eruption, flood, or landslide. The world is filled with these "graveyards" of more than 100,000 different species; some fossil beds have not less than 10 BILLION individual fossils! COAL is a classic example. Trillions of tons of vegetation, much of it perfectly preserved even to flowers and leaves, are buried, with some seams as much as 30-40 feet thick. Forget your grade school image of trees falling into a swamp and "millions of years later" becoming coal. Under the right conditions, coal can be formed in a few DECADES, and plants falling into water only rot unless SUDDENLY compressed and cut off from oxidation by a large dump of soil or clay. No known peat bog in the world grades into coal, and some coal seams have 75 or more stratas each representing up to 300-400 feet of original vegetable matter! And what about large tree trunks that go right through SEVERAL sedimentary strata?

---

15) *Time*, January 29, 1979.
16) Parker, op. cit. 117-118.
17) Men of Galley Hill, Swanscombe, Foxhall, Grimaldi, Oldoway, Wadjak, and others.

A Warning In The Rocks

It looks very much indeed as if the fossil record is one of great CATASTROPHE, an order of DEATH, not an order of ascending life. One creation model much researched today is that of Flood Geology, which postulates that much of the fossil record is an order of DEPOSITION, as a terrible judgment swept the world the first time.[18]

All life was buried by walls of water, and so-called "ages" are actually ecological ZONES that were buried and choked in mud. In the Noarchian Flood, waters swirled over the planet face for 371 days, with tides 5,000 to 10,000 feet high creating tremendous pressure on all buried matter, providing the power to fossilize forests and petrify wood in a matter of months. Recently there have been popularized searches for the location of the last resting place of the Ark (NOAH'S Ark, not the one Indiana Jones was after!). It was a massive vehicle of some 43,300 tons displacement, around 450 X 75 X 45 feet in size, with a total deck area of 101,250 square feet and a carrying capacity equal to **8 freight trains** of 65 cars each! (1,396,000 cubic ft.) Ernest Mayr, leading systematic taxonomist, lists around 1,000,000 different species of modern animal life, of which, (even according to modern "kinds") only some 35,000 were land-based. With around 240 large animals to a standard 2-deck rail car, 2 trains hauling 73 such cars could carry the full load; the Ark had space for 522 cars this size, so there was plenty of room (even for the elephants' bathrooms)! It should be obvious that without supernatural CARE, Noah's little family would never have survived; without supernatural INTERVENTION, our world would STILL be buried in water. (See *Isaiah 54:9-10*.) Scripture indicates a possible mammoth re-structuring of Earth's topology *(Psalm 104:6-9– "The mountains ascend, the valleys descend")*, creating our present deep ocean basins to drain off the floodwaters, and our ancestors finally stepped off into a new world. *(Genesis 6:20, 7:15-16, 8:1)*

---

18) Whitcombe & Morris; **The Genesis Flood;** George Howe, ed: **Speak to the Earth,** Pres. & Reformed Publishing Co.; Duane Gish: **Evolution–The Fossils Say No!** Creation Life Publishers.

How Long Can We Tread Water?

"*For the coming of the Son of Man will be just like the days of Noah,*" said Jesus, "*For as in those days which were before the flood they were eating and drinking, they were marrying and giving in marriage, until the day that Noah entered the ark, and they did not understand until the flood came and took them all away; so shall the coming of the Son of Man be.*" (Matt. 24:37-39) The **first** time He came as a baby; the **next** time He comes as the rightful King of the Earth. The Apostle Peter said: "*Know this first of all, that in the last days scoffers will come with their mocking, following after their own lusts, and saying, 'Where is the promise of His coming?'... For this they willingly are ignorant of... the world that then was being overflowed with water perished; but the present heavens and earth by His Word are being reserved for fire, kept for the day of judgment and destruction of ungodly men.*" (II Peter 3:3-7)

Water then, FIRE next time. It is the considered conviction of thousands of respected researchers and scientists that, based on the evidence, it is time to return to the Lord. They say this not because they are blind, prejudiced, or stupid, but because the FACTS do not fit the alternative. If both the Creationist and Evolutionist picture are, in the final analysis, matters of FAITH, it is better to stick with the faith that best coincides with the facts. It is a big gamble indeed to risk your soul and your future on the hope that you are nothing more than the blind product of time, chance, and matter, when you may have to stand one day before the Creator you rejected–DESPITE THE FACTS–and explain to Him your logic. It is also our conviction that you will not have to wait very long. Time's final drama is about to take place, and as C.S. Lewis put it–"*When the Author walks on stage, the play is over.*" It is time to seek the Lord. The next move is over to you...

This article is available in tract form as LD#31.

Master Book List of Creationist Research

These books can be obtained through your local Christian book store—they are not available through Last Days Ministries.

GENERAL OVERVIEW AND SUMMARY

* **Evolution & The Christian Faith,** Bolton Davidheiser/Baker.
***Creation—The Facts of Life,** Gary E. Parker, Creation Life Publishers, Box 1606, El Cajon, CA 92022
Man's Origin, Man's Destiny, A.E. Wilder-Smith, Harold Shaw Publishers, Wheaton, IL, 1970.
The Remarkable Birth of Planet Earth, Henry M. Morris, Creation Life Publishers, Box 1606, El Cajon, CA 92022
***The Creation—Evolution Controversy,** Randy L. Wysong, Inquiry Press, 4925 Jefferson Ave., Midland, MI 48640, Creation Life Publishers.

FLOOD GEOLOGY

***The Genesis Flood,** Henry Morris, John Whitcomb, Pres. & Reformed Publishing Co., 1967.
Speak to the Earth, Ed. George F. Howe, Pres. & Reformed, 1976.

ANTHROPOLOGY

***Noah's Three Sons,** Arthur C. Custance, Zondervan.

FOSSILS

Genesis & Early Man, Arthur C. Custance, Zondervan, 1975.
***Evolution—The Challenge of the Fossil Record,** Duane T. Gish, Creation Life Publishers, Box 1606, El Cajon, CA 92022
Fossils in Focus, J. Kerby Anderson, Zondervan, 1977.

FLOOD HISTORY

The Flood—Local or Global? Arthur C. Custance, Zondervan, 1979.

HISTORY OF DARWINISM

Evolution or Creation? Arthur C. Custance, Zondervan, 1976.
Darwin—Before and After, R.E.D. Clarke, Moody Press, Chicago, IL, 1967.

POLITICAL IMPLICATIONS

Communism Versus Creation, Francis Nigel Lee, Craig Press, Nutley, NJ 07110, 1969.

PHILOSOPHICAL IMPLICATIONS

Genesis in Space and Time, Francis Schaeffer, IVF Press, Wheaton, IL.

APE-MEN

Ape-Men—Fact or Fallacy? M. Bowden, Sovereign Pubs., Box 88, Bromley Kent, BR2 9PF, 1977.

CYBERNETICS

* **The Creation of Life,** A.E. Wilder-Smith, Harold Shaw Pub., Wheaton, IL, 1970.

DEBATES

The Battle for Creation, Eds. Henry Morris/Duane Gish, 2 Volumes: Creation Life Pub., Box 1606, El Cajon, CA 92022

SCHOLARLY ARTICLES

A Symposium on Creation, Donald Patten Ed. & Various, Baker Vols. 1-6, 1977.

THERMODYNAMICS
Scientific Case for Creation, Henry M. Morris, Creation Life Publishers.

PROBABILITY
* **Evolution—Possible or Impossible?** James F. Coppedge, Zondervan.

SOLAR SYSTEM
Age of the Solar System, Harold Slusher & Stephen Duursma, Institute Creation Research Tech. Monograph (ICRTM).

EARTH
Age of the Earth, Harold Slusher & Thomas Gamwell, ICRTM.

UNIVERSE
Origins of the Universe, Harold Slusher, ICRTM.

ORIGINS OF LIFE
Theories on Origins of Life, Duane T. Gish, ICRTM.

DATING
A Critique of Radiometric Dating, Harold Slusher, ICRTM.

SCHOOL OUTLINES
Origins—Two Models, Richard Bliss, Creation Life Publishers.

Those marked with an asterisk (*) are of special value and content.

If you have technical questions or need futher research materials or information, please contact one of the following creation-research organizations:

Bible–Science Association
2911 E. 42nd St.
Minneapolis, MN 55406
(Bible–Science Newsletter)

Creation Research Society
2717 Cranbrook Rd.
Ann Arbor, MI
(Creation Research Quarterly)

Institute for Creation Research
P.O. Box 2667
El Cajon, CA 92021 (Readers may be interested in the free subscription plus catalogs for books [dozens], tapes, and elementary education materials. All of the information is interesting and very up-to-date and is free.)

PHOTO CREDITS

Page 180 (upper photo): Neg. No.123843, courtesy Department Library Services, American Museum of Natural History.
Page 180 (lower photo): Neg. No. 325025, Photo by Rota, courtesy Department Library Services, American Museum of Natural History.

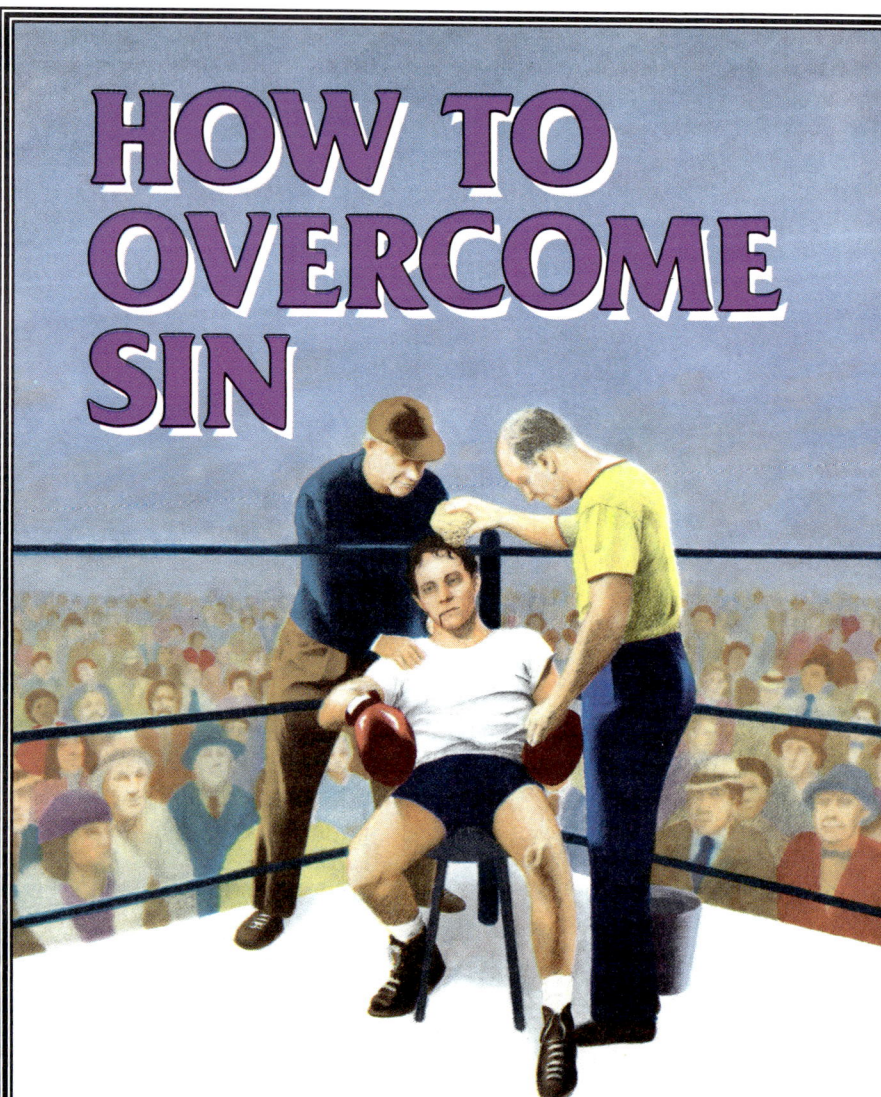

There are multitudes of anxious Christians who are inquiring what they shall do to overcome the world, the flesh, and the devil. They overlook the fact that *"this is the victory that has overcome the world–our faith" (I John 5:4)* that it is with *"the shield of faith"* that they are to *"extinguish all the flaming missiles of the evil one." (Eph. 6:16)* They ask, "Why am I overcome by sin? Why can't I get above its power? Why am I the slave of my appetites and passions and the sport of the devil?" They look all around them for the cause of all this spiritual wretchedness and death. Sometimes they think they have discovered the answer in the neglect of one duty, and at another time in the neglect of another duty. Sometimes they imagine they have found the cause of their wretchedness to be that they have yielded to one sin and sometimes in yielding to another. They put forth efforts in this direction and patch up their righteousness on one side, while they make a tear in the other. Thus they spend years running around in a circle, making dams of sand across the current of their own corruptions. Instead of at once **purifying their hearts by faith** *(Acts 15:9)*, they are engaged in trying to stop the overflow of its bitter waters.

"Why do I sin?" they inquire; and looking around for the cause, they come to the same conclusion: "It is because I neglect such and such a duty!" "But how shall I get rid of sin?" Usual answer: "By doing my duty, that is by ceasing from sin." Now the real question should be: Why do they neglect their duty? Why do they commit sin at all? Where is the foundation of all this mischief? But all this only brings us back to the real question again: How are we to overcome this corrupt nature, this wickedness, and our sinful habits? I answer, **BY FAITH ALONE.** No works of law have the least tendency to overcome our sins, but rather they strengthen the soul in self-righteousness and unbelief.

The great and fundamental sin which is at the foundation of all other sin is unbelief. The first thing to do is to give **that** up–to believe the Word of God. There is no breaking away from one sin without this. *"Whatever is not of faith is sin." (Rom. 14:23) "Without faith it is impossible to please God." (Heb. 11:6)* Thus we see that the backslider and convicted Christian, when agonizing to overcome sin, will almost always try to use the works of law to obtain faith. They will fast and pray and read and struggle and outwardly reform, and thus endeavor to obtain grace. But all this is in vain and wrong. Do you ask, "Shall we not fast and pray and read and struggle? Shall we do nothing but sit down in cheap security and inaction?" I answer: You must do all that God commands you to do; but begin where He tells you to begin, and do it in the manner in which He commands you to do it. That is—in the exercise of that faith that works by love. *(Gal. 5:6)* Purify your hearts by faith. Believe in the Son of God! *(I John 5:10)*

What Is "Faith"?

The first element of saving faith is realizing the truth of the Bible. But this alone is not saving faith, for Satan also realizes the truth of the Bible, which makes him tremble. *(James 2:19)* But a second element in saving faith is the agreement of the heart (or will) to the truth understood by the mind. It is a cordial trust or resting of the mind in those truths, and yielding up the whole being to their influence. Now it is easy to see that without the consent of the will, there can be nothing but an outward obedience to God. A wife without confidence in her husband can do nothing more than outwardly perform her duty to him. Works of law may be performed without faith, that is, we may serve from fear or hope or some selfish motive, but without the confidence that works by love, obedience from the heart is naturally impossible.

By what I've already said, I mean that to seek the grace of faith by mere human works is an utter abomination. It is as abominable as to attempt to purchase the Holy Ghost with money. *(Acts 8:20)* It is to set aside the testimony of God's Word concerning our utter depravity (helplessness) and attempt to pawn off our unbelieving, heartless works upon an infinitely Holy God. It is an attempt to purchase His favor, instead of accepting grace as His sovereign gift.

To give any other answer to one in unbelief, and to tell him to perform any work with the expectation that by it he shall obtain faith, is to confirm him in self-righteousness, to prolong his rebellion, to lead him to settle down in a self-righteous hope to produce in the end, discouragement and blasphemy.

Because repentance, faith, love, and every other holy exercise both **imply** and **proceed** from faith—without confidence in the character and requirements of God, it is impossible to repent. **For what is repentance but heartily to justify God and condemn ourselves.** So it is equally impossible to exercise a trusting love in God without faith. Submission to God implies the exercise of confidence in God and in His requirements.

Faith is the only exercise that receives Christ with all His powerfully sanctifying influences into the heart. The Bible everywhere represents the sanctified soul as being under the influence of an indwelling Christ. Now the exercise of faith is an opening of the door by which Christ is received to reign in the heart. If this is so, the proper direction plainly is to do that which receives Christ. If this is done, all else will be done. If this is neglected, all else will be neglected, of course!

Some Helpful Remarks

1. You see why the Church is not sanctified. They overlook the office and necessity of faith as that which alone can produce acceptable obedience to God. They are engaged in efforts to obtain faith by works, instead of first exercising that faith which will produce within them a clean heart. And in this way they seek in vain for sanctification. How common it is to see Christians bustling about with outward efforts and works—fasting and praying, giving and doing and struggling—and after all this, they do not have the fruits of the Spirit: *"love, joy, peace, longsuffering, gentleness, goodness, faith, meekness, temperance,* **against which there is no law.***"* *(Gal. 5:22-23)*

2. You see why the Bible lays so much stress upon faith.

3. You see what the difficulty is for those who are constantly in a complaining state in their walk with the Lord. They seem to know they are wrong, but do not understand what the foundation of their wrong consists of. They sometimes think that a neglect of a certain duty is the grand difficulty, and sometimes their mind fastens upon something else that is the prime difficulty in their case. They set themselves to break off from one sin and another, they practice **this** self-denial and **that** duty, and all without that faith that fills the heart with love. Thus they go round and round in a circle and do not see that unbelief is their great, their damning sin, without the removal of which **no other sin** can be repented of or forgiven. All their efforts are entirely legal, hypocritical, and vain until they exercise faith.

4. If persons without faith, in an unsanctified state, set themselves to obey the commandments of God, their efforts must necessarily be legal, self-righteous, and destructive. To them the directions of the Gospel, as well as the commandments of the law, are a horrible pit of miry clay. And when you cast a man into a horrible pit of miry clay, the more he struggles the deeper he sinks. Every effort at obedience without faith is sin, and as it confirms self-righteousness, is sinking him further and further from God and rational hope. And the more violently he struggles, the more desperate and alarming his case becomes. The clay surrounds him and cleaves to him, suffocates and kills him. Just so the commands of God to an unbelieving heart are a snare and a pit. Without faith, there is ruin and damnation in them.

5. To the careless, unawakened sinner who knows nothing of his lostness, it might be important and proper to direct his attention to the law of God to bring conviction—not with the expectation of promoting holiness in him, but of convicting him of sin. Thus we find Christ requiring the rich young man who is wrapped up in self-righteousness to keep the commandments, bringing out before his mind his supreme love of the world and of things. *(Luke 18:18-23)*

6. You see how to the Jews and to all unbelievers, the commandments of God are a stumbling block. All outward conformity to them is useless and ruinous. **Love without faith is impossible.** And consequently, the merciful directions and instructions contained in the dos and don'ts of the Bible are made the food of self-righteousness and the snare of death. But to those whose souls are full of faith and love, the commandments of God are just the instruction which they need when, in their ignorance, they earnestly inquire what they shall do to glorify God. "Do this and avoid that," and the like, are just the things upon which hearts of love will seize as the needed directions of their Heavenly Father.

7. But someone may inquire, "Do not men learn to exercise faith by what you call legal efforts and an obedience to the legal directions?" No. They only learn by experience that all such directions are vain, and that they are totally depraved and dependent, which they **ought** to have **believed** before. They set themselves to pray and read and struggle, expecting at every meeting they attend, with every prayer they make, to obtain grace and faith. But they never do until they are completely discouraged and despair of obtaining help in this way. And the history of every self-righteous sinner's conversion and every anxious Christian's sanctification would develop this truth: that deliverance does not come until their self-righteous efforts are proved by their own experience to be utterly vain, and abandoned as useless—and the whole subject thrown upon the sovereign mercy of God. This submitting a subject to the sovereign mercy of God is that **very act of faith** which they should have put forth long before, but which they would not exercise until **every other means had been tried in vain!**

8. But perhaps you will say, "If by this self-righteous struggle they learn their depravity and dependence, and in this matter come to prove by their own experience the truth of God, why not encourage them to make these efforts as at least an indirect way of obtaining faith?" Answer: Blasphemy and drunkenness and any of the most shocking sins may be, and often have been, the means of working conviction which has resulted in conversion. Why not encourage these things to possibly bring about ultimate salvation for some?

The truth is, when a sinner's attention is awakened and he is convicted and puts forth the inquiry, "What shall I do?" and when a Christian, struggling with his remaining corruption, puts forth this same inquiry, why should they be thrown into the horrible pit of which I have spoken? Why not tell them at once, in the language of the text, *"This is the work of God, that you believe in Him whom He has sent"? (John 6:29)*

9. Let me say to you who would make the inquiry, "How can **I** overcome sin?" don't wait to fast, read, pray, or anything else–don't expect to break off from **any sin** in your unbelief! You may break off from the outward commission–you may substitute praying for swearing, reading your Bible for reading magazines, outward employment and honesty for theft and idleness, soberness for drunkenness, and anything you please–but this, without faith, is after all, only exchanging one form of sin for another–it is only varying the **mode** of your rebellion towards God. For remember that in unbelief, whatever your conduct is, you are still in rebellion against God. Faith would instantly sanctify your heart, sanctify all your doings, and render them in Christ Jesus, acceptable to God.

My dear friend, you inquire whether you shall obtain holiness by reading the Bible, or by prayer, fasting, or by all these together. Now let this sermon answer you and know that by **neither** nor by **all** of these, **in the absence of faith,** are you to grow any better or find any relief. You speak of being in darkness and of being discouraged. No wonder you are so, since you have plainly been seeking sanctification by outward works. You have *"stumbled over the stumbling stone." (Rom. 9:32)* You are in that pit of miry clay. **Immediately** exercise faith upon the Son of God! It is the first, the **only** thing you can do to rest your feet upon the Rock–**and it will immediately put a new song into your mouth!**

This article was originally published under the title "Faith" in the OBERLIN EVANGELIST on January 1, 1839. The article in its original form has been reprinted in a book called THE PROMISE OF THE SPIRIT by Charles Finney, edited and compiled by Timothy L. Smith.

This article is available in tract form as LD#32.

LOVE vs ROMANCE

...fact or fantasy?

by Kathleen Dillard

A young girl wrote us and asked, "Don't Christians believe in romance anymore?" This question startled me, and I decided to begin a study to find out the difference between romance and love. My discoveries may appear very heartless, since "romance" has so often been mistakenly called "love." But I have had the opportunity to do much counseling, and I have seen a lot of normally level-headed men and women act completely irrationally when the issue of personal relationships comes up. Therefore, I am convinced that there is a real need for us to take a closer look at the distinction between romance and love. I realize that this article may be probing into a very personal part of your life, but this is one area where we should all do some deep thinking. After all, the whole human race began with a relationship, and for the time being it looks like it is going to continue that way!

Some Definitions

ROMANCE: *A fictitious tale of wonderful and extraordinary events, characterized by much imagination and idealization; without basis in fact; an exaggeration or falsehood.*–Webster's New World Dictionary.

LOVE: *Love, whether exercised toward the brethren or toward men generally, is not an impulse from the feelings, it does not always run with the natural inclinations, nor does it spend itself only upon those for whom some affinity* [or closeness] *is discovered. Love seeks the welfare of all (Rom. 15:2), and works no ill to any (Rom. 13:8-10), love seeks opportunity to do good to "all men…" (Gal. 6:10)* (Also see *I Cor. 13* and *Col. 3:12-14.*)–Vine's Expository Dictionary of New Testament Words.

The Heart Of The Matter

In light of these definitions, it is a drastic mistake to view romance and love as being interchangeable words. My first and most shocking discovery was that romance deals in **fantasy** rather than **reality.** Romance depends on the "setting," the weather, your moods and expectations–it depends on **everything** except commitment. Love, on the other hand, depends on **nothing** but commitment! When you consider the fact that we live in a world that is always changing, it is easy to see how romance cannot meet the demands of real life. Romance is a weak substitute for love. You can see this by the countless number of broken and bitter hearts–not to mention the soaring divorce rate. It is embarrassing to admit that in the Church as well as the world, romance is being called "love." This has only added to the world's low opinion of Christians, as divorce runs rampant through the Church, and so many Christian homes are destroyed.

Cinderella Syndrome–The Effects Of The Media

The media–which includes radio, TV, magazines, billboards, etc.–is really the main stage upon which romance parades itself as "love." Even though I am not saying that these things are evil in themselves, I do want to remind you that fantasy and ungodly values are the pillars of almost all media entertainment and advertising. And it seems like romantic notions and dreams, in the guise of "I love yous," are constantly bombarding us from every direction. Although glass slippers may work on the movie set, they're not very practical in real life. We can get so caught up in looking for our Prince Charming or our Cinderella, that we begin to weigh each other down with unrealistic expectations. (This holds true even for those who are already married.) If someone doesn't MEASURE UP to the media image of what a "**real** man" or a "**real** woman" is, then we have a tendency to be disappointed or frustrated with them. This way of thinking and relating to each other is something that is encouraged from early childhood.

Here you have this tall, bronze, square-chinned figure of a man named Ken, along with his equally flawless and faithful companion Barbie. Both of them are perfect...**perfectly plastic that is!** Already the children have begun to place a special value on certain "measurements and features." And when they grow up, they will encounter endless problems if they still find themselves trying to play Barbie and Ken, only **this** time it's with **real people!**

As I once heard a wise teacher simply say, "Do you want to know what a 'real' man is? A real man is a **male** one! And do you want to know what a 'real' woman is? A real woman is a **female** one." Placing unrealistic demands on one another is not only unfair, but also unloving. We must pull the plug on our media images and begin allowing each other to be who we are.

Do You Play Cupid?

If your answer is "yes," then I'm sure that you would also add that "it is all in fun." Though your intentions may be harmless, I find myself increasingly uneasy about the outcome of these actions. As I discovered in a mythology book:

"*Cupid is a Roman god derived from the Greek god known as Eros. Both in worship and in popular mind Eros* [or Cupid] *was the god of sexual love. He was attributed especially in the later period with the power of firing men with the passion of love by means of his sharp shafts* [arrows] *and stinging tongues of flame.*"*

It grieves my heart when I consider all of the adults who encourage "romance" among the young people in their churches. With comments like, "You two would make such a **nice** couple!" and the constant flood of pressuring questions that are asked of dating and non-dating Christians alike– "When are you getting married?" or "You're getting pretty old to still be single, aren't you?" These questions are not only embarrassing, but unnecessary.

*****The Mythology of All Races–Greek and Roman,** by William Sherwood Fox, A.M., Ph.D.

Yes, marriage can be a great joy, and I suppose that these adults only want to see these young people experience the same happiness and fulfillment they have found from the marriage relationship. But this continual pushing forward of single people into premature or unblessed relationships is very harmful. For this puts a rush on all aspects of a young relationship–a relationship which they should be entering into slowly, with their eyes open, **and with much prayer.** There's not only matchmaking to cope with, but "Christian dating services" (yes, they **do** exist!) and the countless number of activities arranged by the church for the purpose of "bringing single Christians together." It should be alarming to consider that our "good intentions" in matchmaking just might be making a potential disaster. Matchmaking is God's business, not ours! As Jesus said, "What therefore **God** has joined together..." *(Matt. 19:6)*

Romantic Roulette

If you are unmarried and have been facing the possibility of choosing a life-long mate, then let me caution you: **Walk with your feet on the ground and your eyes on the Lord.** Next to making a commitment to follow Jesus, the marriage commitment is without a doubt **the most important decision you will ever make!**

Our attitude toward marriage today seems to be much too casual. "Love at first sight" or "falling in love" is all that is needed to throw out common sense and godly counsel–leaving us at the mercy of our unfaithful emotions to decide for us a life-long commitment. I call this playing "Romantic Roulette." And I can tell you from my experience as a counselor that many people have had to learn this **the hard way.** Sure it sometimes works out...there isn't always a bullet with every pull of the trigger...but more times than not, this selfish and cruel game produces broken homes and bitter, brokenhearted people.

What To Do

Love is a commitment, and no one can make a faithful and unwavering commitment to someone they don't know. Many attractions are completely foolish. Often people find themselves daydreaming about someone they've seen once or twice at school or work. The daydreamer begins carrying on an imaginary relationship in his head with this person. The entire basis of his affections are founded on what he IMAGINES that person to be like, instead of what they really are.

But other times attractions can be more serious. Occasionally these desires toward the opposite sex can seem overpowering, but the only way to control these feelings is by making the right choices and drawing closer to God. Though it is not a sin to be attracted to someone, what you decide to do with that attraction can be. Since our romantic desires are often stronger than we are, the first thing you should do if you like someone is talk to your Father about it. No, I didn't say, "Talk to your best friend about it…" I said, **talk to your Father in heaven** about it. Ask **His** permission. Oftentimes we run to our friends because we want their approval; we long to hear them say, "Oh, the two of you would go so good together!" But what we should really be seeking is God's opinion—**His** counsel. But all too often we are afraid He'll just say "Wait…" or worse, "This person is not the right one for you." Yet if we are not interested in obeying God, all the counsel in heaven will do us no good!

If you really want to do what's right, then don't feed your desire, **yield it to God.** I recently heard somebody say, "The quickest way to let something die is to quit feeding it." You should also go and get counsel from a pastor, or an older brother or sister in the Lord, for *"through presumption comes nothing but strife, but with those who receive counsel is wisdom." (Proverbs 13:10)* Before closing this section of the article, I would like to share the words of a man who has pastored a congregation and counseled many couples: **"Love can wait, lust can't."**

Fickle Not Faithful

No one wants to enter into a relationship with someone who is fickle. Webster tells us that a person who is fickle is **"changeable or unstable in affection and interest."** Yet, at the core of every "true romantic" is fickleness. Of course, romance will say a lot of the same things that real love might say—"I love you **only**," "I'll love you **always**," etc.—but since it is led around by whim rather than commitment, there is really not too much that one can depend on in all this "sweet talk." When romance is the basis of any relationship, all that it takes is a good dose of reality to wreck the whole thing.

Take, for instance, a young, vibrant, and beautiful cheerleader—a girl who has always had everything going for her. She meets #22, a strong, handsome, and "hard to get" football player. He is a real challenge for her, and she invests every feminine wile she can to get his attention. Of course he falls for it, and they eventually get married. Both are starry-eyed for the time being…thinking that they have gotten all that they have ever wanted in a partner. Then the true test begins. The football player receives a serious knee injury and he can no longer play. They already have two kids, with another one on the way. He cannot seem to find a job and the pressure increases. The dishes are piling up, the kids are screaming, and the house is filled with smoke as our ex-football player nervously finishes his second pack of cigarettes for the day. Then BOOM! "The honeymoon is over," and so is the marriage. Romance can't stand the same tests that love can.

No one can be fickle and faithful at the same time. The Scripture says that love *"bears all things, believes all things, hopes all things, endures all things." (I Cor. 13:7)* On the other hand, I would venture to say that "fickleness bears nothing, is suspicious of everything, is always doubting, and can never endure for long!"

Conclusion

After all that I've said, I do not want you to get the idea that a marriage relationship should be a "dry contract," entered into with no loving "feelings" at all. Sure there's a place for "romance" within a true, godly commitment, but this romance **cannot** be the foundation of the relationship itself. You must look at romance within a relationship like the icing on a cake–just try to imagine a cake that was **all** icing! You can understand why Jesus said so much about building on the **rock** instead of the sand.

I realize a lot more can be said about the differences between romance and love, but I do hope you have seen the importance of why the two should not be confused. God has made available to us a love that "never fails," but many of us have mixed it with our foolish romantic notions and desires. If while reading this article you have found yourself guilty of any of the mistakes mentioned, then ask God to forgive you, and change your ways–and for God's sake, become part of the solution! By becoming *"...imitators of God, as beloved children...walk in love, just as Christ also loved you, and gave Himself up for us, an offering and a sacrifice to God as a fragrant aroma." (Eph. 5:1-2)*

AND THEY LIVED HAPPILY **FOREVER** AFTER!

This article is available in tract form as LD#33.

Everything You Should Know Before You Get A DIVORCE

Looking at the Marriage Commitment

by Keith Green

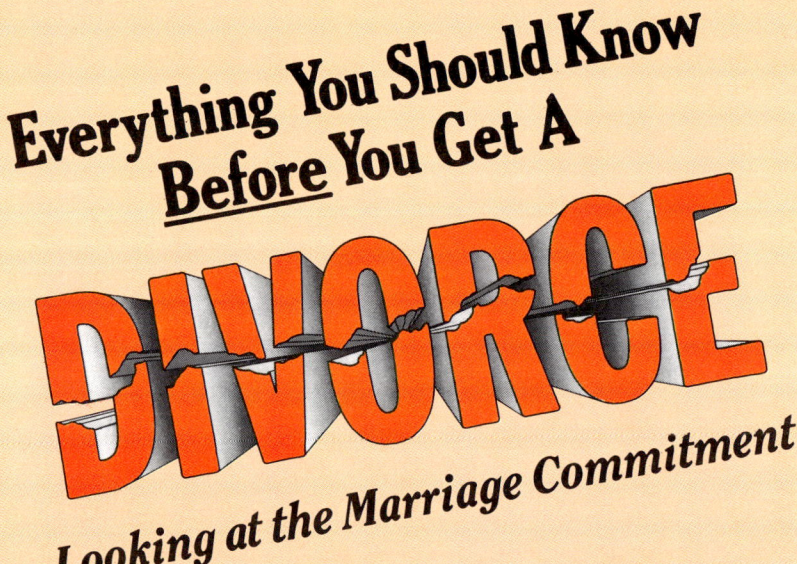

Introduction

*T*his article has been a long time coming. Just about every day we get letters asking us to tackle this subject. On several occasions we have planned to do a whole issue on it, but each time we began, we realized that the subjects and Scriptures involved were so heavily debated, and interpretations so varied, that we would just be stirring up a hornets' nest to put "our" position in print. So we kept putting it off.

But as time has passed, we have become acutely aware of this tragic problem growing in the Church. First of all, my wife and I have many personal friends whose marriages have "fallen apart" during the past few years. These include many well-known Christian musicians and ministers. This has cut Melody and me to the heart as we have watched marriage after marriage disintegrate, hearing one excuse after the other why "we just couldn't live together anymore..." Then we have watched while many of these people quickly got remarried, saying to us, "Oh, **now** I am **really** happy! God has really worked all this out... Maybe it was His will all along!" Meanwhile somewhere, the former husband or wife is still aching, bleeding inside, and wondering, "What happened? Where do I stand now?" And then comes the guilt and torment.

We have also received letters from many wives and husbands begging us for help and advice on what to do. They paint the saddest pictures of fights and mistrust, broken promises, and worst of all—scared children who are innocently caught in the crossfire.

This article is not going to answer all your theological questions concerning divorce or remarriage: "Is it okay to do this?" "Am I allowed to do that?" "What if I'm already remarried?" These questions are among some of the hardest in scriptural study—and have been the cause of no end of debate among Bible scholars. The reason is because the Bible seems to be unclear in many of these areas. Of course "we" have an opinion on all of them (and so does every church on the block!), but we do not want to print merely opinion, we want to share rock-solid truth—ABSOLUTE truth! That is why this article is called "Everything You Should Know **Before** You Get A Divorce."

We know that God clearly said, **"I hate divorce!"** (Malachi 2:16) And so we want to reach you **before** you make that fatal mistake. That is the best time to deal with sin—BEFORE it occurs. Sure God has made provision for repentance and healing, but the "who cans" and "whys" involved in divorce and remarriage are so heavily debated in Church circles, we just want to stay out of the fray. (Please **don't** write us and tell us what you think God will let **you** do; or "such and such a person can get a divorce and still be right with God.") Frankly, the purpose of this article is not to deal with all the "what ifs." We are interested in saving the marriages (and families) that are still able to be saved.

Just as Melody's articles on abortion have been responsible for saving little human lives, we are praying that this article will save the family-lives of many homes, so that many little ones will be protected from the anguish of being brought up by separated parents—completely contrary to God's expressed plan for the family in the Bible. It is never our purpose to "wrangle about words" (II Tim. 2:14), for "the letter kills, but the Spirit gives life." (II Cor. 3:6) We want to spread the Spirit of Christ, who "came so you might have life, and have it more abundantly!" (John 10:10) It is **this** "life," full of victorious battles and overcome trials, that we aim to share in this article.

—Keith Green, January 1982

Marriage—Passion Or Patience?

Some time ago I received a phone call from a very sad brother who had been trying to get ahold of me by phone for many days. He shared that his wife was about to leave him, and she wouldn't listen to him or their pastor, and just didn't want to talk about it anymore. He said that the reason he was calling me was that she really liked our Newsletter and had a lot of respect for me and our ministry. He felt sure that if I was willing, she would talk to me and maybe listen to reason. I told him that I would be glad to try to share with her. So he left the phone, and in a few moments she was there on the other end, sort of giggling nervously.

I said, "I hear you wanna go and get a divorce and end your marriage."

"Yeah," she said.

I said, "Why?"

She said, "Because I just don't love him anymore...anyway, even if we get divorced, I can still serve the Lord, and so can he."

"Well," I said, "concerning 'love,' the Bible says wives should **love** their husbands. It doesn't say you should **'feel'** love, it says you should **LOVE!** Love isn't a feeling, it isn't 'romance.' It's an action based on commitment. In fact, it **is** COMMITMENT!"

There was silence on the other end for a few seconds. Then she said, "No one ever told me that before. I thought that if I didn't FEEL love toward my husband, then what's the use of trying to 'act' loving. What's the use of pretending there's hope for our marriage when I didn't 'love' him anymore?

"I understand," I said. "The world has perverted the concept of love so badly that people go from one relationship to another, one marriage to another, simply because the 'love' feelings are gone. The simple truth is that those feelings were never 'love' in the first place! They were merely 'romantic emotions' that come and go with the wind. They're based on moods and circumstances, but mostly on the excitement and mystique of a 'new' relationship. As soon as the 'newness' wears off, you find yourself sitting across the dinner table from just another human being—and **that's** when the challenge begins. You've made a bunch of promises—and a commitment to love and live together 'till death do us part,'—and now you'd better find out what this word 'love' really means, or there's just no hope for your marriage!"

Just then another long-distance call came in on another line and I had to go, so I prayed with that woman, right there on the phone. In the prayer I asked God to "burn these principles into her mind," so that wherever she turned, all she could see would be God's commandment to "love your husband!"

Well God's power truly fell on us during that prayer! This couple later visited with us and shared that God had really healed their marriage. This woman reported that within one half hour after our phone call, she was weeping and praying with her husband. She said that I had asked God to "burn" my words into her mind, and that's **exactly what He did!** She shared that she had never understood before that love was not a feeling or an option, but a **commandment**—an action and a choice to keep the commitment she had made to her husband and God that she would **always love him.** How free she seemed! She was no longer a slave to her "non-loving" feelings; she now understood that love was something that God had not only commanded her to do, but had **enabled** her to do. **And the feelings came after the obedience!** She said that whenever she did the loving thing, she really FELT love for her husband. How

"But Doc, I just don't love her anymore…"

grateful Melody and I were as we saw their tears and praise to God. And as their two little girls played at our feet, we had more cause to rejoice that God had spared these little ones by keeping their daddy and mommy from destroying the family they had.

The Children

How many times have you heard this: "They're just staying together for the children." I remember the first time I heard that. I wasn't a Christian at the time, and I thought, "What a drag! How can they keep a miserable relationship together just for those kids?" Well, my wife and I now have three little precious ones of our own to bring up in the love and fear of the Lord. I now can see the reasoning of these tormented parents. They might not be able to stand each other, but they both love their children so much that they wouldn't dream of forcing them to relate to two different parents living in two different homes.

In our current "liberated" society, fewer and fewer people have unselfish standards. And unfortunately, this "me first" attitude is spilling over into the Church. Instead of couples having a primary concern for their children, they reason, "If **I'm** not happy, what's the use in keeping my children happy?" "Why, it would be better for the children to live without all this arguing..." More times than not, many of those involved in divorce came from broken homes themselves, and they have promised themselves, "I'll never do that to **my** kids!" And this only adds to the guilt and condemnation later if they get a divorce.

I am not suggesting that couples stay together merely because they have children. This, in itself, is not enough of a reason to keep a shaky marriage together. Many people avoid dealing with the **real** problems in their marriages by using the "children" excuse as the "only" reason to stay together. Then they just continue despising each other in their hearts, and things grow worse. What I want to deal with now are some rules that will help you avoid ever having to deal with this question—"Should we get a divorce or stick it out?"—by replacing it with this question—"What can we do to overcome the problems we're having in our marriage, so we can make a loving home for our family, and glorify God?"

Never Say "DIVORCE!"

Awhile back I was talking with my neighbor David Wilkerson, and he shared with me his burden for all the marriages that were breaking up in the Church. He told me of ministers and church leaders he knew who were throwing in the towel. Then he said something that really hit home. "You know, Keith, God has shown me a principle that would really save a lot of marriages from ending up in divorce. Words are powerful things, and I believe that Christians should be taught that there is **one** word they should avoid at all costs: **Divorce!**"

I can remember when Melody and I first got married, even though we weren't yet Christians, I always said that I never would consider divorce as an option. That way I would always be forced to work through any problem. When Mr. Wilkerson shared his principle with me, I knew it was the truth. *"The tongue is a restless evil, full of deadly poison." (James 3:8)* I believe that married couples should consider "divorce" the dirtiest word in the English language. It should **never** be used. (Better yet, it should never be considered as even a remote possibility!) You wouldn't consider

"I would have left you a year ago if it wasn't for the boy!"

murdering your own child if he was uncontrollable, would you? You would try to work it all out. Oh, things would be trying and difficult, and you might lose your temper, but you would never consider killing him! That's exactly what divorce is—the murder of a marriage and a family. And talking divorce is **talking murder!** Thinking divorce is **thinking murder.** That's the only way to consider it. You must never, NEVER use that word as a weapon in an argument. And if you've already been using it, STOP now! If you have your eye on the door, you'll never be able to straighten things out. The sooner you stop thinking and talking divorce, the sooner an atmosphere of love and trust will begin to form between you and your mate.

Other Things You Shouldn't Say

One of the most destructive things you can say to your husband or wife is, "Bill doesn't do things like that..." or, "Connie keeps **her** house looking **real** nice!" Whatever you do, don't compare your wife or husband to others to make a point. God didn't give you to Bill, He gave you to **your** husband, so you'd better start being grateful and quit looking at and talking about the "greener grass" at Bill's house. And God didn't allow you to marry Connie, so quit using her as an example to make your wife look like a total slob. You must begin by accepting each other the way each of you are, and then work from there in love and patience. Pointing to other people's supposed lack of problems will only hurt. Deal **directly with the problem itself** without bringing **anyone** or **anything** else into it.

But I Married The Wrong Person!

That might be **very** true! It's extremely possible that you went ahead and married the first person you "fell in love with." Or maybe you got married because you felt insecure and were thrilled that somebody actually wanted **you!** Whatever your story is, if you got married for any other reason than obedience to God, to glorify Him, it's more than likely you married the **wrong** person (or at least the right person at the **wrong** time—for all the **wrong** reasons).

Now before you breathe a sigh of relief and call your lawyer, hold on a minute. Even though you might have made your marriage commitment to the wrong person, even for completely selfish reasons, **it is STILL a commitment,** and God wants you to honor it!

"When you make a vow to God, do not be late in paying it, for He takes no delight in fools. Pay what you vow! It is better that you should not vow than that you should vow and not keep it. Do not let your speech cause you to sin, and do not say in the presence of God that 'it was a mistake.' Why should God be angry on account of your words and destroy the work of your hands?" (Eccl. 5:4-6)

Even though it may **be** true that you got married completely out of God's will, you must realize that it is **now** God's will for you to admit your mistake, ask His forgiveness, and then by His grace, make your present marriage A GODLY ONE! Don't think it's okay to get a divorce by using that quasi-religious excuse: "Well, NOW I'm going to obey God and just 'unmarry' the one He didn't want me to marry in the first place!" It might sound like a "spiritual" reason to you, but very few people are going to believe you're getting a divorce to "please God"—especially you! (Not to mention God.)

There is a wonderful promise in Romans: *"And we know that God causes all things to work together for good to those that love God, to those who are called according to **His** purpose." (Rom. 8:28)* How many things? **ALL** THINGS! That's right, even our mistakes, our blunders, our downright stupid errors! God is in the business of taking garbage and making it into jewels—look at Peter (whom the Lord had to rebuke so harshly—*Mark 8:32-33),* look at David (and his adultery with Bathsheba—who later became the mother of Solomon—the next king of Israel!), and look at YOU! Why, if God couldn't take someone's miserable, mistake-filled life and turn it around for blessing and growth, hardly anyone would go to heaven!

The Purpose Of Marriage

When Melody and I first became Christians, we had been married about a year and a half. We began going to a church that had quite a lot of teaching on marriage and the family. We were grateful for this, because we had had quite a few fights during our first year together. One of the things our pastor shared has stuck with us through it all.

He began his marriage series by telling us what God's purpose for a Christian husband was: **To make his wife a success in the Kingdom of God.** And the purpose of the wife? You guessed it: **To make her husband a success in the Kingdom of God!** But what does this mean? Does it mean making sure your husband makes a lot of money, or gets a promotion at work? Not at all. It means that our main function in marriage is to be praying for, encouraging, counseling, and correcting each other in love, so that our mate will fully please God in all they do. This is one of the most exciting teachings about marriage I have heard! After all, love means to serve others for **their** good. We should have as our goal to make our husband or wife the best Christian possible—in prayer, in ministry, in attitude, in service, in giving, and especially, **in loving!** If you truly make this your goal, you will have no time for the selfish attitudes that have caused all the arguments you've ever had.

The Scriptures are full of riches on this subject. *"Husbands, love your wives, just as Christ loved the Church, and gave Himself up for her; that He might sanctify her, having cleansed her by the washing of water with the Word, that He might present to Himself the Church in all her glory, having no spot or wrinkle or any such thing; but that she should be holy and blameless." (Eph. 5:25-27)*

This Scripture shows us that the husband should take the lead in all spiritual things as the head and priest of the household. There should be a daily time of prayer and reading of Scriptures together (as well as a time with the whole family if you have children). No couple can fight and stay bitter long, where there is a deep and sincere time of prayer together. (And beware—when you find you **can't or don't want to** pray, the enemy has got a strangle-hold on your relationship—true prayer is the **surest** way to loosen it!)

But for you wives who now are going to bring out the excuse that your husband is not the spiritual leader he should be, and **that** is why you feel there is no hope for your marriage, the Bible has some medicine for you as well...

*"In the same way, you wives, be submissive to your own husbands so that **even if any of them are disobedient to the Word,** they may be*

won **without a word** by the behavior of their wives, as they observe your chaste and respectful behavior." (I Peter 3:1-2)

Ah, the balance of the Word of God!

Finally... Love, Love And Love Again!

I cannot stress enough the principle that I shared with that woman on the phone who was convinced that divorce was the only answer because she didn't "love her husband anymore." Don't fall for that trap! Love is not a feeling, it's a **commitment.** I pray that God will burn this truth into your mind the same way He burned it into hers. (That's what God means when He says, *"I will write my laws upon their hearts"*—Jer. 31:33. He wants our conscience always to be *"bearing witness to the truth"*—Rom. 2:15.)

Remember, God will not do your loving for you— YOU must love your husband or wife. That means choosing to do what's best for **them.** It means **not** waiting for the right "feelings," but doing the right and loving thing NOW—don't worry, the right feelings will **always** follow the right action. Your marriage, your family, the body of Christ, and the cause of the Gospel depend upon you making the CHOICE to love—in all that you do.

"For love bears all things, believes all things, hopes all things, endures all things... let all that you do be done in love." (I Cor. 13:7; 16:14)

This article is available in tract form as LD#34.

"DEVOTIONS" OR DEVOTION?

by Charles G. Finney
Edited and paraphrased by Keith and Melody Green

"Whether, then, you eat or drink or whatever you do, do all to the glory of God." –I Cor. 10:31

"And whatever you do in word or deed, do all in the name of the Lord Jesus, giving thanks through Him to God the Father...Whatever you do, do it heartily, as for the Lord rather than for men." –Col. 3:17,23

"For not one of us lives for himself, and not one dies for himself; for if we live, we live for the Lord, or if we die, we die for the Lord; therefore whether we live or die, we are the Lord's." –Rom. 14:7-8

These Scriptures reveal the true nature of what devotion to God really is. In discussing this subject, I propose to show:

I. What true devotion to God is not.
II. What true devotion to God is.
III. That devotion, and nothing short of devotion, is true Christianity.
IV. Several mistakes commonly made upon this subject.

"5...4...3...2...1...Amen!"

I. What True Devotion To God *Is Not*.

1. Devotion does not consist of reading the Bible, nor praying, nor attending meetings. These may or may not be specific instances of devotion, but are not to be regarded as devotion itself.

2. Devotion does not consist of a private or public commitment of our lives to God. These are to be regarded as special acts–pledges or promises of devotion–but **not** as devotion itself.

3. Devotion does not consist of individual acts or exercises of any kind. These may indeed be devotional acts, that is, "acts of devotion," but let it be remembered that **no acts or exercises in themselves constitute devotion.**

II. What True Devotion To God *Is*.

Devotion is that state of the heart in which everything–our whole life, being, and possessions–are a continual offering to God, that is, they are **continually devoted to God.** True devotion must be the supreme devotion of the will, extending out to all we have and are–to all times, places, employments, thoughts, and feelings.

Let your own ideas of what a pastor ought to be illustrate my meaning. You most likely believe that a pastor, in preaching the Gospel, should have only **one** purpose in mind–to glorify God by the salvation (and later the sanctification) of sinners. Since he professes to be a servant of God, you feel that he ought to study, preach, and perform all his ministerial duties, not for himself, not for his salary, not to increase his popularity, **but only to glorify God.** Now you can easily see that if he does not have this singleness of eye, his service cannot be acceptable to God. For it is not an offering to God, it is not a devotion to God–but a devotion to himself.

Devotion then, in a pastor, is that state of mind in which all his pastoral duties are performed for the glory of God and where his **whole life** is a continual offering to God.

Again, you feel that a minister ought to be as devoted to God in everything else as he is in praying or preaching–and in this you are right! For he not only **ought** to be, but really **is** only as devoted in the pulpit as he is out of the pulpit. If he is influenced by selfish and worldly motives during the week, then these same motives are surely in his heart on the Sabbath. If during the week his thoughts are centered upon his own interests, endeavoring to promote himself, you can be sure it's the same on the Sabbath.

You most likely also feel that if a minister's devotion is merely an outward farce–that he preaches, prays, visits, and performs all his duties mainly for the purpose of supporting his family, or to get honor and attention for himself–you would say that he was a wicked man, and unless he is converted **he would inevitably lose his soul.**

If these are your views on the subject, they are undoubtedly correct. Here, where you have no personal interest, you form a right judgment and decide correctly concerning the character and destiny of such a man. Now remember, **nothing short of this standard is devotion in you!** Bear it in mind that no particular acts or zeal or gushings of emotion—or resolutions to change, or promises of future obedience—constitute devotion.

For devotion is that state of the will in which the mind is swallowed up in God as the object of its supreme affection—in which we not only live and move **in** God, but **for** God. In other words, devotion is that state of mind in which the attention is diverted from self and self-seeking, and is directed to God—the thoughts, purposes, desires, affections, and emotions all hanging upon, and devoted to, **Him.**

III. Devotion, And Nothing Short Of Devotion, Is True Christianity.

Devotion and true religion are identical.

1. It is impossible for us not to be devoted to the object of our supreme affection. If we love God supremely, He will be the reason for which we live. If an individual loves God supremely, he will be as conscious that he lives for God **as that he lives at all!**

2. Nothing short of this can be acceptable to God. Unless devotion be a habit or a state of mind, unless the whole being be an offering to God, He must have a rival in our hearts. **This** He will not endure. And to attempt to please Him by isolated acts of devotion (when it is not the habit and state of our minds) is far more abominable than for a wife to attempt to please her husband with an occasional smile, while she lives only to please and gain the affections of another man.

3. A departure from this state is **heart-apostasy.** Whatever a man's outward behavior may be, the moment he turns aside from sincere devotion to God—from a supreme consecration of his whole being to the service of God—he has, in his heart, renounced true Christianity. He is no longer in the service of God, but is serving the object upon which his heart is set; and this is the object of his devotion—that is, **it is his god.**

IV. Several Mistakes Commonly Made Upon This Subject.

1. Many imagine that there is a real difference between "devotional" and other kinds of duties—as if a man could be "doing his duty" in that which is not devotion to God. The duties of devotion are generally supposed to be prayer and reading the Scriptures, together with singing and praying in the fellowship of God's House. On the Sabbath, men imagine themselves to be devotional, while on weekdays (except for those few acts they call their "devotions") they are serving themselves and are supremely devoted to their own interests.

Now all such ideas arise out of a total absence of true devotion; and individuals who entertain such views do not yet understand what true Christianity is. **Nothing is "duty" if it is performed for God.** A man that is truly religious is as devotional in his daily business as he is on the Sabbath. The business of the world is performed by him with the same spirit and purpose as he prays, reads his Bible, and attends worship on the Sabbath. If this is not the case, he has no true religion.

2. Now there are some people who really live for God and are obviously in a devotional state of mind, who do not seem to realize that **every act devoted to God is as acceptable to Him as prayer or praise.** If by necessary responsibilities they are kept from spending much time in prayer or going to a lot of meetings, Satan takes advantage of their ignorance and brings them into bondage. He tries to persuade them that they are neglecting their duties to God by attending to other things.

Now you who are devoted to God, should understand that if His providence should confine you at home to nurse the sick, or prevents you from observing those hours of secret prayer that you are used to keeping, you are not to be brought into bondage or condemnation by this—if you are conscious that these other duties are being done for the Lord.

3. Others think that devotion can be sincere, but yet extend only to certain duties. That is, that a man may pray sincerely and from right motives, and yet be worldly in the transaction of business. Now a little reflection will convince any honest mind that this is naturally impossible. **Devotion to God cannot be sincere any further than it annihilates selfishness.** Devotion and selfishness are eternal opposites.

4. Many mistake the religion of emotion for that of the will. You can see this from their lives—they weep and appear to melt and break down. They promise to change and offer entire consecration to God. But attempt to do business with them the very next day, and you will find them supremely selfish—they are not devoted to God at all, but to their own interests. They are ready to take any advantage, even of their brethren, to benefit themselves. Now it is obvious in this case that their melting and breaking down was merely a gushing of their emotions—not a will surrendered and devoted to God.

Some Helpful Remarks

1. A spirit of devotion will turn the most constant cares and the most pressing labors into the deepest and most constant communion with God. The more pressing and tedious our duties—if they are performed for God—the deeper and more continual our communion with Him. **For whatever is done in a spirit of devotion *is* communion with God.**

2. They are not Christians, who do not hold communion with God in their ordinary employments. If you do not hold conscious communion with God in your ordinary business, it is because your business is not performed in a spirit of devotion. If not performed in a spirit of devotion, it is sin. For *"whatever is not of faith is sin."* (Rom. 14:23)

3. They are certainly not in a sanctified state, who cannot attend to the ordinary and lawful business of life without being drawn away from God.

4. Whatever cannot be done in a spirit of devotion is unlawful. If you feel the inconsistency of performing it as an act of devotion to God, **it is unlawful—you yourself being the judge.**

5. Anything not right or wrong in itself may be either right or wrong, according to whether or not it is done in a spirit of devotion. Therefore...

6. A selfish man may condemn a godly person for doing something that would be sinful if he, himself did it—because the motives of his heart are all wrong. The selfish man assumes that the other person's behavior is also wrongly motivated.

On the other hand, a sanctified person may give credit to a selfish person when it is not due, taking it for granted that, "when the act is right, the motive is right."

7. There is no peace of mind but in a state of devotion. No other state of mind is reasonable. In no other state will the powers of the mind harmonize. In any other state than that of devotion to God, there is an inward struggle, and mutiny and strife in the mind itself. The conscience rebukes the heart for selfishness. Hence, *"'There is no peace for the wicked,' says the Lord." (Isaiah 48:22)*

8. They have *"perfect peace whose minds are thus stayed upon God" (Isaiah 26:3)* in an attitude of constant devotion. It is impossible that they should not have peace, **for devotion implies and includes peace.**

And now beloved, do you have the spirit of true devotion? Do not reply, "I hope so," for nothing but a conscious awareness should satisfy you for a moment. If you are devoted to God, you **know it**—and if you are not conscious of being devoted to God, it is because you are *not* **devoted.**

"Do not be deceived, God is not mocked; for whatever a man sows, this he will also reap. For the one who sows to his own flesh shall from the flesh reap corruption, but the one who sows to the Spirit shall from the Spirit reap eternal life." (Gal. 6:7-8)

This article was originally published under the title "Devotion" in the OBERLIN EVANGELIST in 1839. The article in its original form has been reprinted in a book called THE PROMISE OF THE SPIRIT by Charles Finney, edited and compiled by Timothy L. Smith.

This article is available in tract form as LD#36.

SCRIPTURE REFERENCE SOURCES

Breaking Up The Fallow Ground
Pg. 16: Hosea 10:12, NASB

Music Or Missions?
Pg. 29: Luke 9:23, AP; Phil. 1:29, NASB

Holy Bible–Wholly True
Pg. 31: Matt 24:35, NASB
Pg. 33: Isaiah 40:21-22, AP
Pg. 34: Job 26:7, NASB; II Peter 3:10, NASB; II Peter 3:12, NASB; Ezek. 12:25, AP
Pg. 35: Heb. 4:12, NASB

In Search Of Mr. Right
Pg. 37-38: I Cor. 7:9, NASB
Pg. 38: I Cor. 7:7, NASB
Pg. 39: I Cor. 7:28, NASB; I Cor. 7:32, NASB; I Cor. 7:33, NASB; I Cor. 7:35, NASB; I Cor. 7:38, AP
Pg. 40: Heb. 12:2, AP; Phil. 4:19, NASB; Psalm 46:10, KJV

Gossip
Pg. 42: Proverbs 8:13, AP
Pg. 42-43: Lev. 19:16, NKJV
Pg. 43: I Tim. 5:13, NASB; Psalm 101:5, NASB; Matt. 18:15, NASB
Pg. 44: Gal. 6:1, NASB
Pg. 45: Proverbs 6:16-19, NASB; Proverbs 17:4, NASB; I Samuel 24:9, NASB; I Cor. 13:7, AP
Pg. 46: Proverbs 20:19, NASB; Matt. 12:36, NASB; Eph. 4:29, NASB; James 1:26, NASB; Rev. 19:7, NASB

Total Commitment
Pg. 47: Acts 17:6, NASB, Acts 1:8, NASB; Matt. 10:5-6, NASB
Pg. 48: Acts 13:47, NASB
Pg. 51: I Peter 4:17-18, NASB; Mark 3:25, AP
Pg. 52: Mark 16:15, NASB; Matt. 1:21, NASB
Pg. 53: Luke 12:48, AP; James 4:17, AP; Rev. 3:16-17, NASB

Do You Feel Like Giving Up?
Pg. 56: II Cor. 5:4, NASB; II Cor. 1:8, NASB
Pg. 57: Psalm 44:23-24, AP; I Peter 4:12-13, NASB
Pg. 58: Matt. 10:29, NASB; Heb. 11:6, NASB; Jude 24, NASB

Forgiveness–Forgive Or Forget It!
Pg. 60: Heb. 12:15, NASB
Pg. 60-63: Matt. 18:23-35, AP
Pg. 61: Rom. 1:21, NASB; Matt. 6:15, NASB
Pg. 63: Rom. 12:18, NASB; II Cor. 5:18, NASB

Zeal–Love Ablaze!
Pg. 66: Joel 2:17, KJV; Joel 1:13, AP
Pg. 67: Eph. 4:26, NASB; II Tim. 3:5, NASB; Matt. 23:11, NASB
Pg. 68: John 7:24, NASB

Will You Be Bored In Heaven?
Pg. 69: Isaiah 66:2, NASB
Pg. 70: II Cor. 6:2, AP; Heb. 12:14, MLB
Pg. 72: Phil. 1:21-25, NASB; Matt. 24:21, AP; Luke 21:26, AP
Pg. 73: I Thess. 4:17, NASB; Heb. 11:35,38, AP
Pg. 74: John 16:33, AP; Matt. 16:25, AP; II Tim. 3:12, NASB; Matt. 10:28, NASB; Ezek. 33:11, AP; II Cor. 13:5, NASB

The Backslider In Heart
Pg. 76: Matt. 12:34, NASB
Pg. 77: Eph. 2:3, NASB; I Cor. 10:31, NASB
Pg. 79: Proverbs 14:14, NASB

Uncovering The Truth About Modesty
Pg. 82: I Tim. 2:9-10, NASB
Pg. 84: Rom. 12:1, NASB
Pg. 84-85: Luke 17:1-2, NASB
Pg. 86: Proverbs 31:30, NASB
Pg. 87: Ezek. 16:14-15, NASB
Pg. 89: I Chron. 16:29, KJV

Where Are The Elijahs Of God?
Pg. 95: James 5:18, NASB
Pg. 98: Psalm 2:8, KJV; Rev. 3:16, AP

How To Witness...For The Right Side!
Pg. 107: Isaiah 43:10, NASB
Pg. 108: Heb. 12:14, MLB; II Tim. 4:2, NASB
Pg. 110: I Peter 2:23, NASB
Pg. 112: II Cor. 3:2, AP

What's Wrong With The Gospel? Section 1: "The Missing Parts"
Pg. 114: I Cor. 2:2, NASB
Pg. 115: Mark 10:19, TLB; Matt. 19:17, MLB; Rom 3:20, NASB
Pg. 116: Mark 10:21, NASB; Rom 7:7, NASB; Heb. 10:31, NASB

Pg. 117: Proverbs 9:10, NASB; Rom 11:22, NASB; Luke 13:3, NASB
Pg. 118: Proverbs 15:3, NASB; Eph. 4:30, NASB; II Peter 3:15, NASB; Heb. 12:14, MLB; Matt. 5:48, NASB
Pg. 119: I John 1:6, NASB
Pg. 120: Matt. 19:22, AP
Pg. 121: Acts 2:43, NASB; Acts 2:42, NASB

What's Wrong With The Gospel? Section 2: "The Added Parts"

Pg. 126: I John 2:6, AP
Pg. 127: Mark 9:42, AP
Pg. 128: Matt. 7:16, NASB; John 15:16, NASB; Rev. 3:20, NASB; Rev. 3:22, AP
Pg. 131: II Tim. 4:7, NASB; Rom. 15:19, NASB; Matt. 25:21, NIV

Being A Christian At Home

Pg. 134: Phil. 2:3-4, NASB
Pg. 137: Rev. 3:19, NASB
Pg. 138: I Samuel 3:13, NASB

Aggressive Christianity

Pg. 141: Mark 16:15, NASB; Acts 26:15-18, NASB; Psalm 119:136, NASB
Pg. 143: Acts 19:18-19, NASB; Rev. 11:15, KJV; Matt. 24:24, NASB
Pg. 144: I John 3:7-8, NASB; Mark 16:15, NASB
Pg. 145: Acts 26:17-18, NASB; II Cor. 5:11, NASB; Luke 14:23, NASB
Pg. 147: Matt. 10:34, NASB

God Comes To New York

Pg. 149: Rom. 8:7, NASB
Pg. 155: Jer. 29:13, AP

Be Ye Angry...And Sin Not

Pg. 156: Eph. 5:18, KJV; Eph. 4:26, KJV; Ex. 4:14, KJV; Psalm 7:11, KJV; Acts 17:16, KJV; Acts 17:16, Amplified
Pg. 161: Psalm 85:6, KJV

Creation Or Evolution? Part 1

Pg. 163: Gen. 1:1, NASB; Heb. 11:3, Weymouth

Creation Or Evolution? Part 3

Pg. 185: Matt. 24:37-39, NASB; II Peter 3:3-7, NASB

How To Overcome Sin

Pg. 188: John 6:28-29, NASB
Pg. 189: I John 5:4, NASB; Eph. 6:16, NASB; Acts 15:9, KJV; Rom. 14:23, NASB; Heb. 11:6, NIV
Pg. 191: Gal. 5:22-23, KJV

Pg. 193: John 6:29, NASB; Rom. 9:32, NASB

Love vs. Romance...Fact Or Fantasy?

Pg. 197: Matt. 19:6, NASB
Pg. 198: Proverbs 13:10, NASB
Pg. 199: I Cor. 13:7, NASB; Eph. 5:1-2, NASB

Everything You Should Know *Before* You Get A Divorce

Pg. 201: Mal. 2:16, MLB
Pg. 202: II Tim. 2:14, NASB; II Cor. 3:6, NASB; John 10:10, AP
Pg. 205: James 3:8, AP
Pg. 206: Eccl. 5:4-6, AP; Rom. 8:28, NASB
Pg. 207: Eph. 5:25-27, NASB
Pg. 207-208: I Peter 3:1-2, NASB
Pg. 208: Jer. 31:33, AP; Rom. 2:15, AP; I Cor. 13:7; 16:14, RSV

"Devotions" Or Devotion?

Pg. 209: I Cor. 10:31, NASB; Col. 3:17,23, AP; Rom. 14:7-8, NASB
Pg. 212: Rom. 14:23, NASB
Pg. 213: Isaiah 48:22, NASB; Isaiah 26:3, AP; Gal. 6:7-8, NASB

Amplified	Amplified New Testament
AP	Author's Paraphrase
KJV	King James Version
TLB	The Living Bible
MLB	Modern Language Bible
NASB	New American Standard Bible
NIV	New International Version
NKJV	The New King James Version
RSV	Revised Standard Version
Weymouth	Weymouth New Testament In Modern Speech

LAST DAYS MINISTRY MATERIALS FOR WHATEVER YOU CAN AFFORD

Request Our Free Ministry Materials Catalogue
See Page 224

As you know (or maybe you **didn't** know!) Last Days has **many** inspiring ministry materials – including dynamic teachings on audio and video cassettes, over a hundred challenging tracts, the music of Keith Green and Bob Ayala, and life-changing books!

Our "Whatever You Can Afford" Policy

The Lord has given us a unique way to price our ministry materials. From the beginning, the spirit behind our "whatever you can afford" policy was so no one would be deprived of ministry. If they didn't have the money to pay the suggested price – then they could give whatever they could afford – even if that was nothing! We've always been really blessed to serve in this way.

In case you're not familiar with the scope of LDM, in 1987 alone we were able to send out over $100,000 worth of ministry materials for free. We mail materials to 150 countries and some of them are translated into 22 different languages. In the last 11 years we've mailed out over 12 million LDM Magazines, 54 million tracts, 13,000 video programs, 53,000 audio teachings, and 475,000 recordings – all for whatever you can afford!

We Enjoy Serving You

As always, we feel privileged to be a part of your lives. One of our desires is to provide quality ministry materials that glorify Jesus and help Christians grow to be more like Him in every aspect of life. We love you in the Lord!

Melody Green and the staff at Last Days Ministries

Last Days Ministries Box 40, Lindale, TX 75771-0040 (214) 963-8671

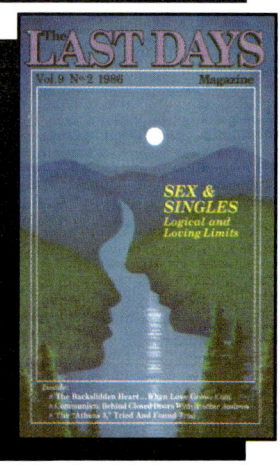

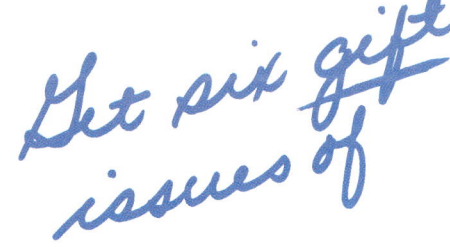

The LAST DAYS MAGAZINE!

In 1977, Keith and Melody Green founded Last Days Ministries. Since that time, millions of lives have been impacted by Keith's powerful music ministry, the Last Days Intensive Christian Training School, and the ever-challenging Last Days Magazine.

The Last Days Magazine reaches hundreds of thousands of people worldwide and we'd like to send you a gift of six issues. It is colorfully illustrated and filled with many challenging articles by dynamic Christian leaders from around the world. Each issue features topics that are not only interesting, but vital to knowing and understanding God for Who He really is.

Through the Last Days Magazine, you'll also have opportunity to order special video programs, audio and video teachings, newly released music, books, and other materials – all for whatever you can afford!

TRACTS

Tracts By The Millions!

We generally reprint the main articles of our Magazine in pamphlet form, but little did we know when we sent out our first tracts in 1979 that we would print over 58 million! As with the Magazine, we have always made every effort to make our tracts attractive, colorful, and easy to read. We have a wide range of dynamic tracts on topics important to our Christian walk. Listed here are just a few of them.

by Keith Green:
"Grumbling And Complaining"
"Why You Should Go To The Mission Field"

by Melody Green:
"Children – Things We Throw Away?"
"Questions About Abortion"
"Being A Christian At Home"
"...But I Can't Forgive Myself!"
"Binding Up The Brokenhearted"
"Pass The Salt"

by Leonard Ravenhill:
"The Judgment Seat of Christ"

by Winkie Pratney:
"Hurt And Bitterness"

by Charles Finney:
"True And False Conversion"

by William Booth:
"How To Find God"

219

MUSIC FROM LDM

KEITH GREEN

Keith's powerfully anointed music has challenged millions and continues as an inheritance to this generation!

For Him Who Has Ears To Hear
Keith sings of the joy and love he found in his new life in Christ.

No Compromise
These songs challenge all believers to live a life of uncompromising obedience to the Lord.

So You Wanna Go Back To Egypt
Dynamic songs that emphasize the unfailing grace of God towards us, His children – even when we blow it!

Songs for the Shepherd
A truly inspiring worship album that will lift your heart to the Lord!

The Prodigal Son
Bringing a message of our Father's love, this album features *"Song For Josiah"* and *"Love with Me (Melody's Song),"* which reveal tender insights into Keith's relationships.

Jesus Commands Us To Go!
This music delivers a challenging message to those who don't know Jesus and to all who've decided to follow Him.

The Complete Musical Legacy of Keith Green

How can you live a holy life in a world filled with compromise? What kind of service is the Lord asking of you? Keith had the guts to ask the questions we all struggle with – and wrestle until he got answers. The answers he found lie not only in Keith's experiences, but in the songs themselves.

Keith Green – The Ministry Years

Volume 1 1977-1979 – **Features 38 songs**
Volume 2 1980-1982 – **Features 33 songs**

Each volume includes its own special booklet with personal insights of the ministry years by Melody Green.

MAKE ME SHINE
by Bob Ayala

Lord I love You more than my –
    I love You more than my life
I'd lay it down if You asked
But what You want of me is a living
    sacrifice
But Lord that's a much harder task

It's so easy to let my feelings take
    control
'Til I'm tossed like a ship on the sea
Keep Your hold on me – don't You
    ever let me go
Lord, You've been so faithful to me

You rescued my life from the
    gathering night
You captured my heart but I gave
    such a fight
But I don't want to fight anymore –
    I just want to surrender
I don't wanna be just another
    pretender

Make me a message – won't You
    make me to shine
It's getting close to the end
Eternity is just a matter of time
It's getting close to the end
So make me a message – won't
    You make me to shine

The music of Bob Ayala *ministers*. God has gifted Bob with rare sensitivity and insight into the needs and feelings of people. Sharing from experience, this powerful album is Bob's tribute to God and His ability to rescue and redeem *every* part of our lives, no matter what we've been through.

We were really blessed to have Bob tour with us on The Keith Green Memorial Concerts; Bob and his wife Pam are on staff and live at Last Days with their son Casey.

SPECIAL VIDEO PROGRAMS

Keith Green -*and*- Melody Green

The KEITH GREEN MEMORIAL CONCERT

Hundreds of thousands of people have been challenged and inspired by *The Keith Green Memorial Concert*. This powerful video includes a half-hour concert by Keith Green, where he delivers the burden of God's heart for the world, and a special message by Melody. It also features many personal slides and movies of Keith and the children, as well as Melody's trip to Asia. It's a life changer! (59 min.)

Baby Choice

with Melody Green

A 10-minute documentary
Many people never think of abortion from the victim's point of view – "Baby Choice" will never let you forget.

President Reagan writes –

Dear Melody:
Nancy and I ran "Baby Choice" and were, as you promised, deeply moved. Thank you for giving it to us and, even more, for making it. I know it was a sad, but necessary task, and I hope millions will see it and hear your words...
Be assured I'll be praying for you... Again, thanks and God bless you.
Sincerely,
Ronald Reagan

AUDIO & VIDEO TEACHINGS

We produce and distribute scores of quality teachings by dynamic men and women of God. We continually receive letters from those who've been touched and challenged by these teachings. Great for home fellowships, Sunday school, and youth meetings. Listed are just a few of the teachings we have available.

"Keith Green: The Man Behind The Message" Keith shares about his early experiences as a new Christian and his struggles at being labeled "a prophet." This message leaves no room for excusing ourselves of any sin under the guise of a "special calling." (75 min.)

"Grumbling And Complaining: So You Wanna Go Back To Egypt" by **Keith Green** Is the journey to the Promised Land causing your endurance to wear thin? Before you start longing for Egypt, you should know there are lessons that only the wilderness can teach. (95 min.)

"The Judgment Seat of Christ" by **Leonard Ravenhill** What will it be like when God takes hold of history and empties it? Challenging us to live our lives in the light of eternity, Leonard portrays that awesome day when everyone will stand before the judgment seat of Christ. (80 min.)

"Hurt And Bitterness" by **Winkie Pratney** You'd be surprised at how many problems and habits have sprung out of forgotten hurts. In this study, Winkie uncovers the steps that lead a person into the depths of bitterness and shines a light on the practical way out. This teaching has set many people free from their past hurts. (120 min.)

"Holy Ground" by **David Wilkerson** Looking back over his own experience, David clings to the absolute necessity of personal consecration to God. It's more important that God wins all of us, than for us to win all the world for Him. (45 min.)

"Relating To The Opposite Sex" by **Dean Sherman** (10-part series) Even though God is the One who designed relationships between men and women, many people in the Church have been influenced by the practices of the world in this area. Dean combines keen insight with humor in this teaching, as he gives practical, biblical guidelines for pure, godly relationships. This is excellent for singles, college, and youth groups. (9 hrs. 15 min.)

"Loving The Battle" by **Brother Andrew** Instead of hiding out in some "safe" place, we as Christians are to charge into the enemy's territory, knowing that Christ is in us. Brother Andrew, author of "God's Smuggler" and founder of Open Doors, confidently proclaims our victory in Christ. (65 min.)

GET OUR FREE MINISTRY MATERIALS CATALOGUE

For a listing of all of our ministry materials, and our pricing guidelines, write and ask for our **free** Ministry Materials Catalogue.

Through it you can order special video programs, life-changing audio-video teachings, newly released music, tracts, books, and many other materials – *all for whatever you can afford!*

FREE MATERIALS COUPON

This coupon must be filled out by the person whom the items are for.

SEND TO:

NAME

ADDRESS

CITY   STATE/PROV.

COUNTRY   ZIP/POSTAL CODE   OLD ZIP CODE
                                           (if you've moved)

Please send me free:

- ☐ **The Last Days Magazine**
  A gift of six issues
- ☐ A sample of your most-ordered tracts
- ☐ A Ministry Materials Catalogue
- ☐ A Missions Opportunities List
- ☐ Information on your ICT School

Mail To: **Last Days Ministries** Box 40, Lindale, TX 75771-0040